WITHDRAWN

DATE DUE			

The Urban Economies, 1985

The Urban Economies, 1985

A Multiregional Multi-Industry
Forecasting Model

Curtis C. Harris, Jr.
University of Maryland

Lexington Books
D.C. Heath and Company
Lexington, Massachusetts
Toronto   London

Library of Congress Cataloging in Publication Data

Harris, Curtis C.
   The urban economies, 1985.

   1. Industries, Location of—Mathematical models. 2. Regional planning—
Mathematical models.
I. Title.
HC79.D5H365   338'.09   73-6593
ISBN 0-669-86934-1

Published simultaneously in Canada.

Printed in the United States of America.

International Standard Book Number: 0-669-86934-1

Library of Congress Catalog Card Number: 73-6593

To My Wife

Contents

List of Figures   ix

List of Tables   xi

Preface   xv

Chapter 1   Introduction   1

A Brief Description of the Multiregional,
  Multi-industry Forecasting Model   3
Review of Forecasting Techniques   3

Chapter 2   The Model   9

The Sectors   9
Notation   15
The Equations   18
Explanation of Equations   22
Relationship with a National Model   31

Chapter 3   Theoretical Framework   33

Industry Location   33
Gross Investment   39
Employment   40
Population Migration   40
Labor Force Participation   44

Chapter 4   Data Estimates   47

Supply   47
Demand   49
Labor   54
Income   57
Population and Migration   59
Transportation Costs   64

Chapter 5	**The Equations**	69
	Statistical Procedures	69
	The Use of Regional Shares	71
	The Government Equations	73
	The Output Equations	74
	The Equipment Equations	75
	The Construction Equations	99
	The Employment Equations	103
	The Population and Labor Force Equations	116
	The Income Equations	117
	Other Equations	121
Chapter 6	**The Forecasts**	135
	Assumptions in the National Model	135
	Assumptions in the Regional Model	136
	The Use of 1970 Data	141
	The Use of Residuals	145
	Summary of Results	147
	Regional Effects of Reduced Defense Expenditures	165
	Future Research	193
	Appendix Table	201
	Index	225
	About the Author	231

List of Figures

1-1   Simplified Flow Chart of Multiregional,
           Multi-industry Forecasting Model   4

3-1   Market Equilibrium with One Market   34

3-2   Market Equilibrium in Three Markets   36

6-1   A Hypothetical Regression Line   145

List of Tables

2-1	Sectors Used in the Forecasting Model	10
3-1	Equilibrium Commodity Flows, Rents, and Shadow Prices	35
4-1	Summary of 1965 and 1966 County Output Estimating Procedures and Data Sources by Input-Output Sectors	48
4-2	Components of Total Demand by Industry	50
4-3	National Employment and Unemployment, 1965 and 1966	55
4-4	Summary of 1965 and 1966 County Estimating Procedures	56
4-5	Allocators Used to Disaggregate 1965 and 1966 Personal Income Data of Large Geographic Areas into the Component Countries	58
4-6	Threshold Population by Population Cell	61
4-7	Upper and Lower Bounds for Distribution of Population by Age Within Each Race Group	62
4-8	Overstatement (Understatement) of Migration by Age Group	64
5-1	Equation (2-2) Explaining the Level of 1966 Government Expenditures	73
5-2	Equations Explaining Change in Output by Industry Sector 1965-1966	76
5-3	Summary of Equation (2-4) by Industry	90
5-4	Equations Explaining the 1966 Level of Equipment by Equipment Purchasing Sector	94

5-5   Equations Explaining the 1966 Level of
Construction by Sector   100

5-6   Equation (2-14) Explaining the 1965-1966
Changes in Employment by Industry Sector   104

5-7   Equations Explaining 1966 Employment by
Sector   111

5-8   Equations Explaining 1966 Births, 1966 Deaths
and 1965-1966 Population Migration   118

5-9   Equation (2-32) Explaining 1966 Earnings by
Industry Sector   122

5-10   Equation (2-40) Explaining the 1966 Personal
Consumption Expenditures by Industry Sector   129

5-11   Substitute Equations for Forecasting Marginal
Transportation Costs   133

6-1   Threshold Level of Output for New Firms by
Industry Sector   138

6-2   National Employment and Unemployment, 1970   142

6-3   Sources of State Employment, 1970, Not Covered
by *County Business Patterns*   143

6-4   Procedures Used to Obtain 1970 County
Employment in Sectors Not Covered by
County Business Patterns   144

6-5   Population Data and Projections by Standard
Metropolitan Statistical Area   148

6-6   Population Data and Projections of SMSA
Counties Summarized by State and Region   156

6-7   Population Projections by State and Region
from Alternative Sources   158

6-8   Job Projections of SMSA Counties Summarized
by State and Region   160

6-9   Per Capita Income of SMSA Counties Averaged
        by State and Region Relative to per Capita
        Income of All SMSA Counties   162

6-10   Average Unemployment Rate Projections of SMSA
        Counties Summarized by State and Region   166

6-11   Selected Projections of SMSA Counties Summarized
        by Region   170

6-12   Selected Projections of Central City and
        Suburban Counties in SMSA's with 1970
        Population Over One Million Summarized
        by Region   178

6-13   Industry Sector Outputs in 1985 Under Normal
        and Minimum Deterrence Defense Budgets   192

6-14   The Effect of the Minimum Deterrence Defense
        Budget on the 1985 Urban Economies Summarized
        by State and Region   194

6-15   The Effect of the Minimum Deterrence Defense
        Budget on the 1985 Economies of the Standard
        Metropolitan Statistical Areas   196

Preface

This book is a sequel to a previous book on locational analysis.[1] The previous book presented an industry location model which tried to explain changes in output by industry at the county level. This book adds many other economic relationships to the locational model to form a Multiregional, Multi-industry Forecasting Model.

Data for the forecasting model have been collected for each county in the United States, although in this application, forecasts were made only for the counties that are classified in Standard Metropolitan Statistical Areas. The model assumes that changes in industry location are the driving force that determines the growth or decline of a region. Regional output changes cause changes in employment and income, which in turn affect the regional demand for goods. The changing location of demand and supply affect the factor costs and competitive position of one region relative to others.

The forecasting model at this stage is still experimental. The model could be improved if more and better data were available. Also, there are a large number of functional relationships in the model, and, consequently, there is a continuing need for improvement in their specifications.

One of the major uses of the model will be for regional impact analysis. Projections are made assuming that the relationships among the variables, as specified by the equations, hold true in the future period as they did in the base period. Then one or a few of the relationships are changed, and regional impacts are measured by comparing the two alternative sets of projections. For example, without prior knowledge, the future regional distribution of defense expenditures is assumed to be the same as the distribution in 1970. If this distribution were changed or if the level of national defense expenditures were changed, the regional impacts could be estimated with the forecasting model.

After a brief introduction, the model with all of its equations is presented in Chapter 2 and the theoretical framework supporting the important equations is given in Chapter 3. The industry location equations discussed in these chapters were discussed in more detail in the previous book. Also, the data estimating procedures given in Chapter 4 were presented in greater detail in the previous book for most of the data items. The parameters that were estimated for the functional relationships given in Chapter 2 are presented in Chapter 5, along with a discussion of the statistical procedures. The forecasts themselves are presented in summary form in Chapter 6. This chapter also includes a study of the regional impacts of reduced defense expenditures. The Appendix Table gives summary forecasts for SMSAs that had a 1970 population greater than one million.

---

[1] Curtis C. Harris, Jr. and Frank E. Hopkins, LOCATIONAL ANALYSIS: AN INTER-REGIONAL ECONOMETRIC MODEL OF AGRICULTURE, MINING, MANUFAC-TURING, AND SERVICES (Lexington, Mass.: Heath Lexington Books, 1972).

The author wishes to thank Professors Clopper Almon, Jr., John H. Cumberland, and Frank E. Hopkins for their advice and council. The regional forecasting model relies on Professor Almon's national input-output forecasts from his Maryland Interindustry Forecasting Project. Professor Almon and his staff, particularly Miss Margaret Buckler, were very helpful.

Mrs. Marianne Russek and Mr. Richard Davis were responsible for writing many of the computer programs required to make the regional model work and to process the vast amounts of data. Kenneth McConnell, William Donnely, III, Stanley Wolfson, and Stephen Merchant provided valuable assistance during various periods of the project's history. The typing of reports and manuscripts was provided by the secretarial staff of the Bureau of Business and Economic Research, University of Maryland.

Financial assistance for the Regional Forecasting Project was provided first by the Economic Development Administration of the U.S. Department of Commerce, then by the National Science Foundation. The computer time was supported in part through the facilities of the Computer Science Center of the University of Maryland.

The Urban Economies, 1985

1 Introduction

Will large metropolitan areas grow even larger or will new ones develop? Will suburban areas grow at the expense of central cities? Will California and Florida continue their rapid expansion? Will manufacturing industries move out of the northeastern manufacturing belt? Will unemployment and low income persist in Appalachia? Will population of the Northeast Corridor grow larger?

These questions and many others like them can be answered with the Multiregional, Multi-industry Forecasting Model presented in this book. Given certain assumptions reflecting events that are likely to take place, a set of reasonable forecasts can be made for each of the 3,111 county-type areas. The forecasts include outputs, employment and earnings by industry sector, unemployment, personal income, consumption, investment, government expenditures, and population by age and race.

The model can do more, however. It can be used to trace out regional economic impacts of exogenous changes in certain variables. The model is first run with the variables forecast endogenously, then it is rerun with certain variables set to predetermined levels. Impacts are measured by comparing the two runs. The following paragraphs discuss a few possible applications of the model, although the results of only one of these applications are presented in this book. Some of the applications could be made with very little effort, while others would require special sets of data to be incorporated in the model.

One of the most frequent uses of forecasting models recently has been to measure the economic impacts of alternative defense expenditures. In a recent study sponsored by the Arms Control and Disarmament Agency, two national models and one regional model were used for this purpose.[1] Assumptions were made as to levels and types of defense expenditures, and the models were run in order to measure economic effects of these alternative assumptions. A section in Chapter 6 shows the regional effects of a large reduction in defense expenditures using the model presented in this book.

Federal government expenditures have an impact on regional economies, whether planned or not. If these regional impacts were known ahead of time, then the federal government could control the regional distribution of its

---

[1] Bernard Udis, editor of ADJUSTMENTS OF THE U.S. ECONOMY TO REDUCTIONS IN MILITARY SPENDING, United States Arms Control and Disarmament Agency, ACDA/E-156 December 1970. The national models used were by Lawrence Klein of the University of Pennsylvania and Clopper Almon of the University of Maryland. The regional model was a simpler forcasting model by the author.

1

expenditures in order to achieve national goals. For example, if it were decided that social costs could be lowered if population were to locate away from the large metropolitan areas, then the expenditures could be planned to influence this population distribution.

The impact of state and local government expenditures could also be studied. One of the principal concerns of state and local governments at this time is the effect of pollution control on the local economies. For example, if an output of an industry were reduced at a given site in order to restrict the amount of pollution, the reduction could affect output in other economic activities and in other local areas. If good estimates of the economic effects of pollution control were available, then the decision makers could measure the benefits and the costs of pollution control. With the forecasting model as presented here, outputs can be predetermined at any given location and the economic effects of these output restrictions can be measured. With additional modifications in the model and with data on pollution emissions, it would be possible to say even more about the effects of pollution control.

The U.S. Department of Commerce has an economic development program to aid depressed areas as measured by their unemployment rates and low income. Aid is in the form of business loans and grants for public works. If the program were successful in locating a business firm in an area that would have located elsewhere what would be the total economic effects of this event? How much additional employment would it take to reduce the unemployment rate in a given area below a certain level? Since new jobs often attract migrants, it is necessary to add more than one job in order to take one worker off the unemployment rolls in the local area. Will a new industry be successful in attracting related industries to the area? Will the number of depressed areas become larger or smaller in the future? These are some of the questions that could be answered with the forecasting model.

The Department of Housing and Urban Development has a program to stimulate the creation of new towns, by guaranteeing loans to developers. Will these new towns survive? Will they become economically independent or will they require continual federal aid? Is the location of the new town a desirable one? Is it within commuting distance of jobs or will it be able to generate its own job opportunites? Will the new towns close to metropolitan areas, such as Reston and Columbia, be able to capture a large enough share of the metropolitan growth? Can new towns in isolated areas offer sufficient economic advantages to attract industries?

The Department of Transportation is studying alternative transportation systems to be built in the future. Once the Interstate highway system is completed, should the tax rate be lowered or should the revenue be used to build another highway system, or should it be used for another type of transportation system? Since transportation systems involve billions of dollars, the regional impacts of any system could be substantial. Certain areas might flourish under one transportation system but decline under another. Being able to estimate the alternative effects before actual decisions are made should be very valuable in the decision-making process.

A Brief Description of the Multiregional, Multi-industry Forecasting Model

The model starts by forecasting the location of each industry. The change in output of each industry sector is explained by two sets of variables: (1) input prices that firms face in each location, and (2) agglomeration variables that help explain location behavior that is not accounted for by the prices. After output has been determined, then employment, population, earnings, and personal income are derived. Also, final demand sectors are forecast—consumption, governmental expenditures, investment, and foreign exports.

The model is recursive. The supply and demand data in the year t are used to forecast variables in the year $t+1$, then the forecasts are used as data to make forecasts for the year $t+2$. A simplified flow chart of the forecasting model is presented in Figure 1-1. The left-hand side of the chart itemizes the data and computations for the year t. The connecting lines show how the data is used to make forecasts in the year $t+1$. After $t+1$ forecasts are made they are realigned as data, as given in the left-hand side of the chart, in order to forecast for year $t+2$. In any given year, predetermined changes may be made in the data, such as changes in the governmental expenditures.

An important set of variables used to determine the location of output is the transportation variables (shadow prices). These variables are the cost of transporting a marginal unit of a commodity either into or out of a region. For example, in explaining the location of the steel industry, explanatory variables include the marginal cost of shipping a unit of steel out of each region and the marginal cost of shipping a unit of iron ore (and other inputs) into each region. The shadow prices are derived by determining the cost of shipping a unit of goods between each pair of regions by rail and truck for each weight class. The least-cost method of shipping goods in each weight class for each commodity is determined and these costs are used in a linear programming transportation algorithm in order to produce the shadow prices.

Review of Forecasting Techniques

Most regional forecasts are based on procedures or models that apply to individual regions. Probably the simplest type of approach involves extending past trends into the future using some judgmental procedure. An example is projecting the region's share of the nation of each variable such as population, income, and employment by industry.[2]

---

[2]This method has been used by the National Planning Association and the Regional Economics Division, Office of Business Economics, U.S. Department of Commerce.

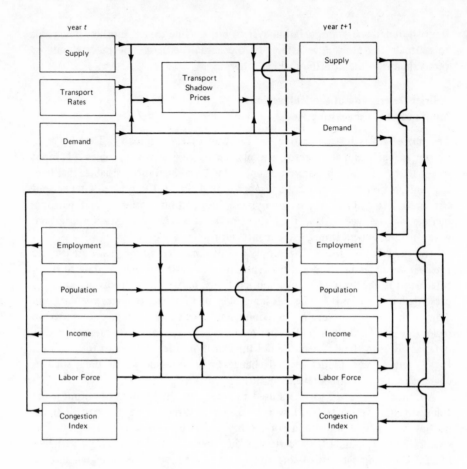

Figure 1-1. Simplified Flow Chart of Multiregional, Multi-industry Forecasting Model

A more mechanical approach involves using the shift-share analysis. A regional competitive effect is computed as the difference between the actual regional employment in an industry (or some other variable) in period t and what the region's employment would be in that industry if it grew at the national rate from period $t-1$. To make forecasts, either the regional competitive effect or the regional competitive effect relative to the base year employment is held constant over time.[3] This method has proven to be unsatisfactory.

---

[3] For applications see National Planning Association "Projection Procedure for Susquehanna Area Economic Base Study" Washington, D.C. 1964 (mimeographed) and Lloyd D. Ashby, "Regional Projections in a National Setting" Regional Economics Division, Office of Business Economics, U.S. Department of Commerce.

In fact, it has been shown that better forecasts can be made by assuming that all regions grow at the national rate, than by assuming that the regional competitive effect remains constant.[4]

The economic base approach is often used in making projections.[5] This approach assumes that all economic activity can be divided into two components—basic and nonbasic. Basic employment is that which is used to produce output for export and the nonbasic employment is that which is used for services. Each industry's employment (or output) is classified between basic and nonbasic, and an employment multiplier is computed as the ratio of total employment to total basic employment. Total employment to forecast by predetermining the level of basic employment and applying the multiplier. Population is also forecast with a similar ratio, one that relates total population to basic employment. This method is very easy to apply, but it has not proven to be very accurate. The employment multiplier does not remain constant over time and it is very difficult to predetermine the level of basic employment.

Econometric techniques with time series data also are used to forecast regional economies. These range from simple regression equations to complicated Keynesian-type macroeconomic models.[6] Relationships established in a historical period often do not continue into the future, and if the economic values of various components are extended using simple unrelated equations, the relationships among the components may become unrealistic. For example, suppose separate equations were derived independently to forecast the output of each industry. There is no guarantee that the relationships among these industries as projected would be realistic when evaluated with interindustry coefficients. Some progress has been made with the macroeconomic models, although they suffer from the lack of good data. To duplicate a national macroeconomic model at the regional level, it is necessary to have a set of regional accounts similar to the national accounts and these data are not readily available.

Another technique being used more frequently is the input-output model.[7] This has an advantage over the other techniques, except for the macroeconomic models, because it can be used to trace out impacts of predetermined changes in some of the variables. Sales of each industry are classified as intermediate products going to other industries and as final products going to persons and governments and for capital formation and export. When this information is set up in a matrix form, the source of each industry's inputs is revealed and the

---

[4]James H. Brown, "Shift and Share Projections of Regional Economic Growth: an Empirical Test," JOURNAL OF REGIONAL SCIENCE, Vol. 9, No. 1 (1969).

[5]See Ralph W. Pfouts, Editor, THE TECHNIQUES OF URBAN ECONOMIC ANALYSIS (West Trenton, N.J.: Chandler-Davis Publishing Co., 1960).

[6]For examples see: Frederick Bell, "An Econometric Forecasting Model for a Region," JOURNAL OF REGIONAL SCIENCE, Vol. 7 (Winter 1967); and Dutta and Su, "An Econometric Model of Puerto Rico," REVIEW OF ECONOMIC STUDIES (July 1969).

[7]For a bibliography, see Phillip J. Bourque and Millicent Cox, AN INVENTORY OF REGIONAL INPUT-OUTPUT STUDIES IN THE UNITED STATES, Occasional Paper No. 22, University of Washington Graduate School of Business Administration, 1970.

interrelationships among industries are apparent. If one industry were to increase its output, it would buy outputs from other industries to be used as inputs and these other industries would be required to buy outputs from still other industries. Therefore, if there is an increase in the demand for final products of one industry of $1, the output generated in the economy would be greater than $1 and changes in output would occur in many industries.

By predetermining the final demand in the region, the input-output model can be used to forecast output. By making different assumptions as to the level and composition of final demand, it is possible to measure the impacts of these alternative assumptions. Input-output models require more information than other models, but they are not without shortcomings. The future final demand is determined exogenously in most models, whereas, in fact, the regional final demand should be endogenous. Moreover, it is necessary to assume that the input-output coefficients reflecting amounts that firms in a region buy from other firms in the region are fixed. Since regions are open economies with a high percentage of imports and exports, the coefficients are not likely to remain stable over time. The movement of an industry into or out of the region would have an effect on most of the coefficients.

All of the above models are applied to individual regions, although the same techniques can be applied to many regions at one time. Some of the above forecasting techniques apply to the region in isolation while forecasts from others are controlled to some degree with national forecasts. Models constructed for an isolated region suffer from a lack of control on the reasonableness of their forecast. Forecasting regional values independent of national values or values in other regions often leads to forecasts that are too optimistic or too pessimistic.

There have been very few regional forecasting models which are interregional in nature. There are several attempts to construct interregional input-output models,[8] but these are difficult to do because of the lack of interregional trade data. The interregional input-output model suffers the same shortcomings as the regional input-output model. Levels of final demand for each region are predetermined and input coefficients are assumed to remain constant. These models fail to allow for the relocation of industry.

Business firms are motivated by the desire to increase profits. They seek locations which will improve profits—areas with low costs and high demands. A firm located in an area near its major buyers and also near its major suppliers would have an advantage over firms in the same industry located elsewhere. At any given point of time, firms are not located optimally; therefore, there will always be a tendency to move to better locations. This process is slowed down

[8]See Leon Moses, "The Stability of Interregional Trading Patterns and Input-Output Analysis," AMERICAN ECONOMIC REVIEW (December 1955); Karen R. Polenske, A MULTIREGIONAL INPUT-OUTPUT MODEL FOR THE UNITED STATES, Economic Development Administration, U.S. Department of Commerce (October 1970); and David Greytak, "Regional Impact of Interregional Trade in Input-Output Analysis," PAPERS OF THE REGIONAL SCIENCE ASSOCIATION, Vol. 25 (1970).

by the fact that once a firm has located, the plant and capital equipment are fixed at that location and the firm would hesitate to relocate. Nevertheless, regional forecasting models should account for the relocation of industry.

The location of industry influences the location of final demand. A firm makes income payments and workers spend this money on consumption items. Therefore, if a new industry were to locate in an area, the consumption expenditures and other components of final demand probably would all increase. The final demand components should not be determined exogenously, but endogenously. The model presented in this book was designed to overcome the shortcomings of an interregional input-output model as a regional forecasting technique, yet it makes use of input-output relationships.

2   The Model

The Multiregional, Multi-industry Forecasting Model, referred to as the regional forecasting model, is presented in this chapter. The theoretical background of important equations and the data estimating procedures are given in later chapters. The chapter is divided into five sections. The first section describes the sectoring scheme used in the equations, the second section gives the notation used, and the third section presents the equations. The equations are explained in the fourth section, and the fifth section relates the regional model to a national model.

The Sectors

The number and names of the sectors used in this study are given in Table 2-1. Since some of the sectors require special handling in the forecasting model, the equations, as presented in this chapter, will use the numbers given in Table 2-1 as subscripts.

Industry sectors used in this study correspond closely to the Office of Business Economics (OBE) input-output sectors.[1] After the publication of the 1958 national input-output table, OBE published additional industry detail in the food and kindred products, the primary nonferrous metals, and the utility sectors. We include this additional detail in our set of industries; and, in addition, the wholesale and retail trade sector is divided into separate sectors, with retail trade further broken down into 11 types of retail outlets. OBE's industry set contains two government enterprises and three dummy industries— (1) business travel, entertainment and gifts, (2) office supplies, and (3) scrap, used and second-hand goods. Because of lack of regional data on these industries, we handle them differently. The government enterprises are considered part of final demand along with the general government. Business travel and office supplies are assumed to be a part of the business service sector and the scrap sector is dropped.

The industry sector classification is used for reporting output, employment, earnings, personal consumer expenditures, defense expenditures, exports, and imports. There are four extra labor sectors used to report employment and earnings, and two extra import sectors for imported goods that do not compete

---

[1] The Office of Business Economics has recently changed its name to the Bureau of Economic Analysis.

Table 2-1
Sectors Used in the Forecasting Model

Industry Sectors	SIC Numbers
1. Livestock	Part 01, Part 02
2. Crops	Part 01, Part 02
3. Forestry and Fishery Products	08, 09
4. Agricultural Services	071, 072, 073, 074
5. Iron Ore Mining	101, 106
6. Nonferrous Ore Mining	102, 103, 104, 105, 108, 109
7. Coal Mining	11, 12
8. Petroleum Mining	13
9. Minerals Mining	141, 142, 144, 145, 148, 149
10. Chemical Mining	147
11. New Construction	Part 15, Part 16, Part 17
12. Maintenance Construction	Part 15, Part 16, Part 17
13. Ordnance	19
14. Meat Packing	201
15. Dairy Products	202
16. Canned and Frozen Foods	203
17. Grain Mill Products	204
18. Bakery Products	205
19. Sugar	206
20. Candy	207
21. Beverages	208
22. Misc. Food Products	209
23. Tobacco	21
24. Fabrics and Yarn	221, 222, 223, 224, 226, 228
25. Rugs, Tire Cord, Misc. Textiles	227, 229
26. Apparel	225, 23, 3992, -239
27. Household Textiles and Upholst.	239
28. Lumber and Prod. Exc. Containers	24, -244
29. Wooden Containers	244
30. Household Furniture	251
31. Office Furniture	25, -251
32. Paper and Prod. Exc. Containers	26, -265
33. Paper Containers	265
34. Printing and Publishing	27
35. Basic Chemicals	281, 286, 287, 289
36. Plastics and Synthetics	282
37. Drugs, Cleaning and Toilet Items	283, 284
38. Paint and Allied Products	285
39. Petroleum Refining	29

Table 2-1 (cont.)

Industry Sectors	SIC Numbers
40. Rubber and Plastic Products	30
41. Leather Tanning	311, 312
42. Shoes and Other Leather Products	31, -311, -312
43. Glass and Glass Products	321, 322, 323
44. Stone and Clay Products	324, 325, 326, 327, 328, 329
45. Iron and Steel	331, 332, 339
46. Copper	3331, 3351, 3362
47. Aluminum	3334, 3352, 3361
48. Other Nonferrous Metals	3332, 3333, 3339, 334, 3356, 3357, 3369
49. Metal Containers	341, 3491
50. Heating, Plumbing, Struc. Metal	343, 344
51. Stampings, Screw Mach. Prod.	345, 346
52. Hardware, Plating, Wire Prod.	342, 347, 348, 349, -3491
53. Engines and Turbines	351
54. Farm Machinery and Equipment	352
55. Construction and Mining Mach.	3531, 3532, 3533
56. Material Handling Equipment	3534, 3535, 3536
57. Metalworking Mach. and Equip.	354
58. Special Industrial Machinery	355
59. General Industrial Machinery	356
60. Machine Shops and Misc. Mach.	359
61. Office and Computing Machines	357
62. Service Industry Machines	358
63. Electric Apparatus and Motors	361, 362
64. Household Appliances	363
65. Electric Light and Wiring Equipment	364
66. Communication Equipment	365, 366
67. Electronic Components	367
68. Batteries and Engine Elec. Equipment	369
69. Motor Vehicles	371
70. Aircraft and Parts	372
71. Ships, Trains, Trailers, Cycles	373, 374, 375, 379
72. Instruments and Clocks	381, 382, 384, 387
73. Optical and Photographic Equip.	383, 385, 386
74. Misc. Manufactured Products	39, -3992
75. Transportation	40, 41, 42, 44, 45, 46, 47
76. Communication	481, 482, 489
77. Radio, TV Broadcasting	483
78. Electric Utility	491, 4931
79. Gas Utility	492, 4932

Table 2-1 (cont.)

Industry Sectors	SIC Numbers
80. Water Utility	494, 495, 496, 497
81. Wholesale Trade	50
82. Finance and Insurance	60, 61, 62, 63, 64, 66, 67
83. Real Estate and Rental	65, -654
84. Motels, Personal and Repair Svc.	70, 72, 76, -7694, -7699
85. Business Services	654, 63, 7694, 7699, 81, 39, -736, -892
86. Automobile Repair Services	75
87. Amusements and Recreation	78, 79
88. Medical and Educational Instit.	736, 80, 82, 84, 86, 892
89. Lumber, Housewares, Farm, Equip. Stores	52
90. General Merchandise Stores	53, -532
91. Food Stores	54
92. Automotive Dealers	55, -554
93. Gasoline Service Stations	554
94. Apparel, Accessory Stores	56
95. Furniture Stores	57
96. Eating, Drinking Places	58
97. Drug and Proprietary Stores	591
98. Other Retail Stores	59, -591
99. Nonstore Retailers	532

Extra Labor Sectors

100. Federal Civilian Government
101. State and Local Government
102. Domestic Services
103. Armed Forces

Extra Import Sectors

100. Noncompetitive Industry Imports
101. Noncompetitive Consumer Imports

Equipment Purchasing Sectors

1. Farm
2. Mining
3. Oil and Gas Wells
4. Construction
5. Ordnance
6. Meat Products
7. Tobacco
8. Fabrics and Yarn
9. Rugs, Tire Cord

Table 2-1 (cont.)

Equipment Purchasing Sectors

10. Apparel
11. Household Textiles and Upholst.
12. Lumber and Prod. Exc. Containers
13. Wooden Containers
14. Household Furniture
15. Office Furniture
16. Paper, Exc. Containers
17. Paper Containers
18. Printing and Publishing
19. Basic Chemicals
20. Plastics and Synthetics
21. Drugs, Cleaning, and Toilet Items
22. Paint
23. Petroleum Refining
24. Rubber and Plastic
25. Leather Tanning
26. Shoes and Other Leather Products
27. Glass and Products
28. Stone and Clay Products
29. Iron and Steel
30. Nonferrous Metals
31. Metal Containers
32. Heating, Plumbing, Struc. Metal
33. Stampings, Screw Mach. Products
34. Hardware, Plating, Wire Prod. and Valves
35. Engines and Turbines
36. Farm Machinery and Equipment
37. Construction and Material Handling Equipment
38. Metal Working Machinery
39. Special Industrial Machinery
40. General Industrial Machinery
41. Machine Shops and Misc.
42. Office and Computing Machines
43. Service Industry Machinery
44. Electric Apparatus and Motors
45. Household Appliances
46. Electric Lighting and Wirings
47. Communication Equipment
48. Electronic Components
49. Batteries, X-Ray, and Engine Elec. Equipment

Table 2-1 (cont.)

Equipment Purchasing Sectors

50. Motor Vehicles
51. Aircraft and Parts
52. Ships, Trains, and Cycles
53. Instruments
54. Optical and Photographic Equip.
55. Misc. Manufacturing
56. Transportation
57. Communication
58. Utility
59. Trade
60. Finance and Insurance
61. Service
62. Dairy Products
63. Canned and Frozen Foods
64. Grain Mill Products
65. Bakery Products
66. Sugar
67. Confectionery
68. Beverages
69. Miscellaneous Foods

Construction Sectors

1. Residential
2. Additions and Alterations to Residences
3. Nonhousekeeping Residential Construction
4. Industrial
5. Offices
6. Stores, Restaurants and Garages
7. Religious
8. Educational
9. Hospital and Institutional
10. Misc. Nonresidential Buildings
11. Farm Construction
12. Oil and Gas Well Drilling and Exploration
13. Railroad
14. Telephone
15. Electric Utility
16. Gas and Petroleum Pipelines
17. All Other Private Construction
18. Highway
19. Military
20. Conservation

Table 2-1 (cont.)

Construction Sectors

21. Sewer Systems
22. Water Systems
23. Public Residential Construction
24. Public Industrial Construction
25. Public Educational
26. Public Hospital
27. Other Public Structures
28. Miscellaneous Public

Government Sectors

1. National Aeronautics and Space Administration
2. Federal Government Not Listed Elsewhere
3. Federal Government Enterprises
4. Expenditures From or Sales To the Livestock Sector
5. Expenditures From or Sales To the Crop Sector
6. Expenditures From or Sales To the Forestry and Fisheries Sector
7. Expenditures From or Sales To the Lumber Sector
8. State and Local Government

Population Age Sectors

1. Ages 14 and under
2. Ages 15–34
3. Ages 35–64
4. Ages 65 and Over

Population Race Sectors

1. White
2. Nonwhite

directly with domestic goods. Equipment is reported by 69 equipment purchasing sectors which either correspond directly to an individual industry sector or to some combination of industry sectors. There are 28 construction sectors; 17 are private, and 11 are public. Eight general government sectors are used to report data on government expenditures, excluding expenditures for construction and employee compensation. There are four population age group sectors and two race sectors used to report population, birth, and death data.

Notation

BIR_{rj}^t Births by race r of residents in region j in year t.

CLF_j^t Civilian labor force by place of residence in region j in year t.

CN_{ij}^t Construction, both private and public, by construction type i located in region j in year t.

COM_j^t Net number of commuters in region j in year t (a positive sign represents commuters coming into region j and a negative sign represents commuters going out of region j).

CPE_j^t Civilian persons employed residing in region j in year t.

CUE_j^t Civilian unemployment of persons residing in region j in year t.

D_{ij}^t Total demand for goods classified by industry i located in region j in year t.

DEF_{ij}^t Defense expenditures, excluding construction and employee compensation, for goods produced in industry i located in region j in year t.

DEH_{arj}^t Deaths by age group a, race r of residents in region j in year t.

DEN_j^t Population density (per square mile) in region j in year t.

EMP_{ij}^t Employment by labor sector i working in region j in year t.

EQ_{ij}^t Equipment purchases by equipment purchasing sector i located in region j in year t.

ERN_j^t Earnings of civilian residents and Armed Forces in region j in year t.

EX_{ij}^t Foreign exports of goods produced by industry i exiting the country through ports in region j in year t.

GOV_{ij}^t General (nondefense) government expenditures, excluding construction and employee compensation, by function type i located in region j in year t.

IM_{ij}^t Foreign imports of goods competing with goods of industry i entering the country through ports in region j in year t.

MB_{ikj}^t Major buying sector k located in region j that bought goods from industry i in year t.

MJH_j^t Number of multijob holders working in region j in year t.

MS_{ikj}^t Major supplying sector k located in region j that sold goods to industry i in year t.

NPM_{arj}^t Net population migration by age group a, race r of persons out of (or into) region j in year t.

NR Number of regions.

NY Number of forecast years.

PAY_{ij}^t Earnings by labor sector i located in region j in year t.

PCE_{ij}^t Personal consumption expenditures of goods classified by industry i in region j in year t.

PEC_j^t Population associated with change in persons employed residing in region j in year t.

PI_j^t Personal income of residents in region j in year t.

PLS_j^t Population associated with labor force surplus (or deficit) residing in region j in year t.

POP_{arj}^t Population by age group a, race r living in region j in year t.

PR_j^t Property income of residents in region j in year t.

Q_{ij}^t Output of industry i located in region j in year t.

QD_{ij}^t Output less defense expenditures of industry i located in region j in year t.

S_{ij}^t Total supply of goods classified by industry i located in region j in year t.

SS_j^t Personal contributions for social insurance of residents in region j in year t.

T_{ikj}^t Transport cost of shipping a unit of commodity i from region k to region j in year t.

TI_{ij}^t Transport cost of obtaining a marginal unit of input from industry i into region j in year t.

TQ_{ij}^t Transport cost of shipping a marginal unit of output from industry i out of region j in year t.

TR_j^t Transfer payments of residents in region j in year t.

VL_j^t Value of land per acre in region j in year t.

WR_{ij}^t Annual earnings per worker in labor sector i working in region j in year t.

c_{ik}^t Construction coefficient (national sales from industry i to construction type k per unit of total construction by type k) in year t.

e_{ik}^t Equipment coefficient (national sales from industry i to equipment purchasing sector k per unit of total equipment purchased by sector k) in year t.

g_{ik}^t Government coefficient (national sales from industry i to government function k per unit total government purchases by function k) in year t.

q_{ik}^t Input-output technical coefficient (national sales from industry i to industry k per unit of output for industry k) in year t.

f_{ik} Denotes the functional relationship in sector i in equation k.

Δ Denotes change between year t and $t-1$ (e.g., $\Delta Q_{ij}^{t} = Q_{ij}^{t} - Q_{ij}^{t-1}$).

$i{\rightarrow}k$ A matching of elements i to elements k.

ϵ Denotes "is an element of."

The Equations

The subscript j is used to denote the region, where $j = 1, \ldots, NR$. In this application of the model, data are acquired for all county-type areas in the United States; therefore, $NR = 3,111$.[2] The model could also be run with the county data aggregated into a fewer number of regions, such as the 173 OBE economic areas. If a variable does not have a subscript j, then it is a national value. The number of sectors in each sector group (see Table 2-1) is unique to the model and some equations give particular sectors special treatment; therefore, sector numbers are used as subscripts in the equations.

In the equations, superscript t ($t = 1, \ldots, NY$) denotes the forecast year, and $t-1$ denotes the prior year for which either data are available or forecasts have already been made. The parameters in the functional relationships will be estimated using counties as observations and with superscript t representing the year 1966 and $t-1$ representing 1965. The model is recursive—data for year $t-1$ are used to make forecasts for year t, then the year t forecasts become data and are used to make forecasts for year $t+1$ and so on. In this application, forecasts are made to the year 1985 with 1970 as the take-off year.

The equations are given below in the logical order needed for making the forecasts.

Government Expenditures, excluding Construction and Employee Compensation:

(2-1) $DEF_{ij}^{t} = DEF_{ij}^{t-1} \cdot DEF_{i}^{t} / DEF_{i}^{t-1}$ $(i = 1, \ldots, 99)$

(2-2) $GOV_{ij}^{t} = f_{i2}(PI_{j}^{t-1})$ $(i = 2, 3, 8)$

(2-3) $GOV_{ij}^{t} = GOV_{ij}^{t} \cdot GOV_{i}^{t} / GOV_{i}^{t-1}$ $(i = 1, 4, 5, 6, 7)$

Output, excluding Construction:

(2-4) $\Delta QD_{ij}^{t} = f_{i4}(TQ_{ij}^{t-1}, TI_{s_k j}^{t-1}, WR_{ij}^{t-1}, VL_{j}^{t-1},$ $(i = 1, \ldots, 88)$
             $Q_{ij}^{t-1}, EQ_{hj}^{t-1}, DEN_{j}^{t-1}, MB_{ijk}^{t-1},$ $(i \neq 11, 12, 75, 81)$
                                     $(k \leqslant 4)$
             $MS_{ijk}^{t-1})$ $(s_k \epsilon \max_{s} q_{si})$
                                        $(h \rightarrow i)^{s}$

---

[2]As defined by U.S. Department of Commerce, Bureau of Census. COUNTY BUSINESS PATTERNS, 1966.

(2-5) $\qquad QD_{ij}^t = \Delta QD_{ij}^t + QD_{ij}^{t-1}$ $\qquad\qquad (i = 1, \ldots, 88)$
$\qquad\qquad\qquad\qquad\qquad\qquad\qquad\qquad\qquad\qquad (i \neq 11, 12, 75, 81)$

(2-6) $\qquad Q_{ij}^t = QD_{ij}^t + DEF_{ij}^t$ $\qquad\qquad (i = 1, \ldots, 88)$
$\qquad\qquad\qquad\qquad\qquad\qquad\qquad\qquad\qquad\qquad (i \neq 11, 12, 75, 81)$

(2-7) $\qquad Q_{ij}^t = Q_{ij}^{t-1} \cdot \sum\limits_{k=1}^{88} Q_{kj}^t \Big/ \sum\limits_{k=1}^{88} Q_{kj}^{t-1}$ $\qquad (i = 75, 81, 89, \ldots, 99)$
$\qquad\qquad\qquad\qquad\qquad\qquad\qquad\qquad\qquad\qquad (k \neq 11, 12, 75, 81)$

Gross Investment:

(2-8) $\qquad EQ_{ij}^t = f_{i8}(\Delta Q_{kj}^t)$ $\qquad\qquad\qquad (i = 1, \ldots, 69)$
$\qquad\qquad\qquad\qquad\qquad\qquad\qquad\qquad\qquad\qquad (k \rightarrow i)$

(2-9) $\qquad CN_{ij}^t = f_{i9}(PI_j^{t-1})$ $\qquad\qquad\qquad (i = 1, 2, 17)$

(2-10) $\qquad CN_{ij}^t = f_{i10}(\Delta Q_{kj}^t)$ $\qquad\qquad\qquad (i = 3, \ldots, 16)$
$\qquad\qquad\qquad\qquad\qquad\qquad\qquad\qquad\qquad\qquad (k \rightarrow i)$

(2-11) $\qquad CN_{ij}^t = f_{i11}(PI_j^{t-1}, GOV_{kj}^{t-1})$ $\qquad (i = 18, \ldots, 28)$
$\qquad\qquad\qquad\qquad\qquad\qquad\qquad\qquad\qquad\qquad (k \rightarrow i)$

Construction Output:

(2-12) $\qquad Q_{11j}^t = \sum\limits_{k=1}^{28} c_{11k}^t CN_{kj}^t$

(2-13) $\qquad Q_{12j}^t = \sum\limits_{k=1}^{99} q_{12k}^t Q_{kj}^t + \sum\limits_{h=1}^{8} g_{12h}^t$ $\qquad (k \neq 12)$

$\qquad\qquad\qquad GOV_{hj}^t + DEF_{12j}^t$

Employment:

(2-14) $\qquad \Delta EMP_{ij}^t = f_{i14}(\Delta Q_{ij}^t, EQ_{kj}^{t-1}, Q_{ij}^{t-1})$ $\qquad (i = 1, \ldots, 99)$
$\qquad\qquad\qquad\qquad\qquad\qquad\qquad\qquad\qquad\qquad (k \rightarrow i)$

(2-15) $\qquad EMP_{100j}^t = f_{100,15}\left(\sum\limits_{k=2}^{7} GOV_{kj}^t\right)$

(2-16) $\qquad EMP_{101j}^t = f_{100,16}(GOV_{8j}^t)$

(2-17) $\qquad EMP_{102j}^t = f_{102,17}(PI_j^{t-1})$

(2-18) $\qquad EMP_{103j}^t = EMP_{103j}^{t-1} \cdot EMP_{103}^t / EMP_{103}^{t-1}$

$$(2\text{-}19) \quad MJH_j^t = \sum_{k=3}^{102} EMP_{kj}^t \cdot MJH_j^{t-1} \Big/ \sum_{k=3}^{102} EMP_{kj}^{t-1} \quad (k \neq 100, 101)$$

$$(2\text{-}20) \quad COM_j^t = \sum_{k=3}^{102} EMP_{kj}^t \cdot COM_j^{t-1} \Big/ \sum_{k=3}^{102} EMP_{kj}^{t-1}$$

$$(2\text{-}21) \quad CPE_j^t = \sum_{k=1}^{102} EMP_{kj}^t - MJH_j^t - COM_j^t$$

Population:

$$(2\text{-}22) \quad BIR_{rj}^t = f_{r22}(POP_{2rj}^{t-1}) \qquad (r = 1, 2)$$

$$(2\text{-}23) \quad DEH_{arj}^t = f_{ar23}(POP_{arj}^{t-1}) \qquad \begin{aligned} &(a = 1, 2, 3, 4) \\ &(r = 1, 2) \end{aligned}$$

$$(2\text{-}24) \quad PLS_j^{t-1} = (CLF_j^{t-1} - CPE_j^{t-1} \cdot CLF^{t-1} \Big/$$
$$CPE^{t-1}) \cdot \sum_{a=1}^{4} \sum_{r=1}^{2} POP_{arj}^{t-1} \Big/ CLF_j^{t-1}$$

$$(2\text{-}25) \quad PEC_j^t = \Delta CPE_j^t \cdot \sum_{a=1}^{4} \sum_{r=1}^{2} POP_{arj}^{t-1} \Big/ CLF_j^{t-1}$$

$$(2\text{-}26) \quad NPM_{arj}^t = f_{ar26}(PLS_j^{t-1}, PEC_j^t, \Delta EMP_{103j}^t, \quad (a = 2, 3; r = 1, 2)$$
$$\sum_{i=1}^{102} PAY_{ij}^{t-1} \Big/ \sum_{i=1}^{102} EMP_{ij}^{t-1})$$

$$(2\text{-}27) \quad NPM_{1rj}^t = f_{r27}\left(\sum_{i=2}^{3} NPM_{irj}^t\right) \qquad (r = 1, 2)$$

$$(2\text{-}28) \quad NPM_{4rj}^t = f_{r28}(POP_{4rj}^{t-1}) \qquad (r = 1, 2)$$

$$(2\text{-}29) \quad POP_{arj}^t = POP_{arj}^{t-1} + (BIR_{arj}^t - DEH_{arj}^t + \qquad \begin{aligned} &(a = 1, 2, 3, 4) \\ &(r = 1, 2) \end{aligned}$$
$$BIR_{arj}^{t-1} - DEH_{arj}^{t-1}) .5 + NPM_{arj}^t +$$
$$(EMP_{103j}^t - EMP_{103j}^{t-1})a_{ar} \qquad \left(\sum_{a=1}^{4} \sum_{r=1}^{2} a_{ar} = 1\right)$$

Labor Force and Unemployment:

$$(2\text{-}30) \quad CLF_j^t = f_{30}\left(\sum_{a=2}^{3} \sum_{r=1}^{2} POP_{arj}^t, PLS_j^{t-1}\right)$$

$$(2\text{-}31) \qquad CUE_j^t \quad = CLF_j^t - CPE_j^t$$

Income:

$$(2\text{-}32) \qquad PAY_{ij}^t \quad = f_{i32}(EMP_{ij}^t, EQ_{ij}^{t-1}) \qquad\qquad (i = 1, \ldots, 99)$$
$$(k \rightarrow i)$$

$$(2\text{-}33) \qquad PAY_{ij}^t \quad = EMP_{ij}^t \cdot PAY_{ij}^{t-1} / EMP_{ij}^{t-1} \qquad (i = 100, \ldots, 103)$$

$$(2\text{-}34) \qquad WR_{ij}^t \quad = PAY_{ij}^t / EMP_{ij}^t \qquad\qquad\qquad (i = 1, \ldots, 103)$$

$$(2\text{-}35) \qquad ERN_j^t \quad = \sum_{i=1}^{103} PAY_{ij}^t - COM_j^t \cdot \sum_{i=3}^{102}$$

$$PAY_{ij}^t / \sum_{i=3}^{102} EMP_{ij}^t$$

$$(2\text{-}36) \qquad TR_j^t \quad = f_{36}\left(\sum_{a=1}^{4} \sum_{r=1}^{2} POP_{arj}, CUE_j^t \right)$$

$$(2\text{-}37) \qquad PR_j^t \quad = f_{37}(ERN_j^t)$$

$$(2\text{-}38) \qquad SS_j^t \quad = CPE_j^t \cdot SS_j^{t-1} / CPE_j^{t-1}$$

$$(2\text{-}39) \qquad PI_j^t \quad = ERN_j^t + TR_j^t + PR_j^t - SS_j^t$$

Personal Consumption Expenditures:

$$(2\text{-}40) \qquad PCE_{ij}^t \quad = f_{i40}(PI_j^t) \qquad\qquad\qquad (i = 1, \ldots, 88; i \neq 81)$$

$$(2\text{-}41) \qquad PCE_{ij}^t \quad = Q_{ij}^t \cdot PCE_i^t / Q_i^t \qquad\qquad (i = 81, 89, \ldots, 99)$$

International Trade:

$$(2\text{-}42) \qquad EX_{ij}^t \quad = f_{i42}(TI_{ij}^{t-1}) \qquad\qquad\qquad (i = 1, \ldots, 99)$$

$$(2\text{-}43) \qquad IM_{ij}^t \quad = f_{i43}(TQ_{ij}^{t-1}) \qquad\qquad\qquad (i = 1, \ldots, 99)$$

$$(2\text{-}44) \qquad IM_{ij}^t \quad = IM_{ij}^{t-1} \cdot IM_i^t / IM_i^{t-1} \qquad (i = 100, 101)$$

Total Supply:

$$(2\text{-}45) \qquad S_{ij}^t \quad = Q_{ij}^t + IM_{ij}^t \qquad\qquad\qquad (i = 1, \ldots, 99)$$

Total Demand:

$$(2\text{-}46) \quad D_{ij}^t \quad = \sum_{k=1}^{99} q_{ik}^t Q_{kj}^t + \sum_{k=1}^{69} e_{ik}^t EQ_{kj} \qquad (i = 1, \ldots, 99)$$

$$+ \sum_{k=1}^{28} c_{ik}^t CN_{kj}^t + \sum_{k=2}^{9} g_{ik}^t GOV_{kj}^t$$

$$+ PCE_{ij}^t + DEF_{ij}^t + EX_{ij}^t$$

Marginal Transport Costs (Shadow Prices):

$$(2\text{-}47) \quad TQ_{ij}^t, TI_{ij}^t = f_{i47}(S_{ik}^t, D_{ik}^t, T_{ikh}^t) \qquad \begin{matrix} (i = 1, \ldots, 74) \\ (i \neq 4, 11, 12) \\ (h, k = 1, \ldots, NR) \end{matrix}$$

Other Variables:

$$(2\text{-}48) \quad VL_i^t \quad = f_{48}(PR_j^t)$$

$$(2\text{-}49) \quad MS_{ikj}^t \in Q_{hj}^t \qquad \begin{matrix} (i, h = 1, \ldots, 99) \\ (k \leqslant 4) \end{matrix}$$

$$(2\text{-}50) \quad MB_{ikj}^t \in Q_{hj}^t, PCE_{hj}^t, DEF_{hj}^t, EX_{hj}^t, EQ_{mj}^t \qquad \begin{matrix} (i, h = 1, \ldots, 99) \\ (m = 1, \ldots, 69) \end{matrix}$$

$$CN_{nj}^t, GOV_{vj}^t \qquad \begin{matrix} (n = 1, \ldots, 28) \\ (v = 2, \ldots, 9) \\ (k \leqslant 4) \end{matrix}$$

Explanation of Equations

Government Expenditures

Government expenditures are, for the most part, exogenous, although without prior information, some of the government functions are allowed to change with income. Equation (2-1) holds the regional distribution of defense expenditures by industry constant over time. Regional defense expenditures in each industry change by the same percentage as the national defense expenditures in that industry. The location of the defense expenditures is defined as the location of the production of the final products.

The forecasts of general federal government expenditures, the federal government enterprises (mostly post offices), and the state and local government expenditures are hypothesized to depend on the prior level of personal income as given in Equation (2-2). In the absence of other knowledge or assumptions about these expenditures, it is assumed that they will grow as personal income grows.

The regional distributions of other nondefense government expenditures are also held constant, with the regional levels changing only as the national levels change, as given in Equation (2-3). These functions include NASA and government purchases of livestock, crops, forestry and fisheries, and lumber. These latter four expenditure categories were given special treatment because the federal government sells as well as buys goods and services to these sectors. The data show for 1966 that the net effect of these transactions was negative for crops and forestry and fisheries. That is, on balance, the federal government sold crops from the Commodity Credit Corporation's inventories and furnished services to the forestry and fisheries industry, mostly in the form of forest management.

The forecast of any of these government sectors can be set at any predetermined level. The three Equations (2-1), (2-2), and (2-3) are used only in the absence of predetermined values. The government expenditures in these three equations do not include expenditures for construction and employee compensation, since they are handled separately.

Output, Excluding Construction

Equation (2-4) forecasts the change in regional output by industry, and it is the principal equation driving the forecasting model. The dependent variable is the change in output after defense expenditures have been subtracted from output. The independent variables are classified either as prices or agglomeration variables. Defense expenditures are subtracted out in the dependent variable because the location of defense expenditures is defined as the location of the production, and because of the practice of using cost plus contracts. The location of the goods for defense is often not influenced by the regional variation of input prices. The theoretical background of Equation (2-4) is presented in the next chapter; therefore, the discussion in this chapter is limited.

The input prices having the most regional variation are the transportation costs; therefore, the independent variables in Equation (2-4) include the marginal transport cost of shipping a unit of output out of each region and the marginal transport cost of obtaining a unit of each of the major inputs into each region. The location of commodity-producing industries is often influenced by the transportation cost of shipping the commodities to markets. Similarly, the location of industries is often influenced by the transportation cost of obtaining its most important inputs. In Equation (2-4) up to four input transportation cost variables were used for each industry, depending on the number of important commodity inputs. These transportation variables are computed using a linear programming transportation algorithm. Since they are important variables in the model, later chapters will explain the theoretical concept of these variables and describe the data that was used to derive them.

Other input prices in Equation (2-4) are the wage rate and the value of land. The wage rate is the annual earnings per worker in each industry, and the value of land is the value of agricultural land per acre. Agricultural land is used since new plants are often built on land that was previously free of structures.

Capital expenditures also can influence industry location. It is possible for interest rates and the construction costs per square foot to vary by region, thus influencing management's decision to locate new plants. Interest rates, however, do not show much regional variation since the money market is essentially a nationwide market.[3] There may be some regional variation in construction costs per square foot; but, unfortunately, we do not have the data on the square footage of construction. Therefore, we cannot use this as a variable in the equation.

Capital stock may be more important in influencing location decisions than the cost of building new plants. Once a plant has been located, it is unlikely that it will be abandoned in the short run. A firm's markets may change location, yet the firm may not change location because of the costs sunk in the existing plant. In order for it to be profitable to abandon the existing plant and build a new one elsewhere, the returns from the new location would have to be greater than the returns from the old location plus the fixed cost associated with the plant. If the plant were abandoned, the firm would still have to incur the fixed costs. In order to capture the influence of capital stock on location, the level of output and the prior equipment investment are entered into Equation (2-4). The theoretical justification for using these two variables is explained in the next chapter.

Other explanatory variables in Equation (2-4) represent agglomeration variables. Firms may locate near principal buyers and suppliers even though the transport costs of shipping output or obtaining the inputs is unimportant. Proximity to other related firms improves the communication between the firms and partially overcomes the uncertainty associated with distance. Moreover, these other firms may share the same labor market. For each industry the important buyers and suppliers of both commodities and services were identified and variables representing up to four buyers and up to four suppliers were used in the equation.

The variables representing major suppliers are the outputs of the other industries. The variables representing major buyers are the outputs of other industries when the other industries are the buyers, or expenditures by final demand sectors when sales are to final demand. For example, if an industry sells to individual consumers, then the value of personal consumption expenditures is

---

[3]Paul A. Meyer, "Price Discrimination, Regional Interest Rates, and the Structure of the Banking Industry," JOURNAL OF FINANCE (March 1967).

used as a variable to represent a major buyer. These variables are given in Equations (2-49) and (2-50).

Population density also is entered as an agglomeration variable in Equation (2-4). The greater the congestion in a region, as measured by population density, the less attractive the region will be for certain industries. On the other hand, other industries would be attracted to dense areas of a high market concentration.

Once the change in output less defense expenditures is estimated, then forecasts of total output are derived as explained in Equations (2-5) and (2-6).

The transportation and trade industries as well as the construction industries are given special treatment. The output in transportation and trade industries is measured by the markup margins of these industries. It is the difference between the value of goods when received by the industries and the value of the goods when sold by these industries. Both the trade and transportation sectors handle all types of goods and both have to be located near the sectors that they serve, although not necessarily in the same region. Therefore, as given in Equation (2-7), the output in the transportation and trade sectors was allowed to change at the same rate at which output in the regular industry sectors changed. The derivation of output in the construction industries will be discussed later.

Gross Investment

The data on gross investment include equipment purchases by 69 equipment purchasing sectors and construction by 28 types of construction. The equipment purchasing sectors are almost identical to the industry sectors, except that some of the industry sectors had to be combined in order to form one equipment purchasing sector. There is, however, a direct mapping of the industry sectors into the equipment purchasing sectors. The construction sectors include 17 private types of construction and 11 public types of construction.

Equipment expenditures by sector are forecast using the change in output of the corresponding industry or industries as given in Equation (2-8). If output increases are expected by an industry, additional equipment purchases will be necessary to produce the additional output.

Equation (2-9) shows that residential construction is forecast by relating it to personal income. The higher the personal income, the higher the expected level of construction. The personal income variable is lagged since the personal income of the current year would not be known to individuals when construction decisions are made.

Equation (2-10) shows the general form of forecasting other private construction. Each individual type of construction is related to the change in output of the appropriate industry sectors. One or more of the industry sectors can be associated with each of these types of private construction. For example, the equation for explaining industrial construction would use the change in output of all manufacturing industries.

Public construction is forecast using Equation (2-11). It is explained by the prior level of personal income, and the prior level of government expenditures in the appropriate government category. As personal income increases, tax revenues increase, and it is more likely that public construction will increase. Also, as other government expenditures increase, it is likely that public construction will increase also.

Construction Output

By definition, new construction output is the value added in the construction industry. For each dollar of construction, a certain proportion is used for buying materials and a certain proportion is in the form of income payments, such as wages to laborers. Using national coefficients for each type of construction that express the value added portion of construction, the region construction output is forecast as given in Equation (2-12). These outputs were summed over all construction types to obtain the regional output level for construction. By definition, the location of output in the construction industry is identical to the location of the demand for the construction services.

The output for maintenance construction is forecast in a similar fashion, as given in Equation (2-13). Maintenance construction sells its services to the industry sectors and to the government sectors; therefore, national coefficients were applied to industry output and the level of government expenditures to forecast output in the maintenance construction industry.

Employment

The change in employment by industry, as shown in Equation (2-14), is a function of the change in output, the lagged equipment purchases of the appropriate equipment sector, and the lagged level of output. The greater the change in output, the greater the demand for employees; although, the greater the level of equipment expenditures, the less the demand for employees, since equipment is often acquired to replace labor.

The employment in federal government as given in Equation (2-15) is a function of the federal government expenditures in the same period. As government expenditures increase, employment is expected to increase. The same type of functional relationship is used to explain the employment in state and local governments as given in Equation (2-16).

Employment of domestic servants in households as given in Equation (2-17) is assumed to be a function of the personal income of the prior period. The greater the personal income, the greater the demand for domestic servants.

The number of armed forces in each region is allowed to grow at the same rate as the level of armed forces in the nation as shown in Equation (2-18). This formula holds the regional distribution of armed forces constant, although the levels of the armed forces, just as with defense expenditures, can be predetermined for each region.

In order to forecast population, income, and unemployment by place of residence, it is necessary to convert the employment from the number of jobs by place of work to the number of persons employed by place of residence. Equation (2-19) derives the number of multijob holders. The number of multijob holders in the prior period is related to the employment in the nonagriculture, nongovernment sectors, and this rate is held constant for the forecast year. The commuters are forecast as given in Equation (2-20) by allowing the commuting rate to be held constant. The commuting rate is the net number of commuters expressed as a percent of the employment in nonagriculture and nonmilitary sectors. The number of civilian persons employed by place of residence is given in Equation (2-21). It is the sum of the jobs in a region minus the multijob holders minus the net commuters. A negative sign on net commuters indicates that residents are commuting out of a region to work in other regions.

Population

Population is forecast by age-race group. As shown in Equation (2-29), the population forecast consists of adding estimates of births, civilian net migration, and the change in military employment to the previous year's population and subtracting estimates of deaths. The births and deaths are forecast as given in Equations (2-22) and (2-23) by relating them to population.

The age breakdown of population is important in explaining population migration. There are four age groups used—namely, 14 and under, 15-34, 35-64, and 65 and over. The migration in the middle two groups, which is the working age population, is explained with the variables representing the labor conditions of the region. Net migration in these two groups, as given in Equation (2-26), is assumed to be a function of (1) the labor force surplus or deficit, modified by the labor force participation rate as defined in Equation (2-24); (2) the change in civilian persons employed, modified by the labor force participation rate as defined in Equation (2-25); (3) the change in the number of armed forces stationed in the region; and (4) the average wage rate in the region.

The change in employment and the labor surplus variables were modified by the labor force participation rate, since labor force participation varies by region. It is assumed that the population migrating into a region has the same employment opportunities as the population already there. For example, one of the reasons for the large regional variation in labor force participation rates is the availability of job opportunities for women. If the labor force participation rate is low, it is likely that there are not a high percentage of women in the labor force and the incoming female migrants are assumed to have the same opportunities as the existing female population.

Net migration for the first age group, those 14 or younger, is related directly to the migration in the working age groups as shown in Equation (2-27). Most individuals in this young age group do not migrate independently, but migrate with their parents.

Population migration in the older age group, those 65 or older, should be explained largely by noneconomic conditions. However, because of the lack of data, migration of these older people is assumed to be a function of the number of people in the age group, as given in Equation (2-28).

Labor Force and Unemployment

Labor force is assumed to be a function of the population in the working age groups, and the population associated with labor force surplus or deficit. This type of equation as given in Equation (2-30) will preserve regional variation in labor force participation rates, but will allow the rates to change with economic conditions. The labor force surplus is defined in relationship to the national unemployment rate. If a region's unemployment rate is greater than the nation's, then the region would have surplus labor. If it is lower than the nation's, then it would have a labor deficit. Studies have shown that participation in the labor force is directly related to the employment opportunities.[4] The higher the employment rate, the higher the labor force participation rate. As the national economy or regional economy slows down and the unemployment rate goes up, then the labor force participation rate goes down.

The civilian unemployment is defined as the difference between the civilian labor force and the number of civilian persons employed.

Income

The earnings by industry sector are hypothesized to be a function of the employment and equipment investment, as shown in Equation (2-32). The greater the employment, the greater the earnings. The equipment investment is used in the employment equations, since as equipment is added, there may be a tendency to reduce or slow down the rate of increase in the amount of employment. Equipment is often added to replace labor, but at the same time, it

---

[4]Sophia Cooper and Denis F. Johnston, "The Outlook for the Labor Force at Mid-Decade," Paper presented before the American Statistical Association, Chicago, Illinois (December 1964).

increases the efficiency or productivity of labor. Therefore, there is a tendency for wage rates in highly productive industries to rise, and a direct relationship between the amount of earnings and the amount of equipment would be expected.

Earnings in the extra labor sectors are directly related to the amount of employment with the wage rate held constant, as given in Equation (2-33). By definition in the national accounting system, there are no productivity changes in government and domestic service; therefore, real wages do not change. Since the forecasts are in constant dollars, these wage rates are held constant.

The earnings by place of residence as given in Equation (2-35) are derived by adjusting the earnings by place of work by assuming that the commuters have the same average wage rate as the noncommuters.

In order to derive the personal income of the region, transfer payments, property income, and military pay are added to the civilian earnings and, in order to be consistent with OBE's definition of personal income, social security payments by the workers are subtracted out. This is shown in Equation (2-39). Transfer payments as given in Equation (2-36) are assumed to be a function of the population and the level of unemployment since they include pensions, unemployment insurance payments, and welfare payments. Property income as given in Equation (2-37) is assumed to be a function of the earnings in the area. A large proportion of the property income is rental income and as earnings increase in a region, rents also have a tendency to increase. The social security payments are estimated by applying the prior year's ratio of social security payments to civilian persons employed to the current year's civilian persons employed, as shown in Equation (2-38).

Personal Consumer Expenditures

Personal consumer expenditures as given in Equation (2-40) are forecast by industry sector and they are assumed to be a function of the level of personal income. As incomes go up, consumption is expected to go up. Personal consumer expenditures in the trade and transportation sectors are related directly to output in these sectors as given in Equation (2-41).

International Trade

Regional exports to foreign countries by industry are measured at the ports of embarkation. Exports of a region are forecast as given in Equation (2-42) by relating them to the marginal transportation cost of obtaining a unit of the commodity into a region from the points of production. For example, if farm machinery is being exported, the marginal transportation variable is the cost of obtaining an additional unit of farm machinery at the port region.

Imports that are competitive with goods produced in the United States are classified by industry sector. Goods that are not competitive, such as natural rubber and mahogany lumber, are grouped into two extra import sectors. The first extra group contains those noncompetitive imports that are used as material inputs for further processing. The noncompetitive goods that are used directly by individual consumers are classified in the second extra import sector.

The competitive imports as given in Equation (2-43) are forecast by assuming them to be a function of the marginal transportation cost of shipping a unit of goods out of the port region. Just as with exports, foreign imports are measured at the ports of disembarkation. The marginal transportation cost is the cost of shipping a unit of goods out of the port region to other consuming regions in the country. The noncompetitive imports in each region are allowed to change at the same rate as the national level of noncompetitive imports as shown in Equation (2-44). That is, the regional distribution is preserved, since we do not have sufficient data to determine the commodity detail of these imports.

Total Supply and Demand

The supply of the commodities produced classified by industry is the sum of the domestic output in that industry and the competitive imports of that commodity as given in Equation (2-45).

The demand for the commodities classified by industry sectors as given in Equation (2-46) is the sum of the demand for using those commodities as intermediate goods and the demand for using them as final goods. Final demand by industry sector is available for personal consumer expenditures, defense expenditures, and exports. The industry demand in other sectors is estimated using coefficients from a national input-output model. National technical coefficients are applied to regional outputs to obtain the intermediate demand, and national equipment coefficients by equipment purchasing sector are applied to equipment expenditures totals to obtain equipment demand by industry sector. Similarly, national construction coefficients by type of construction are applied to the construction totals to obtain construction demand by industry sector, and national government coefficients are applied to government regional totals in order to obtain regional demand for government expenditures.

Marginal Transport Costs

The marginal transportation costs (shadow prices) are expressed in Equation (2-47) as a function of supply, demand, and transport rates; however, they are computed using a linear programming transportation algorithm. In order to obtain these estimates, it is necessary to have total supply and total demand by industry sector for each region and the transport cost of shipping a unit of goods between each pair of regions. Since these computations are among the most important in the model, they will be described in more detail in later chapters.

Other Variables

The value of land is forecast by relating it to the property income of the region as given in Equation (2-48). A proportion of the property income is a return from investment in land. Therefore, there should be a direct relationship between the level of property income and the land value.

The industry location equations include agglomeration variables representing major suppliers and buyers. These major suppliers and buyers were identified with a national input-output model. The major suppliers were selected by examining the columns of the input-output table. The entries in the columns show the amount of goods being supplied by other industries. The major suppliers are represented by their output levels as shown in Equation (2-49).

The major buyers were selected by examining the rows of the national input-output table. They show the sales of domestic output to the various industry and final demand sectors. A major buyer could be represented by the output of another industry, by an equipment purchasing sector, by a government sector, or by other final demand sectors as shown in Equation (2-50).

Relationship with a National Model

The regional forecasting model is designed to be used in conjunction with a national forecasting model. The national forecasts are used as controls to assure that reasonable regional forecasts are produced. Without these controls, the sum of the regional forecasts for the nation may be completely out of line with what would be expected.

Some of the equations as given above make direct use of forecasts of national input-output coefficients; but, it may not be apparent from these equations just how forecasts can be made consistent with the set of national forecasts. When the equations are used in the computer program, the variables are converted to regional shares so that the model allocates national totals. The procedures are explained in Chapter 5.

The national model used here was developed by Professor Clopper Almon of the University of Maryland,[5] and all the data in the regional model have been adjusted so as to be consistent with the data in the national model. The national model is a dynamic input-output model which forecasts the national economy under various assumptions as to final demand spending. It will be described in Chapter 6.

[5] See THE AMERICAN ECONOMY TO 1975 (New York: Harper & Row, 1966).

3

Theoretical Framework

Some of the equations in the model as given in the previous chapter require further explanation. This chapter presents the theoretical framework behind the most important equations in the model. The equations to be discussed are those concerned with industry location, gross investment, employment, population migration, and labor force. A more thorough discussion on industry location was presented in a previous volume.[1]

Industry Location

The theory behind Equation (2-4) is related to the Ricardian theory of rents. The Ricardian theory assumes that each firm supplies the same market and that firms, because of different land qualities, produce at different levels of constant cost. The supply curve of the market would be a stepped function as illustrated in Figure 3-1, with the firms ranked by their costs from the least to the highest.

Given the demand curve of the market, the price and the identity of the producing firms are determined. At the intersection of the supply and demand curves, the price is such that the costs of the marginal firm are just covered. The other firms in the industry receive rents, since their costs are lower. The vertical distance between the price line P_m and the supply curve S illustrates the per unit rent received by any of the firms. If the demand curve were to shift outward, then additional firms would start up production and the existing firms would receive higher rents. If the demand curve were to shift downward, the marginal firms would go out of business, and the remaining firms would receive lower rents.

In our model, it is assumed that the difference in the production costs of these firms is due to the location of the firms and that production in poor locations always has a tendency to move to better locations where rents are higher. The firms at the poor locations see that other firms are receiving higher rents; therefore, they always have an incentive to move to better locations. Or, firms in good locations expand their production, forcing firms in poorer locations out of business. For forecasting purposes it is assumed that equilibrium is never achieved. Rents change over time because the relocation of production

---

[1]Curtis C. Harris, Jr. and Frank E. Hopkins, LOCATIONAL ANALYSIS: AN INTER-REGIONAL ECONOMETRIC MODEL OF AGRICULTURE, MINING, MANU-FACTURING, AND SERVICES (Lexington, Mass.: Heath Lexington Books, 1972).

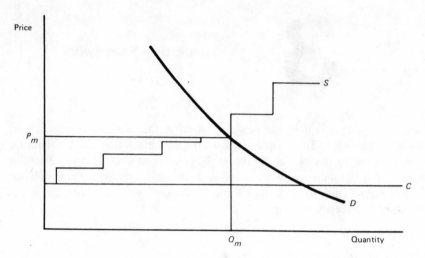

Figure 3-1. Market Equilibrium with One Market

shifts each market's supply curve, and also because the demand curves shift over time.

Now let's look at the cost items that would vary by location. Suppose all costs were the same at each location except for the wage rate. In this case, the vertical distance between the supply curve and the line C would be the per unit wage premium that some firms have to pay above the firm paying the lowest wage rate. If this represented the market situation, then the firms paying the higher wage rates would have incentive to move to locations where the wage rate was lower.[2] Therefore, the wage rate is used as a variable in Equation (2-4) to help explain the change in output. The same reasoning can be applied to other input costs. Other things being equal, firms paying higher prices for inputs will have a tendency to move to locations where the prices are lower. The handling of capital costs and transportation costs will require further explanation.

Transport Costs

If all costs were equal at all locations except for the cost of transporting the product to the market, then Figure 3-1 can be used to illustrate the rents

---

[2]It is possible that locational rents due to a particular industry's wage rate or transport costs may be partially reflected in the agricultural land values. The effect is probably not too great, however, because the land values reflect locational rents of all economic activity in the region. Empirical evidence at the county level shows that correlations between land values and factor prices of individual industries are low.

associated with shipping goods to the market. There is an additional complication, however, because most firms sell their products in more than one market at different locations. In the case of many markets, which transportation cost should be used in explaining the output change of the industry? Fortunately, transportation variables can be derived which are equivalent in concept to the one market situation by using linear programming.

In order to use the linear programming transportation algorithm, it is necessary to know the supply and demand at each location and the transport rates of shipping a commodity between the locations. Table 3-1 illustrates this problem assuming three markets and three supplying firms located in different regions. It is assumed that the firms act as competitors.

The solution to the linear programming transportation algorithm produces marginal transportation costs (shadow prices). The three markets of the example are illustrated in Figure 3-2. Market d_4 is supplied by firms s_2 and s_3. Supplier s_3 is the marginal supplier; therefore, it establishes the market price at $3. In this illustration the $3 is the marginal transportational cost. Since it is being assumed that all other costs are constant, the x-axis has been moved upwards to this constant cost line. Supplier s_2 receives a rent of $2 supplying market d_4, while the marginal supplier s_3 receives zero rent. Supplier s_3 also supplies market d_5, and the rent received there is also zero. Supplier s_1, on the other hand, supplies two markets, d_5 and d_6, and receives a rent of $1 in each market.

Table 3-1
Equilibrium Commodity Flows, Rents, and Shadow Prices

		Markets d_4	d_5	d_6	Supply	Rent α_i	Shadow Price π_i
s u p p l i e r s	s_1	0 $3	2 $4	1 $3	3	$1	$-1
	s_2	4 $1	0 $5	0 $6	4	$2	$-2
	s_3	3 $3	2 $5	0 $8	5	$0	$0
Demand		7	4	1			
Shadow Price $\pi_{\cdot j}$		$3	$5	$4			

x_{ij} ← Commodity flow from supplier i to market j

t_{ij} Unit transport cost from supplier i to market j

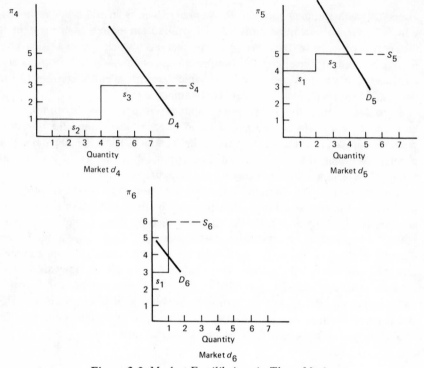

Figure 3-2. Market Equilibrium in Three Markets

As illustrated in Table 3-1, there are two sets of shadow prices. One set is the transportation costs of shipping marginal units of the commodity out of each of the supplying firms $(\pi_i.)$ and the other set is the transportation costs of obtaining marginal units of the commodity into each of the markets $(\pi._j)$. The shadow prices in the illustration have been set so that the most poorly located supplying firm has a shadow price of zero and the other supplying firms have negative shadow prices.

The market shadow prices are then computed using

(3-1) $$\pi._j = t_{ij} - \pi_i.,$$

which holds for all ij with positive shipments from supplier i to market j.

The rents received by each supplying firm as given by the a_i column in Table 3-1 are identical to the supply shadow prices (π_i) except for the change in sign. The equation for the market price (above the constant cost of production) is

(3-2) $$\pi._j = t_{ij} + a_i$$

Therefore, combining Equations (3-1) and (3-2), rent is

(3-3) $\qquad a_i = -\pi_i$.

In explaining the location of the firms in an industry, the rents (or supply shadow prices as computed from the linear programming problem) are used to represent the transportation variable of shipping the final product. Firms that receive low rents will have a tendency to relocate closer to the market in order to receive higher rents. In addition, firms are also concerned about the transportation cost of obtaining the material supplies that are used as inputs. The locations of each of the firms in the above illustration are also markets for material supplies. Therefore, in order to obtain a transportation variable representing the cost of obtaining material supplies, the linear programming algorithm is solved for these material supplying industries. For example, when trying to explain the change in output in the household furniture industry, the transport shadow prices of obtaining an additional unit of lumber at the furniture industry location would be one of the costs that would influence the location of the furniture industry. In Equation (2-4) the marginal transport cost of shipping an additional unit of the product to the market is used as an explanatory variable and up to four transport variables of the material supplying industries are used.

Capital Costs

It is more difficult to handle the cost of capital. In the decision to construct a new plant, a firm would consider the interest rates and the construction costs per square foot. However, there seems to be very little regional variation in interest rates, since the money market is largely a national market. The cost of borrowing money would probably be similar at all locations. There may be regional variation in construction costs, but it would be difficult to determine. For example, some sections of the country may require less in the way of heating equipment, but may require more in the way of air conditioning equipment. Unfortunately, we do not have data on construction costs per square foot; therefore, we cannot incorporate it into the model.

Probably the most important aspect of capital in the location decision is the existence of capital stock. Once a plan has been built, it is used for a long period of time. If market conditions change, making the existing location less favorable, it is more likely that the existing location will be phased out over a long period of time as capital depreciates. It is not likely that the plant will be abandoned in the short run and a new one constructed elsewhere.

The existence of capital stock is handled in the following way. Assume that the production function at location j for industry i is given as

(3-4) $$Q_{ij}^t = g_{i4}\,(K_{ij}^t,\ EMP_{ij}^t)$$

where K^t is defined as the capital stock that is available for use during year t to produce the quantity Q^t. It is assumed that net investment during year t is in the process of being installed during the year and will not be added to the capital stock for purposes of production until the year $t+1$. Since capital stock is fixed in location, its existence will be important in location decisions, i.e., in determining where changes in output will occur. Employment is mobile, therefore the amount of employment used by a firm is determined after output is determined and will not influence the location decision. The price of labor, however, as discussed previously, does affect location decisions. Also, the existence of a labor market may allow external economies at certain locations.

Since output is a function of capital stock and employment, the change in output is assumed to be a function of the change in capital stock and the change in employment as given in

(3-5) $$\Delta Q_{ij}^t = g_{i5}\,(\Delta K_{ij}^t,\ \Delta EMP_{ij}^t).$$

The change in capital stock is equal to net investment and net investment is equal to the gross investment (GI) minus depreciation (D) as given in

(3-6) $$\Delta K_{ij}^t = K_{ij}^t - K_{ij}^{t-1} = GI_{ij}^{t-1} - D_{ij}^{t-1}.$$

Depreciation is assumed to be a function of output as given in

(3-7) $$D_{ij}^{t-1} = g_{i7}\,(Q_{ij}^{t-1}).$$

Therefore, by adding the prior level of output and the prior level of gross investment to Equation (2-4), the influence of the existence of capital stock at various locations should be accounted for.

As given by the above argument, gross investment should enter Equation (2-4) with a positive sign and the coefficient on the prior level of output should be negative. However, the prior level of output may have some agglomeration effects on changes in output which may make the sign of its coefficient positive.

Agglomeration Variables

In addition to variables representing prices of inputs and capital stock, Equation (2-4) has a set of other variables referred to as agglomeration variables. It may be possible that a firm's location decision will be influenced by its association with other economic activity not reflected in prices. One of the variables in the equation is a congestion variable which is measured by the population density.

Some industries may achieve external economies by locating in a highly populated area, while others may achieve diseconomies because of the additional problems in congested areas, such as traffic and crime.

Firms may also wish to locate near other firms in the same industry; therefore, the prior level of output may be an important explanatory variable. The data in the model are for counties and a county may have more than one firm. If a firm has advantages of locating near other firms in the same industry, then it would select a county which has a high level of output in that industry. Firms may also wish to locate near major buyers or suppliers, even though there are no particular transport economies associated with these locations. Proximity often improves communications and reduces uncertainty. The possibility of having more frequent personal contacts with buyers or suppliers may enhance the desirability of a particular location.

Gross Investment

In a firm's decision to relocate plants or in its decision to change output, gross investment is determined simultaneously with the change in output decision. If for some reason a particular location is favorable and increases in output are planned for that location, it is necessary to plan increases in gross investment at that location. If capital stock already exists at that location, depreciated capital would be replaced there and new investment would be added. If a firm is in a poor location, then there would probably be plans to gradually phase-out production at that location. The capital would be allowed to depreciate and the investment to replace depreciated capital will be made at another location by either the same firm or another firm. Since this phasing out process takes time, the gross investment and output decisions are probably planned for several years ahead.

Investment in year t has been assumed not to be ready for use in the production process until $t+1$; therefore, the change in output between years t and $t-1$ and the investment in year t should be the function of the same set of variables as given in Equation (2-4). If prices such as transportation costs and wage rates favor different locations, then these variables will affect not only the change in output, but also the investment decision, since these decisions are essentially one and the same. For purposes of the model, it is not necessary to have gross investment as a function of all the variables as given in Equation (2-4). It is only required that gross investment would be related to changes in output, as given in Equations (2-8) and (2-10). In the model there are separate equations for equipment and construction and Equation (2-10) explains the private construction that is related to industrial production.

Employment

It would be possible to solve Equation (3-4) for employment and state that employment is a function of output and capital stock as given in

(3-8) $$EMP_{ij}^t = g_{i8}\,(Q_{ij}^t, K_{ij}^t).$$

In the previous period, the existing capital stock and employment were combined to produce output. If new equipment is added, it may either be different from the existing equipment, or it may be more of the same equipment, and there may be economies or diseconomies of scale. In either case, it would be possible for the relationship between investment and changes in employment to be different from the relationship between capital stock and the level of employment. Capital is added not only to allow production increases, but also to replace labor; therefore, the change in employment is given as

(3-9) $$\Delta EMP_{ij}^t = g_{i9}\,(\Delta Q_{ij}^t, \Delta K_{ij}^t)$$

Equation (3-6) states that the change in capital stock between years t and $t-1$ is equal to gross investment in year $t-1$ minus depreciation in year $t-1$ and Equation (3-7) states that depreciation would be a function of output; therefore, the change in employment would be a function of the change of output, the prior level of gross investment, and the prior level of output. In Equation (2-4) equipment expenditures are used instead of total gross investment, since detailed identification of construction by industry sector is lacking.

Population Migration

People migrate in order to improve their economic position and satisfaction. An individual compares his estimated income stream at his present location with what he could expect to receive at a different location, and if the present value of the gain in income computed over his working life exceeds the cost of moving, then the individual will gain by making the move.[3] This can be expressed as:

---

[3]The basic theory was developed by Larry Sjaastad, "The Costs and Returns of Human Migration," supplement to THE JOURNAL OF POLITICAL ECONOMY (October 1962), and Gary Becker, HUMAN CAPITAL (New York: National Bureau of Economic Research, 1964). Studies of the returns to migration are by John B. Lansing and Eva Mueller, et al., THE GEOGRAPHIC MOBILITY OF LABOR (Ann Arbor, Michigan: Survey Research Center, Institute for Social Research, 1963), and Richard F. Wertheimer, THE MONETARY REWARDS OF MIGRATION WITHIN THE UNITED STATES, Unpublished Ph.D. Dissertation (College Park, Maryland: University of Maryland, 1971).

$$(3\text{-}10) \qquad G_{ik} = \sum_{t=1}^{L} \frac{R_i^t - R_k^t}{(1+r)^t} - C_{ik} - P_{ik}$$

where G_{ik} is the present value of the expected gain of migrating from region i to region k

R_i^t is the real income in region i in year t

C_{ik} is the monetary cost of moving from region i to region k,

P_{ik} is the psychic cost of moving from region i to region k which may be either negative or positive,

r is the discount rate, and

L is the number of remaining working years of the individual.

In estimating the income stream from both locations, the individual would not only compare the wage rates in both areas for given occupations, but also the opportunities of stepping up on the occupational ladder. Many of the migrants improve their income position by changing occupations when they move. For example, movement from agricultural areas to urban areas usually involves a change in occupation. The chances of changing occupations in a new location would depend on the demand or growth of the occupations and the age, race, and sex of the individual.

The individual would also compare the probability of being fully employed and evaluate the uncertainty of his information. Potential incomes at other locations are often discounted because of the uncertainty as to the information, and uncertainties are often related to distance from the present location and the number of personal contacts that the individual has at the new location. If the individual has relatives at the new location or knows of other people who have migrated to the new location, then he would attach more certainty to his information. The probability of being fully employed would depend on the local unemployment rate and the age, race, and sex of the individual. Young people, because of their lack of experience, and old people, because of the short time they will be in the labor force, usually have less chance of becoming fully employed. The older a person becomes, the less likely he will be able to change occupations because of the cost and time of training necessary for a given occupation. Because of discrimination, black and female individuals often have a harder time changing occupations.

The cost of moving between two points is directly related to the distance of the move, since transport rates are related to distance. The cost of moving also includes the foregone earnings during a move and during the time that the individual needs to locate a new job. Often a mover will suffer a capital loss if he moves, since he has to sell fixed assets; and since assets accumulate with age, the older the person, the greater the likelihood of a capital loss.

The psychic cost of moving is also related to the age, race, and sex of the individual. The longer a person has been at a given location, the deeper the roots and the greater the hardship of moving away from friends. The psychic cost may often be negative, especially for young people. Young people have a desire to move away from their families, even though they may not achieve a monetary gain by moving to a different location.

A number of attempts have been made to explain migration using regression equations.[4] When gross-migration data is used, including data on the origin and destination of the migrants, it is possible to explain migration fairly well. Since the origins and destinations are known, it is possible to compute distances and to obtain measures of relative incomes and employment rates among the regions. Also, with state data from the 1960 census, it is possible to estimate the number of people who are living in region j and who have previously lived in region i.

When only net migration data is available, however, it is more difficult to explain migration. The origin or destination is not identified; therefore, it is impossible to obtain direct measures of distance and of relative incomes and unemployment rates. In a previous paper by the author, a net migration equation was suggested that would provide for some of the important determinations of migration indirectly.[5]

The equation is as follows:

$$(3\text{-}11) \qquad NMR_{ij} = b \left[\left(\frac{PCI_i}{PCI_1}, \frac{EGR_i}{EGR_1} \right), \left(\frac{PCI_i}{PCI_2}, \frac{EGR_i}{EGR_2} \right), \ldots, \right.$$

$$\left. \left(\frac{PCI_i}{PCI_n}, \frac{EGR_i}{EGR_n} \right), D_i \frac{PNW_i}{PNW_1}, \frac{PNW_i}{PNW_1} \right] \qquad j = 1, 2, \ldots, g$$

where

NMR_{ij} = net migration rate of home county i, race-age group j

PCI = per capital income,

[4]Theodore R. Anderson, "Intermetropolitan Migration: A Correlation Analysis," AMERICAN JOURNAL OF SOCIOLOGY, Vol. 56 (March 1956).

Cicely Blanco, "The Determinants of Interstate Population Movement," JOURNAL OF REGIONAL SCIENCE, Vol. 5, No. 1 (Summer 1963).

Ira S. Lowry, MIGRATION AND METROPOLITAN GROWTH: TWO ANALYTICAL MODELS (San Francisco: Chandler Publishing Company, 1966).

M.J. Greenwood, "An Analysis of the Determinants of Geographical Labor Mobility in the United States," REVIEW OF ECONOMICS AND STATISTICS (May 1969).

[5]"A Multiregional, Multi-industry Forecasting Model," PAPERS OF THE REGIONAL SCIENCE ASSOCIATION, Vol. 25 (1970).

EGR = employment growth rate,

PNW = percent nonwhite population,

n   = number of distance groups,

g   = number of race-age groups,

D   = dummy variable having a value of one if the home county is an urban county (included in an SMSA) and zero otherwise.

As discussed above, the age and race of the migrant is important in explaining his movements. The pattern of nonwhite migration has been different from the pattern of white migration and young people have a tendency to be more mobile than older people. Therefore, separate equations are specified for each race-age group. It is also possible that migration is different for males than for females, particularly for the young migrants. In the older age groups, male and female migration is often together as a part of a family move, whereas in the younger groups there would be a higher percentage of unmarried persons who migrate as individuals. The number of race-age groups as previously specified in Equation (3-11) could be expanded to the number of age-race-sex groups.

Relative income and job opportunities are measured in Equation (3-11) by expressing per capita income and employment growth rates relative to per capital income and employment growth rates in other regions. For example, distance group 1 may consist of all counties adjacent to the home county, and the second distance group may be the counties within 200 miles of the county (not including the counties in the first group). It is hypothesized that if per capital incomes in other countries are greater than the home county, then there will be net-migration from the home county, but that the counties closest to the home county would have a stronger influence than counties further away. The same reasoning is applied to the employment growth rate. The stronger the growth in other counties, the greater the out-migration from the home county, but a given relative growth rate would have more weight if it is with counties in the first group than in the other groups. By expressing these relatives in distance groups, the cost of moving and much of the uncertainty is accounted for since both are related to distance. Including the employment growth rates along with the per capital income relatives, serves to discount the relative incomes due to a probability that workers may not be fully employed.

As a measure of psychic costs, the percent nonwhite population in the home county relative to the percent nonwhite population in adjacent counties is included in the equation. Although this variable does not account for many of the psychic costs involved in migration, it may account for some of the nonmonetary influence of movements within metropolitan areas. Since it is expected that the sign on the coefficient of this variable would be different depending on whether or not the home county is an urban or nonurban county, a dummy variable is used to modify the variable. If there is a high percentage of nonwhites in an urban home county relative to the adjacent counties, then it is expected that the white migration will be out of the home county, and that the nonwhite migration will be inward. In nonurban areas, the opposite sign would be expected in explaining the nonwhite migration.

It is expected that the above formulation of a population migration equation will overcome some of the problems inherent in explaining net migration and that the equation would produce results similar to those produced from equations using gross migration. However, there are certain computer problems involved in using the above equation in the forecasting model. Since there is so much data involved in the model, the computer search process of obtaining the data for other counties that are related to the home county would involve procedures that would be too costly to handle. Therefore, in order to accommodate to the computer facilities, Equation (2-26) is used in the forecasting model instead of Equation (3-11). Equation (2-26) has per capita income as an explanatory variable, expressed as earnings per employee, but it is not relative to income of other areas. The equation uses the population associated with labor force surplus (or deficit) of the previous period as another explanatory variable. It is hypothesized that persons will have a tendency to migrate out of areas that have labor surpluses and migrate into areas which have labor deficits. Also, in the equation the population associated with the change in labor force requirements is entered as an independent variable. The final variable in the equation is the change in the number of the armed forces stationed in the region.

Labor Force Participation

Studies of labor force participation have shown that males in the prime working ages have almost 100 percent participation at all times, whereas participation of other categories shows considerable variation depending on economic conditions.[6] Women and older males go in and out of the labor force depending on the job opportunities. If the economy is in a period of expansion and there is a demand for additional labor, then females and older males will enter the labor force. If economic conditions are contracting, these people will drop out of the labor force and remain at home. Similarly, young people also vary labor force participation with economic conditions. The decision of a young person to enter college or post high school training depends on the availability of jobs.

Regional variations in labor force participation also depends on the economic

[6] Alfred Tella, "Labor Force Sensitivity to Employment by Age, Sex," INDUSTRIAL RELATIONS, Vol. 4, No. 2 (February 1965).

Thomas Darnburg and Kenneth Strand, "Hidden Unemployment 1953-62: A Quantitative Analysis by Age and Sex," AMERICAN ECONOMIC REVIEW, Vol. 56 (March 1966).

William G. Bowen and T. Aldrich Finegan, THE ECONOMICS OF LABOR FORCE PARTICIPATION (Princeton: Princeton University Press, 1969).

conditions. If a region has the type of industries that hire many females, then the female participation will be high. If the industries do not hire many females, then the region's labor force participation rate may be low. In some sections of the country women may be less apt to seek jobs because of the customs of the region.

Equation (2-30), which explains labor force, shows that the regional level of labor force can be explained by the level of population in the working age groups and by the surplus or deficit of labor in the region. The labor surplus or deficit is defined as the difference between the actual labor force and what would exist if the region had the same unemployment rate as the nation. It is modified by the labor force participation rate of the region because of the regional variation in these rates due to the regional job opportunities.

4 Data Estimates

This chapter describes the procedures for estimating the 1965 and 1966 county data required in the forecasting model. The chapter is divided into six major sections: (1) Supply, (2) Demand, (3) Labor, (4) Income, (5) Population and Migration, and (6) Transportation Costs.[1]

Supply

Total county supply by industry is the sum of domestic output and foreign imports, measured at the ports of entry. The imports that are added to output by input-output industry sector are those defined as "competitive" with goods produced by domestic industry. Other imports are not classified by input-output sector since the goods have no domestic equivalents.

Domestic Output

County output figures are not directly available for any of the industries for the years 1965 and 1966. In order to make the estimates, it was necessary to apply either output-payroll ratios or output-employment ratios to county payroll or employment figures respectively. In the manufacturing industries, state output-payrolls for 1965 and 1966 were available and were applied to county payroll figures. In some service sectors, county output-employment ratios were obtained for 1963 and used in estimates for 1965 and 1966. Whenever possible, output-payroll ratios were used instead of output-employment ratios because payrolls are more closely related to output, reflecting changes in the number of hours worked.

A summary of the county output estimating procedures is given in Table 4-1.

Foreign Imports

National data by SIC groups were obtained for the value of imports by four methods of entry into the United States—(1) vessel, (2) overland from Canada,

---

[1]Except for population and income, this chapter just summarizes the more detailed description given in Harris and Hopkins, op. cit., Appendixes A, B, and C.

Table 4-1

Summary of 1965 and 1966 County Output Estimating Procedures and Data Sources by Input-Output Sectors*

Input-Output Industry Sectors	Description of Estimating Procedures and Data Sources
Agriculture IO No. 1, 2	State "value of products sold" from *Farm Income Situation* distributed to counties using 1964 county "value of products sold" from 1964 *Census of Agriculture*
Forestry and Fisheries IO No. 3	State output-employment ratios for fishing from *Fishing Statistics* times county employment from *County Business Patterns*; and national forestry output distributed to counties using county payrolls from *County Business Patterns*
Construction IO No. 11, 12	Set equal to demand
Manufacturing IO No. 13-74	State output-payroll ratios from *Annual Survey of Manufactures* times county payrolls from *County Business Patterns*
Telephone and Telegraph IO No. 76	State output estimated from number of telephone calls given in *Statistics of Communications Common Carriers* distributed to counties using employment from *County Business Patterns*
Electric Utilities IO No. 79	State output estimates from *Statistics of Electric Utilities* distributed to counties using employment in *County Business Patterns*
Gas Utilities IO No. 80	State output estimates from *Statistical Abstract of the U.S.* distributed to counties using employment in *County Business Patterns*
Trade and Selected Services IO No. 81, 84, 86, 87, 89-99	County output-employment ratios from 1963 *Census of Business* times 1965 and 1966 employment from *County Business Patterns*
Other Sectors IO No. 4, 5-10, 75, 77, 78, 82, 83, 85, 88	National output distributed to counties using payrolls from *County Business Patterns*

*All output estimates are adjusted to sum to national totals supplied by Almon's Interindustry Forecasting Project. See: Clopper, Almon *The American Economy to 1975* (New York: Harper & Row, 1966).

(3) overland from Mexico, and (4) air. The vessel control totals were allocated to counties using data in the quantity of imports by produce class by port of entry published by the Corps of Engineers in *Waterborne Commerce*. The overland imports from Canada and Mexico were allocated to customs districts along the borders using data from *Highlights of U.S. Export and Import Trade*; then the customs district data were allocated to counties along the border using

employment in the land transportation industry as reported by *County Business Patterns*. The air imports by industry sector were allocated to counties containing major international airports based on the airport's share of imported manufactured goods using data from *Highlights*.

The imports come into the United States through 209 counties. The imported commodities for each county were divided into competitive imports and others, and the competitive imports were classified into the input-output sectors. Competitive imports are those used as intermediate goods and are similar to or compete directly with goods produced in the United States.

Demand

The total county demand for each industry was derived as the sum of the various components of demand as illustrated in Table 4-2. The shaded sections of the table are the sectors for which direct county estimates were made; estimates for other sectors were made by applying national coefficients to county totals.

The intermediate (or interindustry) demand represents demand by the industry sectors for goods and services from other industry sectors that are used as inputs for the production of the outputs. For example, in order to produce steel, the primary metal industry demands iron ore from the metal mining industry. The intermediate demand for each industry's output is obtained by applying national input-output coefficients to the county outputs of all the industry sectors and summing the results.[2]

By using the national coefficients, we are assuming that the input requirements per dollar of output at the county level are the same as at the national level. There are three interrelated principal reasons why this assumption may not be valid. One is that firms in different locations may use different technical production processes, thus requiring different inputs. Another reason is that prices of the inputs may vary by county, resulting in different combinations of inputs as the firms try to minimize costs. The third reason is that since we are working with broad industry sectors, the mix of products within an industry may vary by location. Of the three reasons, the third is probably the most important; therefore, some attempt was made to correct the situation. The national input-output table, as received from Almon's project, is an estimate of a product-to-product table. Secondary products have been taken out of the industry in which they are produced and reassigned to the primary industry. For example, plants in the textile industry may also produce apparel as a secondary product, but this apparel is reassigned to the apparel industry. An industry classification represents a product classification. While this adjustment reduces the multiproduct problem in input-output coefficients, it is necessary to assume

---

[2]Obtained from Almon's Interindustry Forecasting Project, op. cit.

Table 4-2
Components of Total Demand by Industry*

	Intermediate Demand by Industry Sector 1 2 3 4 5 6 7 8 9 10 11 12 . . . 99	Final Demand							Total Demand
		PCE 1 2 . . . 12	Equipment 1 2 3 4 5 6 7 8 9 10 . . . 69	Construction 1 2 3 . . . 28	DEF 1	FG 1 . . . 7	SL 1	EX 1	
1									
2									
3									
4									
5									
6									
7									
8									
9									
10									
11									
12									
.									
.									
.									
99									
Totals									

51

*Direct county estimates are available for shaded sections. Other estimates are made using national coefficients.

Explanation of final demand sections

PCE   Personal Consumption Expenditures by 11 types of retail outlets and one nonretail outlet
Equipment   Gross private equipment by 69 purchasing sectors
Construction   Private and public construction by 28 types
FG   Federal government purchases by seven functional groupings, excluding construction
SL   State and local government purchases, excluding construction
EX   Gross foreign exports
DEF   Federal Defense Expenditures

that regional ratios of primary products to secondary products for each industry are the same as the national ratios. This assumption is necessary since the regional output data are reported on an establishment basis, and they are adjusted proportionally to sum to the national output controls which are on a product basis.

Personal Consumption Expenditures

Total county merchandise sales by 11 types of retail outlets are reported in the 1963 *Census of Business*. In addition, sales classified by 186 merchandise lines for each of the 11 outlets are available for SMSAs and rest-of-the-state areas. The first step in the estimating procedures was to adjust the census data to allow for data not reported, primarily because of the disclosure rules. Next, the sales by merchandise line were converted into sales by input-output sector.

Not all input-output sectors sell directly to consumers, and some sell services that are not reported as merchandise. Sales not going through retail outlets, e.g., medical services, were estimated by assuming that the county ratio of consumption to output for each sector was the same as the national ratio.

The last step was to update the 1963 data to 1965 and 1966. A large matrix of the 1963 data was set up with the national input-output totals as column controls and with county sales by retail outlet as row controls. Since there are 3,112 counties and 11 outlets, there were 34,322 rows in the matrix. The 1963 matrix was balanced; then the controls for 1965 and 1966 controls were substituted for the 1963 controls and the matrix rebalanced. The new control totals for 1965 and 1966 were estimated by applying a sales-payroll ratio for each outlet to the county payrolls as reported in *County Business Patterns*. The sales-payroll ratios were by state, derived from 1963 data.

Investment Expenditures

Construction by 28 different types was estimated for 1965 and 1966 for each county. Seventeen of the types were private construction and the other 11 were public construction. Data for 20 of these types were estimated using county data by type of construction from the F.W. Dodge Division, McGraw-Hill Information Systems Company. The 28 types of construction were converted into construction by the input-output producing sectors using national coefficients.

County equipment purchases were estimated for 69 different sectors for 1965 and 1966. Farm equipment purchases were estimated from farm equipment sales reported in the 1963 *Census of Business* and updated to 1965 and 1966 using the same procedures described for updating personal consumption expenditures. National construction equipment was allocated to counties using the total construction data series.

Estimates of equipment purchases by the manufacturing sectors were first made at the state level, then the county level. State estimates were made by distributing the national figures according to total investment as reported in the *Annual Survey of Manufactures, 1965 and 1966*. The state figures were distributed to countries using Dodge construction data, which were aggregated into manufacturing sectors corresponding to equipment purchasing sectors. National equipment purchases in other sectors were allocated to counties using output that has been aggregated to the appropriate equipment sectors. The county equipment by purchasing sector was converted to input-output producing sector using national coefficients.

Government Expenditures

County data on federal government expenditures by functional category were obtained from the Office of Management and Budget (OMB) for fiscal year 1968. These were used to distribute both 1965 and 1966 national totals to counties for seven types of expenditures. The national totals are for purchases of goods and services and do not include government payrolls and construction expenditures.

Total defense expenditures were distributed to counties using county data on prime defense contracts. In order to obtain the industry sales to defense, a large county-by-industry matrix was set up with the county defense expenditures as row control totals and the national industry totals as column control totals. The initial distribution of the county defense totals to industry producing sectors was made using county output of the producing sectors; then the matrix was balanced to its control totals. This procedure was used instead of using national coefficients, because the various contracts, such as for aircraft and ordnance, require different inputs. Moreover, the location of the demand for defense expenditures is being defined as the location of the prime contractor; therefore, the county defense demand for each industry must be equal to or less than the industry's output.

County estimates for NASA and general government expenditures were made using the OMB data and then converted to input-output producing sectors using the national coefficients. There were four exceptions to this rule, however, since the federal government "sells" some items to the private sectors and these transactions are recorded as negative entries in the sale of industry output to the government sectors. The government sells inventories and performs services such as meat inspection. The national entries for livestock, crops, forestry and fisheries, and lumber were allocated directly to counties using OMB data instead of using the national coefficients.

Data from the 1962 Census of Governments was used to estimate county, state, and local government expenditures. The 1962 county per capita outlays, excluding capital outlays, were applied to 1965 and 1966 populations, and then these first approximations were adjusted proportionally to sum to national controls. The county demand for state and local expenditures by industry producing sector was derived using national coefficients.

Exports

Exports were allocated in a manner similar to the method described for allocating imports. Data on quantities of exports by SIC industry sector and by port obtained from *Waterborne Commerce* were used to allocate national exports by vessel to counties. Overland exports to Canada and Mexico were allocated to customs districts using data from *Highlights of U.S. Export and Import Trade* and then to counties using employment in the land transportation industry. Exports by air for all manufacturing goods were used to allocate commodity exports by air.

Labor

The county data on employment by industry sector are the most complete and reliable data used in the model, and many of the estimates of other data series are related to them. Employment (jobs) has been estimated for the 99 industry sectors plus four additional sectors—Domestic Services, Federal Civilian Government, State and Local Government, and Armed Forces. In addition to Labor Force, other labor sectors are Multijob holders, Net Workers Commuting, and Unemployment. Table 4-3 shows the national values for these labor sectors which are used as control totals in deriving the county data.

The principal source of employment is *County Business Patterns*, which reports employees covered under the Social Security program in March of each year. Employment by industry sectors not covered by *County Business Patterns* includes agriculture, government, household, and railroad employment, and self-employed persons.

Table 4-4 gives a summary of how county estimates of these labor sectors were made. In general, the state data were derived and adjusted to the national control totals and then county data within each state were derived and adjusted to the state control totals.

The employment data in *County Business Patterns* is reported by four-digit SIC codes, but many of the entries are withheld because of the disclosure rules and because of small values. Data are published for an industry only if there are at least 100 employees or ten reporting units. When employment data are withheld because of the disclosure rules, data on the number of reporting units

Table 4-3

National Employment and Unemployment, 1965 and 1966 (Numbers in Thousands)

Job Sector	March 1965	March 1966
Employees under Social Security[a] (Industry Sectors No. 2 - 99)	47,743	50,734
Nonagricultural Self-Employed[c] (Industry Sectors No. 2 - 99)	6,845	6,612
Agriculture[b] (Industry Sectors No. 1, 2)	3,989	3,780
Railroads[d] (Part of Industry Sector No. 75)	729	711
Federal Civilian Government[e] (Labor Sector No. 100)	2,326	2,460
State and Local Civilian Government[e] (Labor Sector No. 101)	7,555	8,207
Domestic Service[c] (Labor Sector No. 102)	2,345	2,415
Armed Forces[g] (Labor Sector No. 103)	(1,616)	(1,793)
Total Civilian Jobs	71,532	74,919
Multijob Holders[h]	1,363	2,896
Net Workers Commuting	–	–
Total Civilians Employed[f]	70,169	72,023
Civilian Unemployment[f]	3,740	3,037
Civilian Labor Force[f]	73,909	75,060

[a]U.S. Department of Commerce, U.S. Bureau of Census, COUNTY BUSINESS PATTERNS, U.S. Summary 1965 and 1966.

[b]U.S. Department of Labor, Bureau of Labor Statistics, EMPLOYMENT AND EARNINGS, Table A-1, June 1965 and 1966.

[c]U.S. Department of Labor, Bureau of Labor Statistics, EMPLOYMENT AND EARNINGS, Table A-16, May 1965 and 1966.

[d]U.S. Department of Labor, Bureau of Labor Statistics, EMPLOYMENT AND EARNINGS, Table B-2, May 1965 and 1966.

[e]U.S. Department of Labor, Bureau of Labor Statistics, EMPLOYMENT AND EARNINGS, Table B-1, June 1965 and 1966.

[f]U.S. Department of Labor, Bureau of Labor Statistics, EMPLOYMENT AND EARNINGS, Table A-1, May 1965 and 1966.

[g]Military stationed in U.S. only, as of June 30, 1965 and 1966. Obtained from Directorate for Statistical Services, Office of Secretary of Defense, U.S. Department of Defense.

[h]Residual: Total Civilian jobs less total civilians employed. This represents multijob holders of employees under social security since the other categories report persons employed. The numbers appear to underestimate the actual multijob holders, probably because of under reporting in COUNTY BUSINESS PATTERNS.

Table 4-4

Summary of 1965 and 1966 County Estimating Procedures

Labor Sector	Description of Estimating Procedures and Data Sources*
Employees under Social Security by industry (No. 2 – 99)	*County Business Patterns* with adjustments for missing items
Nonagricultural Self-Employed by industry (No. 2 – 99)	State total figures from *Social Security Bulletin, Annual Statistical Supplement.* County figures derived by applying national self-employed-employee ratios by industry to county employee figures from *County Business Patterns* and summing. The county totals were adjusted proportionately to state totals, then the county industry figures adjusted proportionately to the new county totals
Agriculture (No. 1, 2)	Total state figures from *Farm Labor* distributed to counties using number of farms reported in 1964 *Census of Agriculture*; county totals divided between livestock and crops by applying national employment-output ratios to county output by sector
Railroads (Part of No. 75)	State figures from *U.S. Railroad Retirement Board* distributed to counties using the number of railroad workers reported in the 1960 *Census of Population*
Federal Civilian Government (No. 100)	*U.S. Civil Service Commission*
State and Local Government (No. 101)	State figures from *Employment and Earnings for States and Areas* distributed to counties using local government employees reported in 1962 *Census of Governments*
Domestic Services (No. 102)	Figure from 1960 *Census of Population* updated by percent change in population
Multijob Holders	Estimated by applying the national ratio of multijob holders to employees under Social Security to the county employees as reported by *County Business Patterns*
Net Workers Commuting	Net commuting rates from the 1960 Census of Population applied to workers working in a county (number of jobs less number of multijob holders)
Total Civilians Employed	Total civilian jobs less multijob holders and net commuters
Civilian Unemployment	State figures from *Area Trends in Employment and Unemployment*; county figures from (1) *Economic Development Administration*, (2) estimates by the state bureaus of employment security, and (3) estimates by applying percent change in population to county unemployment reported in 1960 *Census of Population*; county figures were adjusted to data on 150 labor market areas reported in *Area Trends* before adjustment to state figures

Table 4-4 (cont.)

Labor Sector	Description of Estimating Procedures and Data Sources*
Civilian Labor Force	Sum of total civilians employed and civilian unemployment

*Except for Multijob Holders and Commuters, state estimates were derived first and adjusted proportionately to national totals, then county figures within each state were estimated and adjusted proportionately to the state totals.

by employment size group are given. Therefore, it was possible to develop a procedure to estimate the missing data. It involved assuming average size establishments by size group and balancing industry-by-state and industry-by-county matrices for each level of aggregation given by the SIC codes. Estimated data were balanced first at the state level by major industry group, then by two-digit groups, then three-digit and four-digit groups. The estimates at each higher level were used as controls to derive estimates at the next lower level of aggregation. After state figures were estimated, then the procedure was repeated for counties within each state.

Income

The 1965 and 1966 County Personal income data used in this study are those made available by the Office of Business Economics, (OBE), U.S. Department of Commerce, with some adjustments because of incomplete coverage. The components of OBE's personal income include earnings by 12 major industry sectors, transfer payments, property income, and personal contributions to social insurance. Earnings include wages and salaries, proprietors' income, and other labor income. The data were available for nonurban counties and for Standard Metropolitan Statistical Areas (SMSAs), which may consist of more than one county. The reason given by OBE for not furnishing income for the metropolitan counties has to do with the commuting problem. The earnings data are collected by place of work and the transfer payments and property income are collected by place of residence. If these data were combined in metropolitan counties without adjustment for commuting, they would produce unrealistic personal income totals.

In addition to the lack of county data within SMSAs, there were 15 states that had a "rest-of-state" category which consisted of two or more counties for which individual county data were not reported. These county data were lumped together because converting would make the sum of the personal income components unrealistic for the individual counties. Another problem involved the independent cities in Virginia, and Menominee County in Wisconsin. The forecasting model handles these as separate entities, whereas OBE includes them as part of the surrounding counties.

Since the forecasting model requires data for a particular set of counties, it was necessary to break out the OBE data for the large geographic areas (such as SMSAs) into the component counties. The variables used to do this task are listed in Table 4-5. The county share of each category of personal income of the larger area is assumed to be the same as the county share of variables listed in the table.

Note in Table 4-5 that the two earnings categories "Service" and "Other" are combined for allocation purposes. In some counties the OBE sum of the earnings categories was not equal to the total earnings which was reported separately. This discrepancy was resolved by recomputing the "Other" category as a residual, i.e., by adding the difference between the total earnings and the sum of the components to the "Other" category. Since this procedure sometimes produced unrealistic earnings, the "Other" category was combined with the "Service" category.

Farm earnings in each county was proportioned to the livestock and crops industry sectors using the output shares in each sector. Earnings by OBE industry categories 2 through 9 were expanded to earnings by the 99 industry

Table 4-5

Allocators Used to Disaggregate 1965 and 1966 Personal Income Data of Large Geographic Areas into the Component Counties

OBE's Personal Income Category	Allocator
Earnings	
1. Farm	Output in Industry Sectors 1-2
2. Mining	Payrolls in Labor Sectors 5-10
3. Construction	Payrolls in Labor Sectors 11-12
4. Manufacturing	Payrolls in Labor Sectors 13-74
5. Transportation, Communication and Public Utilities	Payrolls in Labor Sectors 75-80
6. Wholesale and Retail Trade	Payrolls in Labor Sectors 81, 89-99
7. Finance, Insurance, and Real Estate	Payrolls in Labor Sectors 82-83
8. Services (including domestic)	Payrolls in Labor Sectors 3, 4, 84-88
9. Other (Forestry, Fisheries, Agricultural Services, and Rest-of-the-World)	
10. Federal Civilian Government	Employment in Labor Sector 100
11. Armed Forces	Employment in Labor Sector 103
12. State and Local Government	Employment in Labor Sector 101
Property Income	Total Earnings after Adjustment for Commuting
Transfer Payments	Unemployment
Contributions to Social Insurance	Private persons employed (private jobs minus multijob holders and commuters)

sectors using the county payroll data as given by the correspondence in Table 4-5. For example, total earnings in manufacturing was distributed to the individual manufacturing industries based on the distribution of payrolls among the manufacturing industries (No. 13-74).

The county payroll figures, except for domestic services, were obtained from Bureau of Census, *County Business Patterns*. The raw payroll data had the same problems as the employment data; that is, some of the figures were missing because of the disclosure rules or because of their small size. Estimates were made of this missing data by applying appropriate payroll-employment ratios to the employment estimates derived previously. The appropriate ratios were those obtained for the same industry at a higher level of regional aggregation; e.g., state, census region, or nation.[3] The county domestic service payrolls are not included in the data from the *County Business Patterns*; therefore, they were estimated by applying the national wage rate to the county employment in domestic service. Because most workers in domestic service are part-time, their payroll estimates were subtracted from the OBE earnings in the combined service and other earnings category (OBE sectors No. 8 and No. 9) before it was allocated to our industry sectors 3, 4, and 84-88. The county payroll estimates were also used to help derive output and consumption figures as discussed previously.

As given in Equation 2-35, total earnings by place of work was adjusted to total earnings by place of residence. This equation states that earnings by place of residence are equal to the sum of earnings by place of work minus the earnings associated with the net number of commuters. It was assumed that commuters have the same average nonagriculture civilian earnings rate as noncommuters. After the earnings were adjusted to a residence basis, then other components of personal income were added to earnings in order to estimate total personal income by county of residence. As given in Equation 2-39, personal income is equal to earnings plus transfer payments plus property income minus personal contributions to social insurance. The adjusted earnings were also used to allocate property income to the counties within a larger geographic area as indicated in Table 4-5.

Population and Migration

This section describes procedures for estimating 1965 and 1966 county population by 8 age-race categories. The formula for estimating migration between 1965 and 1966 is also given. There are four age groups, 14 and under, 15-34, 35-64, and 65 and older; and two race groups, white and nonwhite. In order to make these estimates, the following sets of data were obtained:

---

[3]For a detailed description, see Harris and Hopkins, op. cit., Appendix A.

1. 1960 county population by age and race, from the 1960 *Census of Population*
2. 1960, 1964-67 deaths by county of residence by age and race, obtained from the U.S. Public Health Service
3. 1965 and 1966 births by county of residence by race obtained from the U.S. Public Health Service
4. 1966 total county population estimated by the U.S. Bureau of Census, *Current Population Reports*, Series P-25, Number 247, July 31, 1969
5. 1965 and 1966 national population totals by age and race, estimated by the U.S. Bureau of Census, *Current Population Reports*, Series P-25, Number 352, November 18, 1966
6. 1965 and 1966 state population totals from *Current Population* Reports

The basic technique for estimating population is the Age-Color-Specific-Death-Rate method.[4] This simple method in at least one application has been proven as accurate as some of the highly sophisticated techniques used by the Bureau of Census.[5] For aggregate data in the United States, death rates have shown long term trends but have exhibited only small random fluctuations in the short run. If the death rates remain relatively constant, then a reasonable estimate of population in county j for age-race group i is as follows:

$$(4\text{-}1) \qquad POP_{ij}^t = POP_{ij}^0 \cdot DEH_{ij}^t \,/\, DEH_{ij}^0$$

The superscript 0 denotes values in a base period.

Estimates of State Population

State estimates of population by age-race group were made first in order to obtain control totals for the county estimates. The first approximation of the 1966 state estimates was derived using Equation 4-1 where the deaths in period t were the average deaths for three years centered on 1966 and the base period deaths and population were for the year 1960. If the reported state deaths in 1960 were zero for a particular age-race group, then the 1966 population was estimated by allowing the population in that age-race group to grow at the same rate as total population in the state.

---

[4]The Age-Color-Specific-Death-Rate method has been used to estimate components of SMSA populations by Robert C. Atchley. See "A Short-Cut Method for Estimating Population of Metropolitan Areas," JOURNAL OF THE AMERICAN INSTITUTE OF PLANNERS, Vol. 34 (1968), pp. 259-262.

[5]Bouvier finds that the Age-Color-Specific-Death-Rate method is more accurate than census methods in estimating the components of population of Rhode Island counties. See Leon F. Bouvier, "Estimating Post-Censal Population of Counties," JOURNAL OF AMERICAN INSTITUTE OF PLANNERS, Vol. 37 (1971), pp. 45-46.

The first approximations were put into a 51 by 8 matrix where the row control totals were the state population totals (including the District of Columbia as a state) and the column controls were the national population estimates by the 8 age-race groups. The matrix was then balanced using an iterative procedure that makes proportional adjustments in the population estimates in the cells first by row, then by column and repeating until the entries in the matrix sum to both the row and column control totals.

The 1965 state population by age-race groups were estimated the same way except that the 1966 estimates were used as the base population instead of 1960, and the base deaths were a three year average centered on 1966.

Estimates of 1966 County Population

When applied to 8 cells of county data, problems are encountered in using Equation 4-1 to estimate population by age-race group because of counties with a small amount of population. In 1966 there were approximately 1,000 counties with population less than 10,000. With population this small, deaths do not occur in all of the cells every year. In any given year there could be either zero deaths reported or a very small number reported. In using the above formula, deaths may be zero in the period t or the death rate in the base period may be completely unreasonable because of the small number of deaths or may be nonexistent because of zero deaths.

In order to determine if the number of deaths by age-race group in a county were reasonable, the following procedure was established. Accepting 50 deaths as the number large enough to be a reliable base on the average, a threshold population for each of the 8 cells was computed by dividing the 1960 national death rate into the number 50. If the 1960 county population in each cell was greater than the threshold population, then the 1960 and 1966 deaths were used. If not, they were rejected. Table 4-6 shows the size of the threshold population that each cell must exceed before the county deaths were used.

If the 1960 county deaths were rejected, then the appropriate state deaths for

Table 4-6
Threshold Population by Population Cell

Age Group	Race White	Nonwhite
14 and Under	21,740	10,638
15–34	45,455	21,739
35–64	6,494	3,623
65 and Older	818	829

1960 and 1966 were used; but before a state's deaths were accepted, the same test of reasonableness was applied. Even at the state level a small number of deaths in some of the cells produce unreasonable death rates. If a state's deaths were rejected, then the national deaths for that cell was used. As a further step to reduce the temporal variations in the number of deaths, the average deaths for 1965 to 1967 were used instead of the 1966 deaths in estimating 1966 population.

Even with the above safeguards, the cell composition of the estimated population in some small counties looked unreasonable, since different cells in the same county may have been estimated using different death rates. To avoid drastic changes in cell composition between 1960 and 1966, each estimate in each cell was restrained initially to an upper and lower bound computed relative to the total population in the county. These bounds were determined arbitrarily after examining means and standard deviations by race for each of the four age groups. Table 4-7 shows these upper and lower bounds, expressed as percents of the total race group. The table shows, for example, that for a given county a first approximation estimate of whites 14 and under was not allowed to be more than 40 percent or less than 20 percent of the first approximation estimate of the total number of white males in that county. If the estimate exceeded these bounds, then it was reset at the limit as specified by the bounds.

After estimates of all cells in all counties had been derived using the above described procedures, then they were readjusted to control totals using the matrix balancing procedure described above for the state estimates. A county-by-population cell matrix was set up for each state with total county population as row controls and state population by the 8 age-race groups as column controls. Then each matrix was balanced, forcing the age-race group estimates in each county to sum to the total county population and to the state totals for each age-race group.

Table 4-7

Upper and Lower Bounds for Distribution of Population by Age Within Each Race Group

	(Numbers are percent of Total Race Group)	
	Race	
Age Group	White	Nonwhite
14 and Under	20–40	25–47
15–34	15–35	17–39
36–64	23–45	15–39
65 and Over	4–16	3–13

Estimates of 1965 County Population

The 1965 county population estimates were made using the same procedure that was used for the 1966 estimates; but before they could be balanced in a county-by-population cell matrix, it was necessary to estimate total county population for 1965 since these data were not available. The first approximation of 1965 total population was estimated using Equation 4-1, but as was the case in estimating the components of population, the number of deaths was so small in some counties that the population estimates were unrealistic. If Equation 4-1 yielded unusable results then the following auxiliary equation was used:

$$(4\text{-}2) \qquad POP_j^{65} = .3POP_j^{60} + .7POP_j^{66}$$

There were two contingencies which led to a substitution of Equation 4-2 for Equation 4-1. If the number of deaths in 1960 (DEH^0) was zero, then clearly Equation 4-1 could not be used. If the growth rate from 1960 to 1965 has a sign different from the growth rate of 1960 to 1966, Equation 4-2 was used. This means that if population declines from 1960 to 1966, and Equation 4-1 estimates an increase from 1960 to 1965, we use Equation 4-2. Or, if population increases from 1960 to 1966, and Equation 4-1 estimates a decrease from 1960 to 1965, we use Equation 4-2.

In making the 1965 estimates by age-race group, the 1966 population estimates were used as the base period in Equation 4-1 instead of 1960; and the three year average of deaths centered on 1965 was used instead of 1960 deaths.

Estimates of Migration

Using the data on births, the net civilian population migration (NPM) for county j population cell i between 1965 and 1966 was computed as follows:

$$(4\text{-}3) \qquad NPM_{ij}^t = POP_{ij}^t - POP_{ij}^{t-1} - .5(BIR_{ij}^t + BIR_{ij}^{t-1} - DEH_{ij}^t - DEH_{ij}^{t-1})$$

$$- a_i(EMP_{103j}^t - EMP_{103j}^{t-1})$$

Births and deaths are averaged for two years since the population estimates are for July 1 of each year. The change in the number of armed forces (EMP_{103}) is subtracted out to obtain civilian net migration. The a_i is the proportion of armed forces in age-race group i.

It should be noted that since the data are by broad age groups and not by each individual age, the migration estimates as computed with the above equation overstate (understate) the actual net migration as given in Table 4-8. The reason for these overstatements is that the formula does not allow for the aging of individuals from one age group to the next age group. For example, persons 14 years old in year $t-1$ would move into the next age group in year t, but this is not allowed for in the equation. The sum of these overstatements is equal to zero for all age groups.

Transportation Costs

This section describes the procedures used to calculate the 1965 unit transportation costs between counties for each commodity. As is well known, the price level of transportation services is not determined by the competitive market, but is regulated by the Interstate Commerce Commission. The ICC does not set prices, but it approves or disapproves rates proposed by the carriers under criteria outlined by Congress.[6] The rate-setting procedure for each carrier is a function of intermode competition, national aims outlined in the National Transportation Acts, and provision for an adequate rate of return for the carrier. For our purposes, we can ignore the political aspects of the nation's transportation policy and concentrate upon the cost incurred by the carrier in transporting a commodity between counties and the markup that the carrier can apply to this cost. This procedure will determine the rates carriers can charge their customers. Fortunately, both the costs and the markup ratios can be obtained through publications of the Bureau of Accounts of the ICC.

There are five principal modes of transportation—rail, highway (common

Table 4-8
Overstatement (Understatement) of Migration by Age Group

Age Group	Overstatement (Understatement)
14 and Under	$POP^{t-1}_{14j} - DEH^{t-1}_{14j}$
15-34	$POP^{t-1}_{34j} - DEH^{t-1}_{34j} - (POP^{t-1}_{14j} - DEH^{t-1}_{14j})$
35-64	$POP^{t-1}_{64j} - DEH^{t-1}_{64j} - (POP^{t-1}_{34j} - DEH^{t-1}_{34j})$
65 and older	$- (POP^{t-1}_{64j} - DEH^{t-1}_{64j})$

[6]Charles F. Phillips, Jr., THE ECONOMICS OF REGULATION (Homewood, Illinois: Richard D. Irwin, Inc., 1966), pp. 441-482, reviews the historical development of transportation rate regulation in the U.S.

carrier and private truck), water, air, and pipeline; but transportation rates are calculated only for rail and highway traffic. The time and effort involved to include transport costs for the water, air, and pipeline modes would be too great considering their relative unimportance.

The rate estimating procedure for the two modes of transportation considered—rail and trucks—is expressed as

$$(4\text{-}4) \qquad {_k}C_{ij}^w = {_k}TER_i^w + {_k}LH_{ij}^w + {_k}TER_j^w$$

where

k = mode of transport, 1 for rail, 2 for truck,

i = region originating shipment,

j = region of destination,

w = weight class of shipment,

TER = terminal cost,

LH = line-haul cost

${_k}C_{ij}^w$ = total cost to carriers of a w weight class shipment between counties i and j by mode of transport k;

and

$$(4\text{-}5) \qquad T_{ij} = \sum_{w=1}^{n} a^w \left[\operatorname*{Min}_{k} \left({_k}\overset{w}{C}_{ij} \; MUP_k \right) \right]$$

where

MUP_k = markup ratio of the kth mode,

a^w = number of shipments in the unit shipment bundle of the wth weight class,

n = number of weight classifications,

T_{ij} = transportation rate of unit shipment bundle between the ith and j^{th} counties.

Equation 4-4 is the general form for calculating the cost incurred by the kth carrier for shipping a commodity between the ith and j^{th} counties. Equation 4-5 specifies the formulation used to calculate the actual rates paid to the carriers. Aggregation over all weight classes of the minimum value of the cost by mode for each weight class multiplied by the markup ratio times the number of shipments in each weight class yields the transport rate used in the forecasting model. Since trucking has lower terminal cost and higher line-haul cost than rail, small shipments will normally be shipped by truck and large shipments by rail. The resultant rates reflect not only the influence of distance between counties, but also the weight of shipment and competition between carriers for the shipment of commodities.

Terminal cost includes the expense of pickup or delivery, platform handling, and billing and collecting. Line-haul cost consists of the expense of the carrier while the shipment is actually in transit. Terminal cost is a function of shipment size, mode of transit, type of container, (e.g., railroad car), and region; while line-haul cost is a function of shipment size, mode of transit, type of container, and distance.

The distance measurements used to calculate line-haul costs were obtained from the Bureau of Public Roads.[7] These measurements are particularly useful for the location model, since they approximate actual land transportation routes, rather than the unsophisticated use of straight airline distances between counties. The weight classification of the shipments by commodity were obtained from a unit shipment bundle as a fixed number of pounds arbitrarily defines so that the pounds of shipments of the bundle by weight class reflect the relative number of shipments in each weight class.

Rail Rate Calculation

The method used to calculate rail transportation rates was derived from a paper by Roberts,[8] who applies a markup ratio classified by commodity type to out-of-pocket costs. Out-of-pocket costs are the expenses incurred by the carrier, both terminal and line haul, to transport a commodity from origin to destination, averaged over an extended time period, excluding allocation of capital equipment depreciation rates and overhead expenses. They are similar to total variable cost where the variation refers to many, not just one shipment. The markup ratios used by Roberts are ratios of revenue to out-of-pocket costs by commodity found in the ICC, Bureau of Accounts, *Distribution of Rail Revenue Contribution by Commodity Group*—1960.

The latest publication of this series is for the year 1961; however, a substitute publication, *Procedures for Developing Rail Revenue Contribution by Commodity and Territory*, is issued yearly. While not providing the ratios, it does provide the necessary statistics and outlines the method used to calculate these

[7]Glenn Brokke, NATIONWIDE HIGHWAY TRAVEL (mimeograph), Bureau of Public Roads, U.S. Department of Commerce, June 9, 1966.

[8]Merrill J. Roberts, "Transport Costs, Pricing, and Regulation," in TRANSPORTATION ECONOMICS. Compiled papers of a conference of the Universities-National Bureau Committee for Economic Research, New York, National Bureau of Economic Research (1965), pp. 3-42.

ratios for 1965. The data were listed by shipments within and between three major regions: Official (New England, Middle Atlantic, Eastern, and Mid-West), South (east of the Mississippi River) and West.

Out-of-pocket costs, rather than fully distributed costs, were used as the base to obtain estimates of the transportation rates, because of the de facto policy of the ICC in settling rate controversies. Roberts reports that in a survey of 350 ICC decisions on rate reduction controversies between March 14, 1960, and May 25, 1962, only eight of 252 that presented cost data used fully distributed cost information; the remainder used out-of-pocket cost information.[9] Thus, by not requiring fully distributed cost in its hearings, the ICC has allowed out-of-pocket costs to be the base upon which rates are formulated.

Highway Rate Calculation

The form used for calculating common carrier trucking costs was derived from *Cost of Transporting Freight by Class I and Class II Motor Carriers of General Commodities for 1965*, compiled by the Interstate Commerce Commission. The out-of-pocket costs of the motor carriers plus a markup adequate to insure sufficient revenue, including a reasonable return on invested capital, are used as the rate the common carrier would charge its customers. We assume that these charges apply to all trucking, including intrastate common carriers, and private trucking not under ICC jurisdiction.

The Motor Carrier cost information is divided into 13 regions. The regional delineation is not a simple disaggregation of the country into 13 contiguous regions, but is a hierarchy of regions, beginning with the nation (Transcontinental) and ending on an elementary level (within New England). The markup ratios that the ICC recommends be applied to out-of-pocket cost differ regionally because of regional differentials in interest rates. The truck transport rates apply to all commodities, assuming average operating conditions. Actual variations in operating conditions that affect rates include circuitry of routes, density of shipment, partial pickup and delivery service, jointness of round-trips, and running speed.

---

[9]Ibid.

5

The Equations

This chapter presents the results of fitting the functional relationships specified in Chapter 2 to 1965 and 1966 county data. The first two sections discuss the statistical procedures and the use of regional shares respectively, then the following sections give the parameters of the equations.

Statistical Procedures

Parameters in the equations used in the forecasting model were estimated using ordinary least squares procedures, although considerable control was exercised in developing the equations. The objective in estimating the parameters was not to maximize the explanatory power (R^2) of the equations, but to have coefficients that would provide an economic interpretation of the model corresponding to the theoretical specifications developed in Chapters 2 and 3.

Theil has suggested two basic procedures in specifying a model.[1] The first procedure begins with a critical set of variables in the initial regression; then additional independent variables are introduced in order of their theoretical importance in a step-wise regression program. Variables are added until a coefficient becomes insignificant, at which point the procedure stops. Theil defines this as "extending the set of explanatory variables."[2]

The second procedure orders all variables according to their theoretical importance and the initial regression includes all of these variables. Subsequent regressions are run eliminating the least important independent variables one-by-one, until the last retained variable is significant. Theil defines this as "reducing the set of explanatory variables."[3]

The procedure utilized in this study is a modification of the first procedure. Variables were ordered according to their hypothesized theoretical importance. The least-squares regression routine was set up to preserve the theoretical order of variables entering the equation, but was not terminated when one variable became insignificant.

As with most, if not all econometric models, there is some degree of linear dependency among the independent variables. If this multicollinearity is severe,

[1] Henri Theil, PRINCIPLES OF ECONOMETRICS (New York: John Wiley & Sons, Inc., 1971), pp. 603-607.
[2] Ibid, p. 604.
[3] Ibid, p. 604.

there can be drastic effects on the values of the coefficients in the model. It can increase the standard errors of the coefficients, it can be the cause of a wrong sign on a coefficient, and it can affect the magnitude of individual coefficients. Any degree of multicollinearity can have some effect on the results. In a step-wise regression, the coefficient on the fourth variable, for example, may be insignificant, but the fifth one may be significant even though the fifth variable has less theoretical importance.

In order for a variable to be retained in a particular equation of the model, it had to pass two tests in addition to the standard "t" test of statistical significance. The sign on the coefficient had to have the postulated theoretical sign and the entering variable itself could not have severe multicollinearity with other variables in the equation.

The regression routine also reexamines variables that had been rejected. Suppose the first two variables have entered the equation and the third one is rejected either because the coefficient was not significant or had the wrong sign. Now suppose the fourth variable enters the program; then before examining the fifth variable, the third one would be reexamined to see if it now passes all the tests. If the third variable had been rejected because of multicollinearity with preceding independent variables, then it would not be reexamined again since the multicollinearity cannot be reduced by the addition of another variable. If a new variable to be entered causes a previously entered variable to become insignificant or violate its sign restriction, then the new variable is dropped since the variable already in the equation is preferred by its greater theoretical importance.

The decision rule used for dropping a multicollinear variable from an equation is that a variable was rejected if the coefficient of determination (R^2) of the independent variable to be entered with those independent variables already in the equation exceeded 0.70. This rule should eliminate drastic effects on the coefficients from severe multicollinearity, but it would not eliminate all effects. Remaining multicollinearity still would cause an entering variable to affect the significance and sign of its coefficient or other coefficients in the equation. The decision rule used for the test of significance was that the "t" ratio had to be greater than one; i.e., the standard error could not exceed the coefficient.

These decision rules were designed to ease the burden in estimating the equations. The order procedure, however, in a few industry location Equations (2-4) greatly reduced the efficiency of the estimates. This occurred when a variable was accepted with a low "t" ratio and many of the subsequent variables were prevented from entering the equation because the initial variable became insignificant. Given an economic justification, the order rule was violated when this occurred in order to improve the explanatory power of the equation.

The number of observations in each equation is fewer than the number (3,111) of counties. In all equations, counties were eliminated as observations if the value of the dependent variable was zero. In addition, observations in the location equations were eliminated in some industries because of two data problems. Because of the computer limitations the transportation variables were computed directly only for those counties that had a large excess of supply or demand, and counties not in this set were assigned values of the transportation variables of the closest counties that had direct estimates. In industries where this was a severe problem, the set of observations was limited to the set that had direct estimates of the output transportation variables (TQ). The other data problem had to do with estimating missing data not reported by the Bureau of Census because of disclosure rules. After our data had been estimated, errors in the County Business Patterns data were found; and because of these errors, our matrix balancing procedure to estimate undisclosed data created some unrealistic extreme estimates of employment (and thus output) in small counties. There-fore, counties with these extreme estimates for particular industries were eliminated as observations.

The parameters for each equation were estimated independently using ordinary least squares. The structure of the model, however, indicates the possibility that some other estimating procedures may be more appropriate. For example, current output is a function of lagged variables, and current employ-ment is a function of current output. Output could be estimated using ordinary least squares, since it depends only on lagged variables; then the predicted value of output, rather than the actual value, could be used in estimating employment. This two-stage procedure was not applied since it was decided to make use of the residuals when forecasting. A discussion of the use of residuals is given in the next chapter.

The Use of Regional Shares

Given the state of regional economic forecasting at this time, it seems appropriate that regional forecasts be allocations of national forecasts. If the regional forecasts were made independently of national forecasts, it is quite possible that the sum of the regional values of particular variables would be unrealistic national numbers. There is particular danger in regional forecasting when only one region is under study since national controls cannot be used. It seems that national controls with a set of regions that includes all parts of the nation would allow more reasonable forecasts to be obtained.

It is possible that a different regional distribution of economic activity would result in different national values of economic activity. For example, if there were a perfect match between labor force and employment in all areas of the country, it is likely that the total economy would be more efficient. As it now stands, some regions have very low unemployment rates and others have very high unemployment rates. The effects of different regional distributions on the national economy would be very difficult to study. At some future time it may be possible to construct a national-regional model which would include feedbacks of regional forecasts on the national economy, but at this time it is advisable to predetermine national forecasts for use in a regional model. Therefore, the variables used in the equations are adjusted in order to make the regional forecasts of each variable sum to predetermined national forecasts of the variables.

The regional model can allocate any set of detailed national forecasts; but the only existing national models capable of producing the detail needed for the regional model are input-output forecasting models. An input-output model has advantages over other models because it consistently accounts for the interrelationships among different industries and between industry output and other economic variables. If the output of each industry were forecast separately, there is no assurance that the interrelationships would be consistent and realistic.

Maintaining consistency among industries does not necessarily mean that the interindustry relationships are held constant over time. It is possible to construct a national input-output forecasting model in which the technical coefficients change with expected technological progress. The national model best suited to use as controls for the regional model is the one developed by Professor Clopper Almon of the University of Maryland. The Almon Model is comprehensive in scope and coefficients are allowed to change over time. Moreover, the model is continually being improved with recent data and new techniques.[4]

In order to make the regional model allocate national totals, certain adjustments had to be made in the equations. If X_j^t represents the level of a variable in year t in region j, it is entered in the equations as a relative regional share, X_j^t/NX^t, where the regional value is divided by the national value. If ΔX_j^t denotes change in a variable between the year $t-1$ and t, then the variable is entered into the equation either as the absolute regional share or as the change in the relative regional share. The absolute regional share is defined as ($X_j^t - X_j^{t-1}$ $\cdot NX^t/NX^{t-1}$), and the change in relative shares is ($X_j^t/NX^t - X_j^{t-1}/NX^{t-1}$). With these adjustments, the regional shares of level variables always sum to one, and the change variables sum to zero.

Dividing the regional level by the national total will not affect the fit of the equation since the national total is a constant which is being applied to each of the regional observations. The modification of the change variable, however, may have a slight effect on the fit of the equation. If there is no change in the national total between year $t-1$ and year t, then the absolute regional share variable would be identical to the regional change. However, the larger the percent change in the national totals, the more likely that the absolute regional share variable will be different from the change variable. Experience has shown

---

[4]The model used in this study has base year of 1969. It is an updated version of the model presented in THE AMERICAN ECONOMY TO 1975, op. cit. A brief discussion of the model and its assumptions is given in the next chapter.

that these two variables when used as dependent variables in equations yield almost identical sets of coefficients on the independent variables. There is no empirical basis for choosing one or the other as dependent variables based on the fit of the equation.

When the ratio of two variables is used as an independent variable, such as the wage rate, the national total that is used to divide into the regional value is the sum of the regional ratios (wage rates). It is *not* the national value of the numerator (earnings) divided by the national value of the denominator (employment).

When a variable is entered in an equation as some form of a regional share, the sum of the regional values is always known—it is either zero or one. If the coefficients of an equation are determined in a historical period, as was done with 1965 and 1966 data, and the equation is used for forecasting, the sum of the dependent variable in the forecast year will always be equal to the sum of the dependent variable in the historical year, as long as the sums of the independent variables in the forecast year are the same as the sums of the independent variables in the historical period. This procedure assures that the regional values always sum to the national values. A less satisfactory procedure would be not to use regional shares and make proportional adjustments in the regional values after forecasts have been made.

The Government Equations

The nondefense government expenditures were divided into eight sectors as given in Table 2-1. For five of these sectors and the defense expenditures, we hold the regional distribution constant for the forecast period; and for the other three sectors, the government expenditures are explained by the personal income in the prior year. The results of Equation (2-2) are given in Table 5-1. Both the dependent and independent variables are expressed as relative regional shares.

Table 5-1
Equation (2-2) Explaining the Level of 1966 Government Expenditures

Type	No. Obsv.	R^2	Constant	1965 Personal Income
3. General Federal	950	.6223	.00017 (.00006)	.79225 (.02005)
4. Federal Govt. Enterprises	1223	.9022	−.00010 (.00003)	1.12930 (.01064)
9. State and Local Govt.	873	.8493	.00010 (.00004)	.86747 (.01239)

The Output Equations

The output equations are the driving force of the model but they also can be evaluated alone in explaining the location of industry. In an earlier book, these equations were described in detail by industry.[5] The equations presented here were developed in the same way as discussed in the previous book except that all of the variables have been expressed as regional shares.

The dependent variable is either the absolute regional share or the change in the relative regional share. If an independent variable is a level variable, then it is expressed as a relative regional share, and if it is a change variable, it is expressed as an absolute regional share. The demand for defense expenditures was assumed to be at the same location as the production, therefore, the defense expenditures have been removed from output before computing the dependent variable.

The results of Equation (2-4) are given in Table 5-2. If the dependent variable is the absolute regional share it is denoted by $\triangle QA$; if it is the change in the relative regional share the symbol is $\triangle QR$. There are no equations given for the transportation and trade sectors since the output in these sectors is measures of markup margins. Equation (2-7) show how trade and transportation outputs are forecast. Construction expenditures are estimated with 28 separate equations and the results of these equations, which will be discussed later, are used to compute the construction output as given in Equations (2-12) and (2-13).

Although the dependent variable in the location equations is the change in output, the objective in many applications of the model would be to explain the location of output levels; therefore, we compute the coefficients of determination measuring how well the regional variation in output is explained by the independent variables in the regression equation. The coefficients, also presented in Table 5-2, are computed as follows:

$$R^2\,(QD) = 1 - \frac{\sum_{i=1}^{n}(QD_i^t - \hat{QD}_i^t)^2 \cdot (n-1)}{\sum_{i=1}^{n}(QD_i^t - \overline{QD}^t)^2 \cdot (n-k)}$$

where

$$\hat{QD}_i^t = QD_i^{t-1} + \triangle\hat{QD}_i$$

and $\triangle\hat{QD}_i$ is the predicted change in output using Equation 2-4, $\overline{QD}^t$ is the mean level of output less sales to defense in year t, n is the number of observations and k is the number of variables in Equation (2-4).

---

[5] Harris and Hopkins, op. cit.

The results as given in Table 5-2 are presented in summary form in Table 5-3. The symbols + or − in the table indicate the signs on the coefficients. The signs on Q and DEN could be either + or −, whereas the signs on TI, TQ, WR, and VL were restricted to − and the signs on EQ, MB, and MS were restricted to +. The numbers in the TI columns refer to the industry numbers identifying the source of the inputs. The major buyers and suppliers are identified by symbols with industry subscripts in the MB and MS columns.

The results in Table 5-3 show that the output shadow price TQ was significant in 22 of the industry equations and at least one input shadow price, TI, was significant in 43 equations. The wage rate entered in 20 equations and value of land in 39 equations. Value of land is highly correlated with population density, therefore density with a negative coefficient entered in only 3 equations. It was significant with a positive coefficient in 10 equations.

The level of output was allowed to enter with either sign and it was significant in 69 equations. It had a negative coefficient in 47 cases and a positive coefficient in 22 cases. The level of equipment expenditures was partially responsible for explaining changes in output in 28 equations.

At least one major buyer variable was significant in 50 equations and of these equations seven contained more than one major buyer. At least one major supplier variable was significant in 32 equations with 8 equations having two major supplier variables.

The location of Basic Chemical industry, No. 35, and the Iron and Steel industry, No. 45, strongly influenced the location of other industries. The marginal transport cost of obtaining chemicals partially explained changes in output in 6 industries, and the Basic Chemical industry was significant as a major supplier in three other industry equations. The Iron and Steel industry helped explain changes in output in 6 industry equations.

The Equipment Equations

According to the reasoning presented in Chapter 2, the level of investment is related to the change in output. The same variables that explained change in output should also be used to explain investments, since these are determined simultaneously in the decision-making process.

Equation (2-8) explaining equipment by 69 purchasing sectors is given in Table 5-4. The change in output did not prove to be a very reliable explanatory variable. In 27 of the sectors the change in output either had the wrong sign or was not significant. Because of these poor results, substitute equations were run, using the level of output to explain the level of equipment investment. The fit of the substitute equation, as measured by the R^2, was an improvement over Equation (2-8) in every case; therefore, they are used in the forecasting model.

Note that there is not an equation for every equipment purchasing sector. Original county data on equipment investment were not available for the mining

Table 5-2
Equations Explaining Change in Output by Industry Sector, 1965-1966
(Constraints on the Entry of Hypothesized Variables)

1 LIVESTOCK
****
$$\Delta QR(1,T) = .0000 - .0161\ TQ(1,T-1) - .0204\ TI(17,T-1) - .0046\ WR(1,T-1) - .0439\ VL(T-1) + .1375\ Q(1,T-1)$$
$$(.0000)\quad (.0032)\quad\quad (.0031)\quad\quad (.0016)\quad\quad (.0029)\quad\quad (.0010)$$
$$+ .0012\ EQ(1,T-1) + .0027\ Q(15,T-1) + .0078\ Q(4,T-1)$$
$$(.0008)\quad\quad (.0004)\quad\quad (.0007)$$

NO. OBSV. = 1582   R-SQUARE = .9427   R-SQUARE (LEVEL OF OUTPUT) = .9991

2 CROPS
****
$$\Delta QR(2,T) = .0001 - .1149\ Q(2,T-1) - .0346\ TI(35,T-1)$$
$$(.0000)\quad (.0018)\quad\quad (.0132)$$

NO. OBSV. = 1095   R-SQUARE = .8078   R-SQUARE (LEVEL OF OUTPUT) = .9959

3 FORESTRY & FISHERY PRODUCTS
****
$$\Delta QR(3,T) = .0010 - 4.5214\ TQ(3,T-1) + .0324\ Q(3,T-1) + 1.0495\ EQ(1,T-1) - .0174\ DEN(T-1)$$
$$(.0013)\quad (4.2619)\quad\quad (.0195)\quad\quad (.5195)\quad\quad (.0163)$$

NO. OBSV. = 59   R-SQUARE = .1933   R-SQUARE (LEVEL OF OUTPUT) = .9854

4 AGRICULTURAL SERVICES
****
$$\Delta QR(4,T) = .0002 - .7549\ TI(52,T-1) - .0312\ Q(4,T-1) + .0179\ EQ(1,T-1) + .0034\ DEN(T-1) + .0121\ Q(1,T-1)$$
$$(.0001)\quad (.3677)\quad\quad (.0062)\quad\quad (.0160)\quad\quad (.0018)\quad\quad (.0093)$$
$$+ .0055\ Q(52,T-1) + .0054\ Q(17,T-1)$$
$$(.0032)\quad\quad (.0038)$$

NO. OBSV. = 376   R-SQUARE = .1032   R-SQUARE (LEVEL OF OUTPUT) = .9930

5 IRON ORE MINING
****
$$\Delta QR(5,T) = .0123 - 36.0609\ TI(55,T-1) - .1571\ VL(T-1) - .2864\ Q(5,T-1) + 1.7052\ EQ(2,T-1)$$
$$(.0072)\quad (18.3521)\quad\quad (.1567)\quad\quad (.0486)\quad\quad (.4687)$$

NO. OBSV. = 26   R-SQUARE = .6240   R-SQUARE (LEVEL OF OUTPUT) = .9651

6 NON-FERROUS ORE MINING
****
$$\Delta QR(6,T) = .0010 - 1.4175\ TQ(6,T-1) - .0969\ Q(6,T-1) + .0931\ DEN(T-1)$$
$$(.0006)\quad (1.4072)\quad\quad (.0229)\quad\quad (.0352)$$

NO. OBSV. = 125   R-SQUARE = .1640   R-SQUARE (LEVEL OF OUTPUT) = .9371

77

7 COAL MINING
****
$\Delta QR(7,T) = $ .0004 $-$ 1.4720 TI(53,T-1) $-$ .0894 VL(T-1) $-$ .0204 Q(7,T-1) $+$ .0704 Q(35,T-1)
   (.0003)   (1.1689)   (.0688)   (.0089)   (.0207)
NO. OBSV. = 110   R-SQUARE = .1395   R-SQUARE (LEVEL OF OUTPUT) = .9918

8 PETROLEUM MINING
****
$\Delta QR(8,T) = $ $-$.0000 $-$ 1.0539 TI(35,T-1) $+$ .1181 Q(8,T-1)
   (.0002)   (.6701)   (.0204)
NO. OBSV. = 357   R-SQUARE = .0919   R-SQUARE (LEVEL OF OUTPUT) = .8948

9 MINERALS MINING
****
$\Delta QR(9,T) = $ .0001 $-$ .2409 TQ(9,T-1) $-$ .2217 TI(55,T-1) $-$ .0102 Q(9,T-1) $+$ .0113 DEN(T-1) $+$ .0029 Q(40,T-1)
   (.0001)   (.0808)   (.1012)   (.0058)   (.0017)   (.0017)
NO. OBSV. = 351   R-SQUARE = .1 10   R-SQUARE (LEVEL OF OUTPUT) = .9914

10 CHEMICAL MINING
****
$\Delta QR(10,T) = $ .0153 $-$ 54.0858 TI(55,T-1) $+$ 1.4609 Q(45,T-1)
   (.0116)   (33.9587)   (1.3359)
NO. OBSV. = 13   R-SQUARE = .2123   R-SQUARE (LEVEL OF OUTPUT) = .9688

13 ORDNANCE
****
$\Delta QR(13,T) = $ .0364 $-$ 34.0472 TQ(13,T-1) $-$ 75.6839 TI(67,T-1) $+$ .0507 EQ(5,T-1) $-$ 1.2633 DEN(T-1) $+$ .1346 Q(66,T-1)
   (.0103)   (16.8725)   (25.6512)   (.0383)   (.6743)   (.0431)
NO. OBSV. = 51   R-SQUARE = .4041   R-SQUARE (LEVEL OF OUTPUT) = .9939

14 MEAT PACKING
****
$\Delta QR(14,T) = $ .0001 $-$ .0523 Q(14,T-1) $-$ .0108 VL(T-1) $+$ .0081 EQ(6,T-1) $+$ .0040 EX(14,T-1)
   (.0000)   (.0052)   (.0063)   (.0056)   (.0018)
NO. OBSV. = 361   R-SQUARE = .2655   R-SQUARE (LEVEL OF OUTPUT) = .9929

15 DAIRY PRODUCTS
****
$\Delta QA(15,T) = $ 136.6639 $-$ 231573.3203 Q(15,T-1) $-$ 307191.5508 WR(15,T-1) $-$ 100734.3301 VL(T-1) $+$ 181574.8594 EQ(62,T-1)
   (190.0027)   (41162.8398)   (261698.1797)   (21632.5459)   (29772.5210)
   $+$ 274380.4492 GOV(3,T-1) $+$ 110484.0195 Q(1,T-1)
   (38856.6050)   (55984.2349)
NO. OBSV. = 664   R-SQUARE = .1418   R-SQUARE (LEVEL OF OUTPUT) = .9974

Table 5-2 (cont)

16 CANNED & FROZEN FOODS
****
NO. OBSV. = 386   R-SQUARE (LEVEL OF OUTPUT) = .9582

$$\Delta QR(16,T) = .0023 - 1.5481\ TQ(16,T-1) - .1020\ Q(16,T-1) - .9324\ WR(16,T-1) + .0073\ Q(3,T-1)$$
$$(.0004)\quad(.9231)\qquad\qquad(.0102)\qquad\qquad(.0946)\qquad\qquad(.0058)$$

17 GRAIN MILL PRODUCTS
****
NO. OBSV. = 275   R-SQUARE (LEVEL OF OUTPUT) = .9869

$$\Delta QR(17,T) = .0003 - .7432\ TI(2,T-1) - .0313\ VL(T-1)$$
$$(.0002)\quad(.6569)\qquad\qquad(.0265)$$

18 BAKERY PRODUCTS
****
NO. OBSV. = 295   R-SQUARE (LEVEL OF OUTPUT) = .9969

$$\Delta QR(18,T) = -.0000 - .0062\ VL(T-1) + .0057\ Q(18,T-1) + .0139\ Q(17,T-1)$$
$$(.0000)\quad(.0037)\qquad\qquad(.0047)\qquad\qquad(.0060)$$

19 SUGAR
****
NO. OBSV. = 31   R-SQUARE (LEVEL OF OUTPUT) = .9929

$$\Delta QR(19,T) = .0006 - 1.7455\ TI(34,T-1) + .0335\ Q(19,T-1) + .0343\ EQ(66,T-1) - .2415\ VL(T-1)$$
$$(.0007)\quad(1.2096)\qquad\qquad(.0219)\qquad\qquad(.0128)\qquad\qquad(.1475)$$

20 CANDY
****
NO. OBSV. = 159   R-SQUARE (LEVEL OF OUTPUT) = .9969

$$\Delta QR(20,T) = .0003 - 1.2750\ TQ(20,T-1) - .0361\ VL(T-1) - .0430\ Q(20,T-1) + .0589\ PCE(20,T-1) + .1232\ Q(2,T-1)$$
$$(.0002)\quad(.8639)\qquad\qquad(.0131)\qquad\qquad(.0056)\qquad\qquad(.0231)\qquad\qquad(.1040)$$

21 BEVERAGES
****
NO. OBSV. = 372   R-SQUARE (LEVEL OF OUTPUT) = .9903

$$\Delta QR(21,T) = .0001 - .2176\ WR(21,T-1) - .0100\ VL(T-1) + .0462\ Q(21,T-1) + .0064\ Q(19,T-1)$$
$$(.0001)\quad(.1389)\qquad\qquad(.0063)\qquad\qquad(.0060)\qquad\qquad(.0057)$$

22 MISC. FOOD PRODUCTS
****
NO. OBSV. = 406   R-SQUARE = .1628   R-SQUARE (LEVEL OF OUTPUT) = .9840

ΔQA(22,T) = 3407.9449 - 5180978.5000 TI(2,T-1) - 571670.2891 WR(22,T-1) - 530776.2031 Q(22,T-1) - 81342.5156 DEN(T-1)
       (1530.1174)   (4290865.1250)   (216333.1406)   (65597.1182)   (66652.8076)

       + 169979.6504 Q(85,T-1)
         (54891.5771)

23 TOBACCO
****
NO. OBSV. = 100   R-SQUARE = .4918   R-SQUARE (LEVEL OF OUTPUT) = .9839

ΔQR(23,T) = .0015 - .2427 EMP(23,T-1) + .0735 EQ(7,T-1)
       (.0005) (.0253)   (.0148)

24 FABRICS & YARN
****
NO. OBSV. = 150   R-SQUARE = .0694   R-SQUARE (LEVEL OF OUTPUT) = .9914

ΔQR(24,T) = .0002 - .7753 TI(36,T-1) - .0582 VL(T-1) + .0208 Q(24,T-1) + .0127 Q(27,T-1)
       (.0002) (.6134)   (.0349)   (.0079)   (.0123)

25 RUGS, TIRE CORD, MISC. TEXTILES
****
NO. OBSV. = 71   R-SQUARE = .1553   R-SQUARE (LEVEL OF OUTPUT) = .9926

ΔQR(25,T) = .0001 + .0215 Q(25,T-1) - .7483 TI(36,T-1) + .0153 DEN(T-1) + .0140 Q(24,T-1)
       (.0002) (.0117)   (.7290)   (.0096)   (.0099)

26 APPAREL
****
NO. OBSV. = 756   R-SQUARE = .1331   R-SQUARE (LEVEL OF OUTPUT) = .9960

ΔQR(26,T) = .0000 - .0369 VL(T-1) + .0113 Q(24,T-1)
       (.0000) (.0035)   (.0037)

27 HOUSEHOLD TEXTILES & UPHOLST.
****
NO. OBSV. = 150   R-SQUARE = .7959   R-SQUARE (LEVEL OF OUTPUT) = .9977

ΔQR(27,T) = .0006 - .2835 TI(24,T-1) - .1205 Q(27,T-1) + .2369 WR(27,T-1) + .0533 DEN(T-1) + .0467 PCE(27,T-1)
       (.0002) (.2797)   (.0067)   (.1096)   (.0066)   (.0119)

       + .0079 Q(25,T-1)
         (.0063)

80

Table 5-2 (cont.)

---

28 LUMBER & PROD. EXC. CONTAINERS   NO. OBSV. = 798   R-SQUARE = .0138   R-SQUARE (LEVEL OF OUTPUT) = .9948
****
$$\Delta QR(28,T) = \underset{(.0000)}{.0001} - \underset{(.1370)}{.1813}\, TI(3,T\text{-}1) - \underset{(.0293)}{.0601}\, WR(28,T\text{-}1)$$

29 WOODEN CONTAINERS   NO. OBSV. = 55   R-SQUARE = .4210   R-SQUARE (LEVEL OF OUTPUT) = .9784
****
$$\Delta QR(29,T) = -\underset{(.0003)}{.0007} + \underset{(.0374)}{.1303}\, Q(29,T\text{-}1) + \underset{(.0155)}{.0161}\, EQ(13,T\text{-}1)$$

30 HOUSEHOLD FURNITURE   NO. OBSV. = 431   R-SQUARE = .0254   R-SQUARE (LEVEL OF OUTPUT) = .9758
****
$$\Delta QR(30,T) = \underset{(.0003)}{.0004} - \underset{(.2931)}{.5892}\, TQ(30,T\text{-}1) - \underset{(.5260)}{.5669}\, TI(28,T\text{-}1) - \underset{(.0072)}{.0120}\, VL(T\text{-}1) + \underset{(.0057)}{.0093}\, EQ(14,T\text{-}1)$$

31 OFFICE FURNITURE   NO. OBSV. = 206   R-SQUARE = .5415   R-SQUARE (LEVEL OF OUTPUT) = .9972
****
$$\Delta QR(31,T) = \underset{(.0002)}{.0005} - \underset{(.0062)}{.0663}\, Q(31,T\text{-}1) + \underset{(.3790)}{.9455}\, TI(45,T\text{-}1) - \underset{(.3930)}{.5302}\, TI(28,T\text{-}1) + \underset{(.0050)}{.0212}\, EQ(15,T\text{-}1) + \underset{(.0030)}{.0078}\, DEN(T\text{-}1)$$
$$+ \underset{(.0050)}{.0069}\, Q(52,T\text{-}1)$$

32 PAPER & PROD. EXC. CONTAINERS   NO. OBSV. = 354   R-SQUARE = .0997   R-SQUARE (LEVEL OF OUTPUT) = .9958
****
$$\Delta QR(32,T) = \underset{(.0000)}{.0000} - \underset{(.0841)}{.1386}\, TI(33,T\text{-}1) - \underset{(.0033)}{.0034}\, VL(T\text{-}1) + \underset{(.0051)}{.0135}\, Q(32,T\text{-}1) + \underset{(.0033)}{.0186}\, Q(34,T\text{-}1)$$

33 PAPER CONTAINERS   NO. OBSV. = 309   R-SQUARE = .0245   R-SQUARE (LEVEL OF OUTPUT) = .9602
****
$$\Delta QR(33,T) = \underset{(.0002)}{.0003} - \underset{(.5192)}{.7536}\, TI(35,T\text{-}1) - \underset{(.0178)}{.0389}\, Q(33,T\text{-}1) + \underset{(.0283)}{.0713}\, Q(15,T\text{-}1)$$

81

```
34  PRINTING & PUBLISHING
************************
                                        NO. OBSV. =  522    R-SQUARE = .0398    R-SQUARE (LEVEL OF OUTPUT) = .9996
ΔQR(34,T) = .0000 - .0425 TQ(34,T-1) - .0657 WR(34,T-1) - .0034 VL(T-1) + .0030 Q(34,T-1) + .0012 Q(73,T-1)
          (.0000)  (.0270)            (.0579)             (.0021)          (.0013)           (.0004)

35  BASIC CHEMICALS
************************
                                        NO. OBSV. =  256    R-SQUARE = .1348    R-SQUARE (LEVEL OF OUTPUT) = .9933
ΔQR(35,T) = .0002 - .5647 TI(49,T-1) - .0318 Q(35,T-1)
          (.0002)  (.4792)            (.0051)

36  PLASTICS & SYNTHETICS
************************
                                        NO. OBSV. =  358    R-SQUARE = .0 95    R-SQUARE (LEVEL OF OUTPUT) = .9095
ΔQR(36,T) = .0004 - .2749 WR(36,T-1) + .0204 EQ(20,T-1)
          (.0004)  (.2043)            (.0066)

37  DRUGS, CLEANING & TOILET ITEMS
************************
                                        NO. OBSV. =  223    R-SQUARE = .1394    R-SQUARE (LEVEL OF OUTPUT) = .9405
ΔQR(37,T) = .0028 - 1.6988 TQ(37,T-1) - .0823 Q(37,T-1) - .0523 VL(T-1) - 6.1036 TI(49,T-1)
          (.0013)  (1.0847)            (.0162)           (.0237)          (3.8985)

38  PAINT & ALLIED PRODUCTS
************************
                                        NO. OBSV. =   59    R-SQUARE = .1650    R-SQUARE (LEVEL OF OUTPUT) = .9976
ΔQR(38,T) = .0016 - 4.7143 TQ(38,T-1) + .0192 Q(38,T-1)
          (.0015)  (4.0226)            (.0068)

39  PETROLEUM REFINING
************************
                                        NO. OBSV. =  240    R-SQUARE = .0371    R-SQUARE (LEVEL OF OUTPUT) = .9872
ΔQR(39,T) = .0007 - .5994 TQ(39,T-1) + .0236 PCE(39,T-1)
          (.0002)  (.4967)            (.0208)

40  RUBBER & PLASTIC PRODUCTS
************************
                                        NO. OBSV. =  414    R-SQUARE = .2387    R-SQUARE (LEVEL OF OUTPUT) = .9813
ΔQR(40,T) = .0002 - .4642 TI(36,T-1) + .0863 Q(40,T-1) + .0089 EQ(24,T-1) + .1157 PCE(40,T-1)
          (.0001)  (.4216)            (.0079)           (.0088)            (.0187)
```

82

Table 5-2 (cont.)

41 LEATHER TANNING
****
ΔQR(41,T) = .0004 - 1.6934 TI(35,T-1) + .0110 Q(26,T-1)
         (.0007)   (1.5188)   (.0085)
NO. OBSV. = 46   R-SQUARE = .3244   R-SQUARE (LEVEL OF OUTPUT) = .9982

42 SHOES & OTHER LEATHER PRODUCTS
****
ΔQR(42,T) = -.0001 + .0086 Q(42,T-1) + .0060 EQ(26,T-1) + .0173 DEN(T-1)
          (.0000)   (.0055)   (.0041)   (.0041)
NO. OBSV. = 211   R-SQUARE = .2608   R-SQUARE (LEVEL OF OUTPUT) = .9965

43 GLASS & GLASS PRODUCTS
****
ΔQR(43,T) = .0002 - 1.1762 TQ(43,T-1) + .0170 Q(43,T-1) + .0117 Q(69,T-1)
         (.0002)   (.5685)   (.0080)   (.0046)
NO. OBSV. = 141   R-SQUARE = .1186   R-SQUARE (LEVEL OF OUTPUT) = .9923

44 STONE & CLAY PRODUCTS
****
ΔQA(44,T) = 636.0934 - 2150962.8125 TI(32,T-1) - 184869.7109 Q(44,T-1) + 23885.6531 EQ(28,T-1) + 34357.2241 DEN(T-1)
         (283.3909)   (861478.9531)   (51257.7310)   (23731.6150)   (21331.6970)
        + 86207.7061 CN(18,T-1) + 78821.9473 Q(35,T-1)
         (70839.6865)   (37073.9600)
NO. OBSV. = 688   R-SQUARE = .0339   R-SQUARE (LEVEL OF OUTPUT) = .9932

45 IRON & STEEL
****
ΔQR(45,T) = .0011 - 1.5778 TI(5,T-1) - .4397 TI(35,T-1) - .3765 WR(45,T-1) + .0054 Q(69,T-1)
         (.0005)   (1.0802)   (.4251)   (.2362)   (.0047)
NO. OBSV. = 377   R-SQUARE = .0185   R-SQUARE (LEVEL OF OUTPUT) = .9844

46 COPPER
****
ΔQR(46,T) = .0006 - 4.5443 TI(48,T-1) - .0268 Q(46,T-1) + .0659 EQ(30,T-1)
         (.0007)   (2.3333)   (.0169)   (.0389)
NO. OBSV. = 61   R-SQUARE = .1177   R-SQUARE (LEVEL OF OUTPUT) = .9863

83

47 ALUMINUM
****
NO. OBSV. = 81   R-SQUARE = .4991   R-SQUARE (LEVEL OF OUTPUT) = .9812

$\Delta QR(47,T) = .0011 - 1.8827\ TQ(47,T-1) - .1419\ Q(47,T-1) + .0401\ Q(50,T-1)$
$\qquad\quad (.0005)\ (1.3384)\qquad\qquad (.0177)\qquad\qquad (.0208)$

48 OTHER NON-FERROUS METALS
****
NO. OBSV. = 84   R-SQUARE = .4090   R-SQUARE (LEVEL OF OUTPUT) = .9922

$\Delta QR(48,T) = .0007 - .4047\ WR(48,T-1) + .0759\ Q(48,T-1) + .0162\ Q(45,T-1)$
$\qquad\quad (.0005)\ (.1981)\qquad\qquad (.0131)\qquad\qquad (.0161)$

49 METAL CONTAINERS
****
NO. OBSV. = 46   R-SQUARE = .2494   R-SQUARE (LEVEL OF OUTPUT) = .9964

$\Delta QR(49,T) = .0001 - .1682\ VL(T-1) - .0440\ Q(49,T-1) + .0517\ Q(21,T-1) + .0356\ Q(37,T-1)$
$\qquad\quad (.0003)\ (.0867)\qquad (.0172)\qquad\quad (.0263)\qquad\quad (.0202)$

50 HEATING, PLUMBING, STRUC METAL
****
NO. OBSV. = 477   R-SQUARE = .0237   R-SQUARE (LEVEL OF OUTPUT) = .9866

$\Delta QR(50,T) = .0000 - .0134\ VL(T-1) - .0264\ Q(50,T-1) + .0135\ Q(52,T-1) + .0083\ Q(85,T-1)$
$\qquad\quad (.0000)\ (.0064)\qquad (.0096)\qquad\quad (.0072)\qquad\quad (.0043)$

51 STAMPINGS, SCREW MACHINE PROD.
****
NO. OBSV. = 168   R-SQUARE = .4295   R-SQUARE (LEVEL OF OUTPUT) = .9957

$\Delta QR(51,T) = .0004 - 2.5248\ TQ(51,T-1) - .0160\ VL(T-1) + .0127\ Q(51,T-1) + .0424\ Q(69,T-1)$
$\qquad\quad (.0002)\ (.7963)\qquad\qquad (.0139)\qquad\quad (.0067)\qquad\quad (.0054)$

52 HARDWARE, PLATING, WIRE PROD.
****
NO. OBSV. = 221   R-SQUARE = .3488   R-SQUARE (LEVEL OF OUTPUT) = .9967

$\Delta QR(52,T) = -.0000 - .0979\ Q(52,T-1) - .0250\ VL(T-1) + .0209\ EQ(34,T-1) + .0535\ Q(50,T-1) + .0399\ Q(48,T-1)$
$\qquad\quad (.0000)\ (.0102)\qquad (.0064)\qquad\quad (.0051)\qquad\qquad (.0099)\qquad\quad (.0063)$
$\qquad\quad + .0165\ Q(85,T-1)$
$\qquad\qquad (.0041)$

53 ENGINES & TURBINES
****
NO. OBSV. = 142   R-SQUARE = .2401   R-SQUARE (LEVEL OF OUTPUT) = .9367

$\Delta QR(53,T) = .0040 - 10.2779\ TI(45,T-1) - .4442\ WR(53,T-1) - .0533\ VL(T-1) - .1068\ Q(53,T-1) + .2392\ EQ(58,T-1)$
$\qquad\quad (.0016)\ (3.1101)\qquad\qquad (.3898)\qquad\qquad (.0438)\qquad (.0224)\qquad\quad (.0557)$

Table 5-2 (cont.)

54 FARM MACHINERY & EQUIPMENT
****
NO. OBSV. = 118   R-SQUARE = .3483   R-SQUARE (LEVEL OF OUTPUT) = .9967

$\Delta QR(54,T) = -.0002 + .0415\ Q(54,T-1) + .0181\ Q(53,T-1)$
     (.0001)   (.0058)   (.0119)

55 CONSTRUCTION & MINING MACHINES
****
NO. OBSV. = 120   R-SQUARE = .3441   R-SQUARE (LEVEL OF OUTPUT) = .9944

$\Delta QR(55,T) = .0000 - .0613\ Q(55,T-1) + .0646\ EQ(3,T-1) + .0776\ Q(53,T-1)$
     (.0001)   (.0102)   (.0186)   (.0101)

56 MATERIAL HANDLING EQUIPMENT
****
NO. OBSV. = 64   R-SQUARE = .1792   R-SQUARE (LEVEL OF OUTPUT) = .9933

$\Delta QR(56,T) = .0004 - 1.7668\ TI(63,T-1) - .0358\ VL(T-1) - .0490\ Q(56,T-1) + .0296\ EQ(37,T-1) + .0488\ Q(63,T-1)$
     (.0004)   (1.1915)   (.0236)   (.0211)   (.0203)   (.0237)

57 METALWORKING MACHINERY & EQUIP
****
NO. OBSV. = 183   R-SQUARE = .2215   R-SQUARE (LEVEL OF OUTPUT) = .9983

$\Delta QR(57,T) = .0002 - .8451\ TQ(57,T-1) - .0371\ Q(57,T-1) + .0185\ EQ(38,T-1) + .0077\ EQ(30,T-1) + .0029\ Q(70,T-1)$
     (.0002)   (.7349)   (.0056)   (.0049)   (.0045)   (.0025)
$+ .0154\ Q(63,T-1)$
     (.0055)

58 SPECIAL INDUSTRIAL MACHINERY
****
NO. OBSV. = 268   R-SQUARE = .1473   R-SQUARE (LEVEL OF OUTPUT) = .9647

$\Delta QR(58,T) = .0005 - .7206\ TQ(58,T-1) - .0242\ VL(T-1) - .0898\ Q(58,T-1) + .0111\ EX(58,T-1) + .0234\ Q(63,T-1)$
     (.0001)   (.4080)   (.0209)   (.0159)   (.0067)   (.0135)
$+ .0111\ Q(57,T-1)$
     (.0104)

59 GENERAL INDUSTRIAL MACHINERY   NO. OBSV. = 165   R-SQUARE = .0427   R-SQUARE (LEVEL OF OUTPUT) = .9891
****
$\Delta QR(59,T)$ = .0001 - .6035 TI(63,T-1) - .0116 Q(59,T-1) + .0180 EQ(19,T-1) + .0030 EX(59,T-1) + .0074 Q(54,T-1)
(.0002)   (.5025)   (.0097)   (.0136)   (.0028)   (.0052)

60 MACHINE SHOPS & MISC MACHINERY   NO. OBSV. = 187   R-SQUARE = .1184   R-SQUARE (LEVEL OF OUTPUT) = .9934
****
$\Delta QR(60,T)$ = -.0001 - .0081 VL(T-1) + .0174 Q(70,T-1)
(.0001)   (.0073)   (.0036)

61 OFFICE & COMPUTING MACHINES   NO. OBSV. = 231   R-SQUARE = .0394   R-SQUARE (LEVEL OF OUTPUT) = .8213
****
$\Delta QR(61,T)$ = .0030 - 4.1552 TI(47,T-1) - .7258 WR(61,T-1) + .0573 DEF(61,T-1)
(.0018)   (3.5895)   (.4465)   (.0216)

62 SERVICE INDUSTRY MACHINES   NO. OBSV. = 210   R-SQUARE = .1145   R-SQUARE (LEVEL OF OUTPUT) = .9158
****
$\Delta QR(62,T)$ = .0001 - .0368 Q(62,T-1) + .0403 EQ(43,T-1) + .0096 EX(62,T-1) + .0620 Q(45,T-1)
(.0002)   (.0248)   (.0166)   (.0067)   (.0199)

63 ELECTRIC APPARATUS & MOTORS   NO. OBSV. = 127   R-SQUARE = .0373   R-SQUARE (LEVEL OF OUTPUT) = .9935
****
$\Delta QR(63,T)$ = .0026 - 7.5130 TI(67,T-1) - .1475 WR(63,T-1)
(.0013)   (3.5401)   (.1372)

64 HOUSEHOLD APPLIANCES   NO. OBSV. = 88   R-SQUARE = .6232   R-SQUARE (LEVEL OF OUTPUT) = .9956
****
$\Delta QR(64,T)$ = .0009 - 2.0025 TI(63,T-1) - .2184 WR(64,T-1) - .0619 VL(T-1) - .0809 Q(64,T-1) + .0122 EQ(45,T-1)
(.0005)   (1.2178)   (.1340)   (.0120)   (.0104)   (.0097)
+ .2367 PCE(64,T-1)
(.0229)

Table 5-2 (cont.)

65 ELECTRIC LIGHT & WIRING EQUIP.   NO. OBSV. = 119   R-SQUARE = .3471   R-SQUARE (LEVEL OF OUTPUT) = .9969
****

$$\Delta QA(65,T) = 636.4214 - 2733730.3125\ TI(48,T-1) - 90956.3994\ VL(T-1) - 141861.9004\ Q(65,T-1) + 49441.8169\ EQ(46,T-1)$$
(488.8353)   (1901134.2969)   (22688.9910)   (29073.5701)   (15758.0150)

$$+\ 112848.1299\ PCE(65,T-1)$$
(58986.0479)

66 COMMUNICATION EQUIPMENT   NO. OBSV. = 131   R-SQUARE = .2221   R-SQUARE (LEVEL OF OUTPUT) = .9981
****

$$\Delta QA(66,T) = 5805.5354 - 15584730.0000\ TQ(66,T-1) - 2103552.0937\ WR(66,T-1) - 381255.1719\ VL(T-1) + 74510.2539\ Q(66,T-1)$$
(4219.1925)   (1181697z.0000)   (1833085.2969)   (107353.7197)   (59301.1069)

$$+\ 822428.1406\ EQ(57,T-1)$$
(221768.4609)

67 ELECTRONIC COMPONENTS   NO. OBSV. = 121   R-SQUARE = .3186   R-SQUARE (LEVEL OF OUTPUT) = .9929
****

$$\Delta QR(67,T) = -.0000 - .0874\ Q(67,T-1) + .0272\ EQ(48,T-1) + .0225\ Q(84,T-1) + .0164\ Q(13,T-1)$$
(.0001) (.0131)   (.0072)   (.0153)   (.0043)

68 BATTERIES & ENGINE ELEC EQUIP.   NO. OBSV. = 89   R-SQUARE = .4076   R-SQUARE (LEVEL OF OUTPUT) = .9927
****

$$\Delta QR(68,T) = .0004 - .9110\ TQ(68,T-1) - .1004\ WR(68,T-1) - .0634\ Q(68,T-1) + .0150\ EQ(49,T-1) + .1097\ PCE(68,T-1)$$
(.0004) (.7024)   (.0985)   (.0123)   (.0043)   (.0285)

$$+\ .0293\ Q(69,T-1)$$
(.0192)

69 MOTOR VEHICLES   NO. OBSV. = 166   R-SQUARE = .1805   R-SQUARE (LEVEL OF OUTPUT) = .9985
****

$$\Delta QR(69,T) = .0001 - .6003\ TQ(69,T-1) - .0169\ Q(69,T-1)$$
(.0001) (.2291)   (.0030)

70 AIRCRAFT & PARTS
****

$$\Delta QA(70,T) = 1434.1489 - 5601714.6250\ TQ(70,T-1) - 535030.9687\ WR(70,T-1) - 530134.0625\ VL(T-1) + 1501500.7031\ Q(70,T-1)$$
$$(1626.7201)\quad (4248260.6875)\quad\quad (458625.0586)\quad\quad (183442.8301)\quad\quad (26807.8000)$$
$$+\ 99855.9102\ EX(70,T-1)$$
$$(61228.0781)$$

NO. OBSV. = 168   R-SQUARE = .9732   R-SQUARE (LEVEL OF OUTPUT) = .9997

71 SHIPS, TRAINS, TRAILRS, CYCLES
****

$$\Delta QA(71,T) = 1453.4594 - 3416994.0000\ TI(28,T-1) - 507112.0508\ Q(71,T-1) + 55771.5020\ DEN(T-1) + 336057.2187\ PCE(71,T-1)$$
$$(808.5146)\quad (1962300.2031)\quad\quad (41726.0239)\quad\quad (47234.6880)\quad\quad (70879.0879)$$
$$+\ 54589.5908\ Q(45,T-1)$$
$$(29142.4209)$$

NO. OBSV. = 171   R-SQUARE = .5253   R-SQUARE (LEVEL OF OUTPUT) = .9966

72 INSTRUMENTS & CLOCKS
****

$$\Delta QA(72,T) = -498.1777 - 73249.1895\ Q(72,T-1) - 112960.1797\ VL(T-1) + 326058.4609\ PCE(72,T-1)$$
$$(490.0446)\quad (47483.9341)\quad\quad (56780.0801)\quad\quad (87608.2158)$$

NO. OBSV. = 104   R-SQUARE = .1318   R-SQUARE (LEVEL OF OUTPUT) = .9933

73 OPTICAL & PHOTOGRAPHIC EQUIP.
****

$$\Delta QR(73,T) = .0005 - .9775\ TQ(73,T-1) - .0428\ VL(T-1) - .0207\ Q(73,T-1) + .0295\ EQ(61,T-1)$$
$$(.0003)\quad (.8949)\quad\quad (.0203)\quad\quad (.0041)\quad\quad (.0156)$$

NO. OBSV. = 139   R-SQUARE = .1675   R-SQUARE (LEVEL OF OUTPUT) = .9981

74 MISC. MANUFACTURED PRODUCTS
****

$$\Delta QR(74,T) = .0001 - .1127\ WR(74,T-1) - .0358\ VL(T-1) - .0241\ Q(74,T-1) + .0153\ EQ(55,T-1) + .0248\ PCE(74,T-1)$$
$$(.0001)\quad (.0790)\quad\quad (.0057)\quad\quad (.0052)\quad\quad (.0052)\quad\quad (.0086)$$
$$+\ .0090\ Q(36,T-1) + .0092\ Q(40,T-1) + .0051\ Q(48,T-1)$$
$$(.0056)\quad (.0035)\quad\quad (.0044)$$

NO. OBSV. = 259   R-SQUARE = .5197   R-SQUARE (LEVEL OF OUTPUT) = .9984

76 COMMUNICATION
****

$$\Delta QR(76,T) = .0000 - .0141\ Q(76,T-1) - .0464\ VL(T-1) + .0056\ Q(66,T-1)$$
$$(.0000)\quad (.0094)\quad\quad (.0055)\quad\quad (.0036)$$

NO. OBSV. = 964   R-SQUARE = .1266   R-SQUARE (LEVEL OF OUTPUT) = .9633

Table 5-2 (cont.)

77 RADIO, TV BROADCASTING
****
NO. OBSV. = 1263   R-SQUARE = .8081   R-SQUARE (LEVEL OF OUTPUT) = .9074

$$\Delta QA(77,T) = -193.8982 - 2498176.3125\ Q(77,T-1) + 500041.3281\ DEN(T-1) + 2487444.0937\ Q(85,T-1)$$
$$(147.7410) \qquad (50461.8540) \qquad\qquad (51404.9878) \qquad\qquad (41659.9692)$$

78 ELECTRIC UTILITY
****
NO. OBSV. = 768   R-SQUARE = .2743   R-SQUARE (LEVEL OF OUTPUT) = .9942

$$\Delta QR(78,T) = -.0000 + .0268\ PI(T-1) - .0441\ TI(7,T-1) - .0135\ VL(T-1) + .0064\ Q(39,T-1) + .0087\ Q(79,T-1)$$
$$(.0000) \quad (.0050) \qquad (.0421) \qquad\quad (.0024) \qquad (.0015) \qquad\quad (.0030)$$

79 GAS UTILITY
****
NO. OBSV. = 428   R-SQUARE = .0822   R-SQUARE (LEVEL OF OUTPUT) = .9944

$$\Delta QR(79,T) = -.0000 + .0415\ PI(T-1) - .0089\ VL(T-1)$$
$$(.0000) \quad (.0074) \qquad (.0048)$$

80 WATER UTILITY
****
NO. OBSV. = 123   R-SQUARE = .5529   R-SQUARE (LEVEL OF OUTPUT) = .9969

$$\Delta QR(80,T) = .0001 + .0366\ PI(T-1) - .0835\ Q(80,T-1) - .4754\ TI(39,T-1) + .0613\ Q(35,T-1) + .0235\ Q(39,T-1)$$
$$(.0002) \quad (.0159) \qquad (.0073) \qquad\quad (.4544) \qquad\quad (.0252) \qquad\quad (.0081)$$

82 FINANCE & INSURANCE
****
NO. OBSV. = 649   R-SQUARE = .1163   R-SQUARE (LEVEL OF OUTPUT) = .9993

$$\Delta QR(82,T) = .0000 - .0427\ TI(34,T-1) - .1277\ TI(32,T-1) + .0096\ Q(82,T-1)$$
$$(.0000) \quad (.0364) \qquad\quad (.0852) \qquad\quad (.0011)$$

83 REAL ESTATE & RENTAL
****
NO. OBSV. = 392   R-SQUARE = .6437   R-SQUARE (LEVEL OF OUTPUT) = .9992

$$\Delta QR(83,T) = .0001 - .0118\ VL(T-1) - .0315\ Q(83,T-1)$$
$$(.0000) \quad (.0033) \qquad (.0021)$$

84 HOTELS, PERSONAL & REPAIR SVC.
****
NO. OBSV. = 832   R-SQUARE = .4385   R-SQUARE (LEVEL OF OUTPUT) = .9987

$$\Delta QR(84,T) = .0002 - .4010\ TI(67,T-1) - .0381\ TI(74,T-1) - .0162\ VL(T-1) - .0242\ Q(84,T-1) + .0056\ Q(67,T-1)$$
$$(.0001) \quad (.2029) \qquad\quad (.0291) \qquad\quad (.0016) \qquad (.0024) \qquad\quad (.0014)$$
$$+ .0056\ Q(37,T-1)$$
$$(.0012)$$

85 BUSINESS SERVICES
****
$\Delta QR(85,T) = .0001 + .0430\ PI(T-1) - .0827\ TI(34,T-1) - .3680\ WR(85,T-1) + .0297\ DEF(85,T-1)$
$\quad\quad\quad (.0000)\ \ (.0041)\quad\quad (.0618)\quad\quad\quad (.1364)\quad\quad\quad (.0016)$

NO. OBSV. = 354   R-SQUARE = .7474   R-SQUARE (LEVEL OF OUTPUT) = .9994

86 AUTOMOBILE REPAIR SERVICES
****
$\Delta QR(86,T) = .0000 - .0164\ VL(T-1) + .0059\ Q(86,T-1)$
$\quad\quad\quad (.0000)\ \ (.0017)\quad\quad (.0022)$

NO. OBSV. = 655   R-SQUARE = .1261   R-SQUARE (LEVEL OF OUTPUT) = .9975

87 AMUSEMENTS & RECREATION
****
$\Delta QR(87,T) = -.0000 + .0326\ PI(T-1) - .0574\ VL(T-1) + .0302\ Q(77,T-1)$
$\quad\quad\quad (.0000)\ \ (.0052)\quad\quad (.0032)\quad\quad (.0029)$

NO. OBSV. = 503   R-SQUARE = .4706   R-SQUARE (LEVEL OF OUTPUT) = .9985

88 MEDICAL & EDUCATIONAL INSTIT.
****
$\Delta QR(88,T) = .0001 - .2528\ TI(37,T-1) - .0135\ VL(T-1) - .0337\ Q(88,T-1) + .0069\ Q(37,T-1)$
$\quad\quad\quad (.0001)\ \ (.1997)\quad\quad (.0090)\quad\quad (.0109)\quad\quad (.0062)$

NO. OBSV. = 725   R-SQUARE = .0503   R-SQUARE (LEVEL OF OUTPUT) = .9696

Table 5-3
Summary of Equation (2-4) by Industry

Industry	TQ	TI	WR	VL	Q*	EQ	DEN	MS	MS
1. Livestock	−	17	−	−	+	+		Q_{15}	Q_4
2. Crops		35			−				
3. Forestry and Fishery Products	−				+	+	−		Q_{17}, Q_{52}
4. Agricultural Services		52		−	+	+	+	Q_1	Q_1
5. Iron Ore Mining		55			−	+			
6. Nonferrous Ore Mining	−				−		+		
7. Coal Mining		53		−					Q_{35}
8. Petroleum Mining		35			+				
9. Minerals Mining	−	55					+		Q_{40}
10. Chemical Mining		55		−					Q_{45}
13. Ordnance	−	67		−		+	−		Q_{66}
14. Meat Packing					−	+		EX_{14}	
15. Dairy Products	−		−	−	+			GOV_3	Q_1
16. Canned and Frozen Foods		49	−	−	+				Q_3
17. Grain Mill Products		2							
18. Bakery Products					+	+			Q_{17}
19. Sugar		34			+				
20. Candy	−			−				PCE_{20}	Q_2
21. Beverages			−	−	+				Q_{19}
22. Misc. Food Products		2	−				−		Q_{85}
23. Tobacco				−		+			
24. Fabrics and Yarn		36			+			Q_{27}	
25. Rugs, Tire Cord, Misc. Textiles		36	−	−	+		+	Q_{24}	
26. Apparel									Q_{24}

#	Industry								Symbols
27.	Household Textiles and Upholst	−	−		−	+			PCE_{27} Q_{25}
28.	Lumber and Prod. Exc. Containers	−	−		+				
29.	Wooden Containers			+	+				
30.	Household Furniture	−	−	+	+				
31.	Office Furniture	45,28	−	+	+	+			Q_{52}
32.	Paper and Prod. Exc. Containers	33	−	−				Q_{34}	
33.	Paper Containers	35	−					Q_{15}	
34.	Printing and Publishing	−	−	+	+				Q_{73}
35.	Basic Chemicals	49	−	−					
36.	Plastics and Synthetics	−	−	+					
37.	Drugs, Cleaning and Toilet Items	49	−	−	+				
38.	Paint and Allied Products	−	+	+					
39.	Petroleum Refining	35	−	−				PCE_{39}	
40.	Rubber and Plastic Products	36	+	+				PCE_{40}	
41.	Leather Tanning	35	+	+				Q_{26}	
42.	Shoes and Other Leather Products	+	+	+	+				
43.	Glass and Glass Products	−	+	+	+			Q_{69}	
44.	Stone and Clay Products	32	−	+	+	+		CN_{18}	Q_{35}
45.	Iron and Steel	35,5	−	+	−	+		Q_{69}	
46.	Copper	48	−						
47.	Aluminum	−						Q_{50}	
48.	Other Nonferrous Metals	+	+					Q_{45}	
49.	Metal Containers	−	−					Q_{21} Q_{37}	
50.	Heating, Plumbing, Struc. Metal	−	−						Q_{52}, Q_{85}
51.	Stampings, Screw Mach. Prod.	−	+						
52.	Hardware, Plating, Wire Prod.	−	−	+				Q_{69}	Q_{48}, Q_{85}
53.	Engines and Turbines	45	−	−	+			Q_{50}	

Table 5-3 (cont.)

Industry	TQ	TI	WR	VL	Q^*	EQ	DEN	MS	MS
54. Farm Machinery and Equipment					+				Q_{53}
55. Construction and Mining Mach.					−			EQ_3	Q_{53}
56. Material Handling Equipment	−	63	−	−	−	+			Q_{63}
57. Metalworking Mach. and Equip.	−				−	+		EQ_{30}, Q_{70}	Q_{63}
58. Special Industrial Machinery				−	−			EX_{38}	Q_{63}, Q_{57}
59. General Industrial Machinery	−	63	−		−			EQ_{19}, EX_{59}, Q_{54}	
60. Machine Shops and Misc. Mach.				−				Q_{70}	
61. Office and Computing Machines		47			−	+		DEF_{61}	
62. Service Industry Machines			−		−	+		EX_{62}	Q_{45}
63. Electric Apparatus and Motors		67	−		−				
64. Household Appliances		63	−		−	+		PCE_{64}	
65. Electric Light and Wiring Equip.		48	−			+		PCE_{65}	
66. Communication Equipment	−			−	+	+			
67. Electronic Components				−	+	+		Q_{84}, Q_{13}	
68. Batteries and Engine Elec. Equip.	−		−			+		PCE_{68}, Q_{69}	
69. Motor Vehicles	−				−				
70. Aircraft and Parts	−	28	−		+			EX_{70}	
71. Ships, Trains, Trailers, Cycles			−		−		+	PCE_{71}	Q_{45}
72. Instruments and Clocks			−		−			PCE_{72}	
73. Optical and Photographic Equip.	−		−	−	−			EQ_{61}	

Industry							Deflator	Q-source
74. Misc. Manufactured Products			+	—		—	Q_{36}, PCE_{74}	Q_{40}, Q_{48}
76. Communication				—	—	—		Q_{66}
77. Radio, TV Broadcasting		+			—	+	Q_{85}	
78. Electric Utility	7			—	—	—	PI	Q_{39}, Q_{79}
79. Gas Utility					—	—	PI	
80. Water Utility	39				—		PI	Q_{35}, Q_{39}
82. Finance and Insurance	34,32				+			
83. Real Estate and Rental					—	—		
84. Hotels, Personal and Repair Svc.	67,74		—		—	—		Q_{67}, Q_{37}
85. Business Services	34				—		PI DEF_{85}	
86. Automobile Repair Services					+	—		
87. Amusements and Recreation					+	—	PI	
88. Medical and Educational Instit.	37				—	—		Q_{37}

*Employment was substituted for output in industry 23

Table 5-4
Equations Explaining the 1966 Level of Equipment by Equipment Purchasing Sector

Equipment Sector	No. Obsv.	Equation (2-8)			Industry No.	Substitute Equation		
		R^2	Constant	1965-66 Change in Output[a]		R^2	Constant	1965 Output
1. Farm	2647	.000	.00038 (.00001)	WS	1–4	.2664	.00024 (.00001)	.41065 (.01325)
2. Mining	—	—	—	—	9–10	—	.00000 (.00000)	1.0000[b]
3. Oil and Gas Wells	—	—	—	—	8	—	-.00000 (.00000)	1.0000[b]
4. Construction	—	—	—	—	—	—	.00000 (.00000)	1.0000[c]
5. Ordnance	821	.0391	.00122 (.00031)	.00181 (.00031)	13	.4894	.00009 (.00023)	1.40689 (.05021)
6. Meat Products	440	.0000	.00227 (.00024)	NS	14	.2277	.00139 (.00023)	.56545 (.04976)
7. Tobacco	95	.0000	.01052 (.00465)	WS	23	.8178	.00185 (.00204)	1.07170 (.05245)
8. Fabrics and Yarn	279	.0037	.00353 (.00058)	.00016 (.00016)	24	.2060	.00163 (.00057)	.76878 (.09070)
9. Rugs, Tire Cord	213	.0486	.00447 (.00083)	.00184 (.00056)	25	.2738	.00237 (.00076)	.83523 (.09364)
10. Apparel	432	.0000	.00231 (.00032)	NS	26	.0278	.00194 (.00033)	.31124 (.08879)
11. Household Textiles and Upholst.	202	.0245	.00468 (.00103)	.00729 (.00325)	27	.0562	.00347 (.00109)	.55786 (.16166)
12. Lumber and Prod. Exc. Wooden Containers	487	.0000	.00205 (.0036)	WS	28	.3410	.00090 (.00030)	2.06133 (.13012)
13. Wooden Containers	245	.0103	.00401 (.00068)	.01967 (.01238)	29	.1207	.00269 (.00068)	1.00673 (.17430)

Industry							
14. Household Furniture	259	.0000	.00385 (.0065)	WS	30 .3615	.00179 (.00055)	.99866 (.08280)
15. Office Furniture	178	.0000	.00561 (.00095)	WS	31 .2581	.00340 (.00087)	.78713 (.10059)
16. Paper Exc. Containers	264	.0070	.00381 (.0047)	.00151 (.00111)	32 .1399	.00221 (.00050)	.72235 (.11067)
17. Paper Containers	183	.0090	.00544 (.0064)	.00101 (.00078)	33 .4100	.00266 (.00056)	.75520 (.06734)
18. Printing and Publishing	602	.0047	.00167 (.00021)	.00104 (.00062)	34 .0937	.00138 (.00021)	.21443 (.02722)
19. Basic Chemicals	342	.0000	.00292 (.00043)	NS	35 .2651	.00101 (.00041)	.98586 (.08902)
20. Plastics and Synthetics	290	.0787	.00323 (.00072)	.00294 (.00059)	36 .3614	.00036 (.00064)	1.44965 (.11354)
21. Drugs, Cleaning and Toilet Items	244	.0000	.00410 (.00052)	WS	37 .3929	.00230 (.00043)	.51401 (.04107)
22. Paint	192	.0000	.00521 (.00071)	NS	38 .3206	.00327 (.00062)	.41254 (.04357)
23. Petroleum Refining	246	.0456	.00355 (.00140)	.00222 (.00065)	39 .8424	−.00082 (.00058)	2.60169 (.07203)
24. Rubber and Plastic	260	.0000	.00385 (.00052)	NS	40 .2240	.00262 (.00048)	.51014 (.05911)
25. Leather Tanning	112	.2174	.00711 (.00198)	.05584 (.01010)	41 .1712	.00601 (.00210)	.49804 (.10449)
26. Shoes and Other Leather Products	153	.0590	.00552 (.00156)	.01064 (.00346)	42 .1224	.00372 (.00159)	1.10380 (.24048)
27. Glass Products	280	.0000	.00357 (.00068)	WS	43 .2694	.00138 (.00062)	.92495 (.09136)
28. Stone and Clay Products	599	.0394	.00162 (.00018)	.00320 (.00065)	44 .1610	.00100 (.00018)	.70640 (.06601)
29. Iron and Steel	334	.0000	.00299 (.00054)	WS	45 .3435	.00144 (.00046)	.66642 (.05056)

Table 5-4 (cont.)

Equipment Sector	Equation (2-8)				Industry No.	Substitute Equation		
	No. Obsv.	R^2	Constant	1965-66 Change in Output[a]		R^2	Constant	1965 Output
30. Nonferrous Metals	317	.0229	.00298 (.00055)	.00108 (.00040)	46–48	.2419	.00170 (.00051)	.87297 (.08708)
31. Metal Containers	151	.0384	.00626 (.00141)	.00254 (.00104)	49	.6937	.00182 (.00083)	.96644 (.05261)
32. Heating, Plumbing Struc. Metal	348	.0049	.00287 (.00035)	.00105 (.00081)	50	.5291	.00084 (.00026)	.98010 (.04971)
33. Stampings, Screw Mach. Products	261	.0832	.00380 (.00064)	.00433 (.00089)	51	.7894	.00074 (.00032)	.97723 (.03136)
34. Hardware, Plating, Wire Prod. and Valves	282	.0000	.00355 (.00051)	NS	52	.5615	.00113 (.00036)	.90962 (.04804)
35. Engines and Turbines	177	.0000	.00565 (.00089)	NS	53	.2478	.00334 (.00083)	.51707 (.06809)
36. Farm Machinery and Equipment	301	.0000	.00332 (.00060)	NS	54	.1223	.00244 (.00058)	.35727 (.05535)
37. Construction and Material Handling Equip.	231	.0431	.00429 (.00079)	.00310 (.00097)	55–56	.2242	.00211 (.00076)	.72151 (.08870)
38. Metal Working Machinery	284	.0000	.00352 (.00060)	WS	57	.4393	.00117 (.00048)	.74212 (.04993)
39. Special Industrial Machinery	236	.0060	.00418 (.00056)	.00112 (.00094)	58	.2265	.00222 (.00055)	.61833 (.07469)
40. General Industrial Machinery	318	.0108	.00315 (.00043)	.00152 (.00082)	59	.4268	.00096 (.00036)	.79188 (.05162)
41. Machine Shops and Misc.	380	.0281	.00260 (.00037)	.00593 (.00180)	60	.6591	.00076 (.00023)	.87561 (.03239)
42. Office and Computing Machines	283	.0000	.00353 (.00058)	NS	61	.4602	.00125 (.00045)	.77011 (.04975)

97

43. Service Industry Machinery	127	.0155	.00758 (.00132)	.00204 (.00146)	62	.3001	.00419 (.00121)	1.10585 (.15105)
44. Electric Apparatus and Motors	229	.0097	.00433 (.00059)	.00075 (.00050)	63	.3723	.00200 (.00051)	.75248 (.06485)
45. Household Appliances	183	.0000	.00546 (.00101)	NS	64	.4613	.00229 (.00079)	.81247 (.06526)
46. Electric Lighting and Wirings	167	.0131	.00604 (.00114)	.00253 (.00171)	65	.2770	.00239 (.00108)	.80887 (.10173)
47. Communication Equipment	333	.0624	.00291 (.00053)	.00121 (.00026)	66	.6561	.00099 (.00033)	.87824 (.03495)
48. Electronic Components	319	.0000	.00313 (.00055)	NS	67	.2407	.00149 (.00050)	.71436 (.07126)
49. Batteries, X-ray and Engine Elec. Equip.	175	.0000	.00571 (.00090)	WS	68	.3493	.00204 (.00082)	.91346 (.09479)
50. Motor Vehicles	240	.0000	.00417 (.00088)	WS	69	.5956	.00156 (.00058)	.77338 (.04130)
51. Aircraft and Parts	484	.3238	.00156 (.00039)	.00181 (.00012)	70	.4809	.00105 (.00034)	.70440 (.03333)
52. Ships, Trains, and Cycles	353	.0279	.00279 (.00058)	.00122 (.00038)	71	.5184	.00085 (.00042)	1.36783 (.07037)
53. Instruments and Clocks	185	.0428	.00510 (.00103)	.00476 (.00166)	72	.1057	.00374 (.00105)	.50723 (.10909)
54. Optical and Photographic Equipment	143	.0000	.00699 (.00284)	NS	73	.8874	.00156 (.00097)	.95448 (.02863)
55. Misc. Manufacturing	492	.0093	.00204 (.00021)	.00140 (.00066)	74	.3137	.00134 (.00018)	.38450 (.02569)
56. Transportation	—	—	—	—	75	—	.00000	1.00000[b]
57. Communication	—	—	—	—	76–77	—	.00000	1.00000[b]
58. Utility	—	—	—	—	78–80	—	.00000	1.00000[b]
59. Trade	—	—	—	—	81	—	.00000	1.00000[b]

Table 5-4 (cont.)

Equipment Sector	No. Obsv.	Equation (2-8)				Industry No.	Substitute Equation		
		R^2	Constant	1965-66 Change in Output[a]			R^2	Constant	1965 Output
60. Finance and Insurance	—	—	—	—		82	—	.00000	1.00000[b]
61. Service	—	—	—	—		83–88	—	.00000	1.00000[b]
62. Dairy Products	464	.0177	.00212 (.00020)	.00137 (.00047)		15	.2723	.00110 (.00019)	.71567 (.05443)
63. Canned and Frozen Foods	393	.0000	.00254 (.00029)	WS		16	.4062	.00132 (.00024)	.66652 (.04075)
64. Grain Mill Products	400	.0000	.00250 (.00036)	WS		17	.2139	.00139 (.00034)	.67627 (.06499)
65. Bakery Products	410	.0222	.00241 (.00030)	.00249 (.00082)		18	.7239	.00061 (.00017)	.89661 (.02742)
66. Sugar	160	.1400	.00486 (.00145)	.01181 (.00233)		19	.3413	.00192 (.00133)	1.12038 (.12383)
67. Confectionery	259	.0000	.00386 (.00115)	WS		20	.9227	.00048 (.00033)	1.03661 (.01872)
68. Beverages	448	.0766	.00218 (.00024)	.00173 (.00028)		21	.5671	.00097 (.00017)	.72263 (.02990)
69. Miscellaneous Food	417	.0000	.00240 (.00034)	WS		22	.5461	.00069 (.00024)	.88139 (.03944)

[a]Coefficients Scaled: divide by 10,000 to obtain actual coefficient.
[b]No Equation: used 1966 regional output to allocate national equipment to regions.
[c]Used 1966 total construction as allocator.
Symbols: WS = wrong sign, NS = not significant

(No. 2-3) and service sectors (No. 56-61); therefore, they were estimated using the level of output. Both the 1965 and 1966 equipment investment in these sectors were derived by allowing the county distribution of equipment to be the same as the county distribution of output. The forecasts of equipment investment in these sectors are made the same way as indicated in Table 5-4 where the constant term is set at zero and the coefficient on the level of output is set at one. This means that the relative regional share in equipment investment is the same as the relative regional share in output.

The construction equipment is also handled in a special way, since there were no original construction equipment data by county. The data were estimated by assuming that the construction equipment investment had the same regional distribution as the total amount of construction. Thus, in making forecasts, the relative regional share of construction equipment is determined by the relative regional share of total construction expenditures.

The Construction Equations

The 28 construction sectors have been divided into three groups for the purpose of estimating parameters. The three sectors pertaining to construction activities of individuals are in the first group. These are residential construction (No. 1), additions and alterations to residences (No. 2), and all other private construction (No. 17). The 1965 personal income was used to explain the 1966 level of construction in these sectors. The equations are given in Table 5-5. Note that the equations for sectors 1 and 2 are identical. This is because the county estimates for additions and alterations were made by assuming that the relative regional distribution of additions and alterations was the same as the regional distribution of residential construction. Data on additions and alterations were not available for all sections of the county.

The next group of construction equations in Table 5-5 include the other private construction sectors (No. 3-16). The construction in these sectors can be associated with industry sectors. Therefore, the same type equation that is used for equipment is used for construction. It was hypothesized that the level of construction investment could be explained with the change in output as given by Equation (2-10). But as was true with the equipment equations, these construction equations did not work out very well. Therefore, a substitute equation was used which explains construction with the level of output. In every case the substitute equation was an improvement over the one hypothesized. All the variables are expressed as regional shares. The level variables are expressed relative to the nation, and the change variables are expressed as absolute regional shares.

The public construction sectors are grouped together in the third section of Table 5-5. Public construction is explained by personal income and government

Table 5-5
Equations Explaining the 1966 Level of Construction by Sector

Private Sectors Related to Income	Equation (2-9)			
	1965 Personal Income	Constant	R^2	No. Obs.
1. Residential	.57532 (.00867)	.00014 (.00001)	.5905	3055
2. Additions and Alterations to Residences	.57532 (.00867)	.00014 (.00001)	.5905	3055
17. All Other Private Construction	.67228 (.02094)	.00036 (.00006)	.4744	1144

Private Sectors Related to Output	Substitute Equation				Equation (2-10)			
	1965 Output	Constant	R^2	Industry No.	1965-66 Change in Output[a]	Constant	R^2	No. Obsv.
3. Nonhousekeeping Residential Construction	.42620 (.01843)	.00065 (.00006)	.3606	84	WS	.00105 (.00008)	.0000	950
4. Industrial	.62600 (.01782)	.00034 (.00005)	.5028	13–74	.00496 (.00107)	.00082 (.00006)	.0173	1223
5. Offices	.68066 (.00797)	.00021 (.00003)	.8228	81–83	WS	.00064 (.00008)	.0000	1573
6. Stores, Restaurants and Garages	.34094 (.01213)	.00049 (.00004)	.3654	85.86 89–99	WS	.00073 (.00005)	.0000	1375
7. Religious	.36185 (.01050)	.00048 (.00003)	.4635	88	WS	.00073 (.00005)	.0000	1376
8. Educational	.72419 (.01879)	.00059 (.00009)	.7028	88	WS	.00159 (.00016)	.0000	630
9. Hospital and Institutional	.51069 (.01664)	.00063 (.00007)	.5195	88	.00365 (.00300)	.00115 (.00009)	.0017	873

Private Sectors	No. Obsv.	R²		Constant				1965 Govt. Expend.		Govt. No.
10. Misc. Nonresidential	523	.0033	.00190 (.00033)	.01770 (.01344)	WS	75,77 87	.3203	.00061 (.00028)	.77806 (.04966)	8
11. Farm Construction	2647	.0000	.00038 (.00001)	—	WS	1-4	.2664	.00024 (.00001)	.41065 (.01325)	DEF
12. Oil and Gas Well Drilling and Exploration	—	—	—	—	—	8	—	.00000	1.00000^b	
13. Railroad	—	—	—	—	—	75	—	.00000	1.00000^b	
14. Telephone	—	—	—	—	—	76	—	.00000	1.00000^b	
15. Electric Utility	—	—	—	—	—	78	—	.00000	1.00000^b	
16. Gas and Petroleum Pipelines	—	—	—	—	—	—	—	—	—	

Equation (2-11)

Public Sectors	No. Obsv.	R²	Constant	1965 Personal Income	1965 Govt. Expend.	Govt. No.
18. Highway	2845	.4095	.00023 (.00001)	.34331 (.00773)	M	8
19. Military	369	.0029	.00262 (.00027)	—	.04785 (.04626)	DEF
20. Conservation	931	.0109	.00089 (.00022)	.24299 (.07601)	NS	6
21. Sewer Systems	1141	.5252	.00031 (.00006)	.74700 (.02104)	M	8
22. Water Systems	1364	.3819	-.00012 (.00012)	1.33260 (.05123)	M	8
23. Public Residential Construction	665	.1443	.00125 (.00010)	.39324 (.04013)	-.12204 (.02962)	DEF
24. Public Industrial Construction	1810	.3085	.00024 (.00005)	.41816 (.03126)	.18952 (.02299)	DEF

Table 5-5 (cont.)

Public Sectors	No. Obsv.	R^2	Equation (2-11) Constant	1965 Personal Income	1965 Govt. Expend.	Govt. No.
25. Public Educational	1938	.6478	.00024 (.00002)	.56433 (.00946)	M	8
26. Public Hospital	521	.5251	.00010 (.00024)	1.48817 (.06212)	M	8
27. Other Public Structures	1298	.3222	.00024 (.00008)	.78937 (.03180)	NS	2
28. Miscellaneous Public	1822	.2834	.00024 (.00005)	.56197 (.03710)	.04840 (.03699)	2

[a]Coefficients Scaled: Divide by 1,000,000 to obtain actual coefficient.

[b]No equation: Used 1966 regional output to allocate national construction to regions.

Symbols:

WR = = wrong sign
NS = = not significant
M = = multicollinearity
DEF = = defense expenditures

expenditures. The poorest equation was the one explaining military construction. This would be expected since the decisions to construct military facilities presumably are not based on economic factors. Defense government expenditures are used in three of the equations—19, Military; 23, Public Residential; and 24, Public Industrial Construction. Most of the construction in these later two categories are for military purposes. However, in recent years there has been an increase in public residence construction for private individuals. The construction sector showing the greatest correlation with personal income is public education.

Note that there are no equations for Sectors 12-16. The historical regional data for Sectors 12-15 had been estimated using the regional distribution of our appropriate output sector. The number of the output sector is given in the table in the fifth column. There is no equation for gas and petroleum pipeline construction, No. 16, since the location of this construction is between the source of materials and their markets. In the absence of other knowledge, the regional distribution of pipeline construction is held constant in the forecast years.

The Employment Equations

The results of fitting Equation (2-14) are given in Table 5-6. The dependent variable, the change in employment, and the independent variable, the change in output, are absolute regional shares and equipment and output are expressed as relative regional shares.

The changes in employment equations appear to be acceptable in terms of their fit, but early experiments with the forecasting model indicated that the employment forecasts did not always behave well. Therefore, substitute equations were used which explained the level of employment. The new equation is

$$EMP_{ij}^t = g_{j14}\left(Q_{ij}^t, EQ_j^{t-1}\right) \qquad \begin{aligned}&(i = 1, \ldots, 99)\\&(i{\rightarrow}k)\\&(j = 1, \ldots, NR)\end{aligned}$$

The fit of the substitute equation is reported in Table 5-7. As would be expected the overall fit as measured by the R^2 was higher when the level of employment was used as a dependent variable than when the change in employment was used. The prior level of equipment did not enter in 41 of the 99 equations either because of multicollinearity or because of insignificance. The output level variable completely dominated the equations, explaining most of the variance in the level of employment. In most equations where the equipment variable did enter the equations the standard errors of the coefficient were large. Equipment was multicollinear in the mining and service sectors because, as explained above, the equipment data estimates of these sectors depended on the output data.

Table 5-6
Equation (2-14) Explaining the 1965-66 Changes in Employment by Industry Sector

Industry Number and Name	No. Obsv.	R^2	Constant	1965-66 Change in Output	1965 Equipment	No.	1965 Output
1. Livestock	3049	.0466	35.46 (14.60)	.00829 (.00088)	-109993 (24951)	1	M
2. Crops	3037	.0419	-42.21 (12.46)	.00651 (.00153)	-71133 (23979)	1	198309 (17990)
3. Forestry and Fishery Products	572	.8022	4.26 (.94)	.01781 (.00039)	NS	1	-715 (119)
4. Agricultural Services	2274	.4608	-.43 (.87)	.08022 (.00182)	3034 (1242)	1	NS*
5. Iron Ore Mining	160	.7148	-10.38 (7.33)	.02296 (.00143)	5178 (2288)	2	1237 (363)
6. Nonferrous Ore Mining	439	.7725	3.11 (2.91)	.02059 (.00056)	-2040 (1231)	2	M
7. Coal Mining	445	.2237	.87 (5.40)	.01142 (.00109)	6609 (3175)	2	-2063 (1155)
8. Petroleum Mining	650	.1544	3.09 (3.31)	.00216 (.00020)	NS	3	NS
9. Minerals Mining	1544	.5396	5.18 (1.14)	.01020 (.00030)	1925 (705)	2	-6081 (783)
10. Chemical Mining	93	.5111	5.28 (9.60)	.01117 (.00119)	NS	2	343 (329)
11. New Construction	2971	.1590	37.92 (8.44)	.00939 (.00042)	-111690 (7389)	4	M
12. Maintenance Construction	2682	.0979	9.92 (3.57)	.01504 (.00169)	-26410 (3110)	4	M
13. Ordnance	799	.7833	14.45 (5.22)	.02536 (.00053)	-6375 (665)	5	-9471 (665)

Industry							
14. Meat Packing	1332	.4075	5.38 (2.33)	.00514 (.00018)	-3950 (812)	6	NS*
15. Dairy Products	1489	.6894	1.00 (.91)	.01647 (.00029)	-657 (331)	62	675 (505)
16. Canned and Frozen Food	911	.4822	5.29 (3.93)	.01445 (.00053)	-1603 (965)	63	NS
17. Grain Mill Products	1177	.7922	.96 (.92)	.00993 (.00015)	290 (235)	64	NS*
18. Bakery Products	934	.5563	3.77 (2.04)	.02553 (.00077)	2947 (841)	65	-5402 (905)
19. Sugar	161	.3708	12.08 (7.44)	.00711 (.00074)	NS	66	-1184 (609)
20. Candy	531	.6298	-2.34 (2.51)	.03712 (.00129)	1720 (242)	67	M
21. Beverages	1308	.7104	-.05 (1.28)	.01275 (.00025)	-2134 (453)	68	3662 (450)
22. Misc. Food Products	1068	.6155	2.83 (1.29)	.01063 (.00029)	-881 (285)	69	-1253 (412)
23. Tobacco	223	.9231	-5.77 (9.18)	.01499 (.00029)	1397 (336)	7	M
24. Fabrics and Yarn	739	.3065	12.39 (14.50)	.00872 (.00051)	-29430 (3628)	8	22686 (4209)
25. Rugs, Tire Cord, Misc. Textiles	489	.5457	21.59 (8.36)	.01507 (.00073)	4611 (1482)	9	-12561 (1987)
26. Apparel	1549	.3628	2.09 (5.04)	.02186 (.00074)	1745 (1190)	10	NS*
27. Household Textiles and Upholst.	547	.5994	10.95 (4.72)	.02246 (.00115)	1575 (514)	11	-5591 (691)
28. Lumber and Prod. Exc. Containers	1984	.4865	5.30 (1.75)	.03072 (.00080)	1745 (571)	12	-8882 (1206)
29. Wooden Containers	684	.6649	3.94 (1.08)	.05303 (.00150)	862 (181)	13	-2159 (352)

Table 5-6 (cont.)

Industry Number and Name	No. Obsv.	R^2	Constant	1965-66 Change in Output	1965 Equipment	No.	1965 Output
30. Household Furniture	828	.5575	6.73 (4.54)	.04585 (.00161)	1530 (1120)	14	−5193 (1483)
31. Office Furniture	510	.1580	−6.00 (5.26)	.01947 (.00243)	−5416 (942)	15	9353 (1117)
32. Paper and Prod. Exc. Containers	873	.4203	−.82 (3.77)	.02542 (.00101)	NS	16	NS
33. Paper Containers	471	.3331	−4.41 (6.39)	.01473 (.00098)	2042 (1069)	17	2369 (1440)
34. Printing and Publishing	2082	.7046	.18 (1.63)	.05322 (.00077)	1129 (438)	18	NS
35. Basic Chemicals	1194	.7657	.64 (2.80)	.01817 (.00029)	1348 (691)	19	NS
36. Plastics and Synthetics	656	.8887	−5.58 (3.38)	.02496 (.00036)	−893 (388)	20	3957 (907)
37. Drugs, Cleaning and Toilet Items	494	.2761	21.51 (8.53)	.00362 (.00047)	4397 (2005)	21	−12795 (1896)
38. Paint and Allied Products	253	.8939	−1.91 (2.79)	.02350 (.00051)	855 (258)	22	NS
39. Petroleum Refining	447	.2627	4.74 (4.85)	.00272 (.00022)	NS	23	NS
40. Rubber and Plastic Products	928	.6643	4.54 (5.16)	.02550 (.00067)	1727 (1507)	24	−3618 (1430)
41. Leather Tanning	188	.6495	7.41 (4.21)	.03894 (.00218)	−388 (285)	25	−797 (290)
42. Shoes and Other Leather Products	558	.6484	−5.91 (7.88)	.05957 (.00187)	3540 (1181)	26	NS

Industry							
43. Glass and Glass Products	570	.4772	3.75 (3.43)	.02433 (.00112)	27	-945 (283)	NS*
44. Stone and Clay Products	1673	.6725	2.35 (1.62)	.03386 (.00058)	28	NS	-1531 (889)
45. Iron and Steel	1111	.5447	25.24 6.59	.01064 (.00044)	29	4063 (963)	-28111 (1488)
46. Copper	272	.7134	7.74 (6.08)	.00864 (.00035)	30	1242 (886)	-1421 (557)
47. Aluminum	518	.6926	11.55 (5.48)	.01631 (.00048)	30	-1453 (910)	NS*
48. Other Nonferrous Metals	452	.4240	3.29 (6.61)	.00802 (.00044)	30	NS	NS
49. Metal Containers	232	.2596	17.23 (13.03)	.00840 (.00104)	31	-2429 (900)	M
50. Heating, Plumbing, Structural Metal	924	.6571	2.16 (2.87)	.03263 (.00078)	32	NS	NS
51. Stamping, Screw Mach. Prod.	527	.7539	2.30 (4.18)	.02842 (.00071)	33	NS	NS
52. Hardware, Plating, Wire Prod.	844	.8153	1.86 (3.14)	.04605 (.00077)	34	2203 (812)	-2457 (979)
53. Engines and Turbines	346	.9250	4.92 (4.61)	.03408 (.00053)	35	-719 (491)	NS
54. Farm Machinery and Equipment	715	.8675	9.28 (2.27)	.02987 (.00046)	36	-3190 (571)	-2817 (511)
55. Construction and Mining Machinery	556	.6492	5.28 (4.66)	.02920 (.00094)	37	-2266 (654)	NS*
56. Material Handling Equipment	349	.8846	2.92 (2.60)	.02746 (.00053)	37	NS	NS
57. Metal Working Mach. and Equipment	562	.7550	6.98 (3.35)	.04024 (.00108)	38	1653 (767)	-4910 (809)
58. Special Industrial Machinery	507	.8342	6.65 (3.42)	.03608 (.00077)	39	-943 (706)	-1437 (859)

Table 5-6 (cont.)

Industry Number and Name	No. Obsv.	R^2	Constant	1965-66 Change in Output	1965 Equipment	No.	1965 Output
59. General Industrial Machinery	545	.6225	2.14 (4.67)	.02990 (.00101)	3111 (927)	40	-2979 (1182)
60. Machine Shops and Misc. Mach.	787	.8238	-1.86 (1.60)	.05860 (.00098)	2726 (285)	41	M
61. Office and Computing Machines	500	.8949	5.00 (6.72)	.02032 (.00032)	-3174 (707)	42	1799 (1150)
62. Service Industry Machinery	387	.5652	9.10 (6.78)	.01696 (.00082)	3889 (873)	43	-5264 (1325)
63. Electrical Apparatus and Motors	593	.8337	7.44 (6.63)	.04113 (.00076)	-3312 (848)	44	NS*
64. Household Appliances	424	.7478	.52 (8.90)	.03363 (.00096)	1467 (941)	56	NS*
65. Electric Light and Wiring Equipment	363	.8923	8.06 (4.90)	.03956 (.00077)	1135 (604)	46	-3352 (789)
66. Communication Equipment	761	.8835	6.01 (7.41)	.03753 (.00050)	-2607 (1789)	47	-9476 (1738)
67. Electronic Components	692	.8998	-6.27 (5.59)	.03809 (.00049)	-4091 (1053)	48	8044 (1312)
68. Batteries and Engine Elec. Equipment	372	.7713	3.39 (5.69)	.04088 (.00125)	-3173 (456)	49	2292 (1060)
69. Motor Vehicles	893	.4519	.50 (15.57)	.01472 (.00055)	-4656 3235	50	8284 (3859)
70. Aircraft and Parts	1106	.3427	-7.62 (16.81)	.01096 (.00057)	20662 (2396)	51	NS
71. Ships, Trains, Trailers, Cycles	860	.8702	1.66 (7.71)	.04898 (.00067)	2205 (1152)	52	-2691 (1947)
72. Instruments and Clocks	444	.6438	11.98 (6.34)	.02971 (.00109)	727 (692)	53	-4910 (1099)

73. Optical and Photographic Equip.	319	.3684	-12.67 (10.99)	.01632 (.00258)	54	6170 (482)	M
74. Misc. Manufactured Products	1018	.7291	2.21 (2.54)	.05186 (.00099)	55	-1125 (694)	NS*
75. Transportation	2974	.4298	7.36 (3.77)	.02660 (.00058)	56	-21671 (1585)	M
76. Communication	2748	.9448	-4.23 (1.32)	.05591 (.00026)	57	11528 (831)	M
77. Radio, TV, Broadcasting	1221	.9235	-8.53 (3.14)	.02976 (.00026)	57	5842 (2184)	7813 (1141)
78. Electric Utility	2466	.3045	-.76 (2.05)	.00911 (.00033)	58	11870 (1051)	-8818 (2101)
79. Gas Utility	1490	.2944	2.88 (2.75)	.01473 (.00075)	58	-7629 (1055)	2666 (1289)
80. Water Utility	431	.8296	1.11 (.82)	.01208 (.00027)	58	158 (113)	NS*
81. Wholesale Trade	2985	.5215	-.94 (2.52)	.03802 (.00067)	59	-18201 (2963)	20315 (1354)
82. Finance and Insurance	3016	.6538	8.08 (1.85)	.03933 (.00058)	60	12029 (1135)	-36243 (858)
83. Real Estate and Rental	2576	.7310	1.07 (1.12)	.00496 (.00010)	60	-635 (570)	-1906 (534)
84. Hotels, Personal and Repair Svc.	3016	.4168	6.06 (3.08)	.04647 (.00137)	61	24303 (1516)	-42262 (2334)
85. Business Service	2844	.6255	-16.48 (3.15)	.00158 (.00015)	61	-8737 (1369)	56923 (1149)
86. Automobile Repair Service	2519	.4610	-.39 (.75)	.01637 (.00036)	61	1090 (370)	800 (617)
87. Amusements and Recreation	2690	.7903	.02 (.98)	.05056 (.00054)	61	-1153 (441)	2074 (436)
88. Medical and Educational Instit.	3024	.0245	4.15 (3.93)	WS	61	-12263 (1407)	NS

Table 5-6 (cont.)

Industry Number and Name	No. Obsv.	R^2	Constant	1965-66 Change in Output	1965 Equipment	No.	1965 Output
89. Lumber, Houseware, Farm Equip. Stores	2954	.3366	.15 (.66)	.03443 (.00089)	NS	59	NS
90. General Merchandise Stores	3020	.8259	-7.21 (1.64)	.12781 (.00108)	21798 (1216)	59	M
91. Food Stores	3023	.7966	-2.83 (1.02)	.09224 (.00087)	8744 (764)	59	M
92. Automotive Dealers	2950	.5273	-1.41 (.82)	.06860 (.00121)	4100 (601)	59	M
93. Gasoline Service Stations	2979	.8199	-.47 (.37)	.12478 (.00107)	1811 (263)	59	M
94. Apparel, Accessory Stores	2855	.8683	-.44 (.56)	.11340 (.00083)	-5090 (635)	59	6599 (336)
95. Furniture Stores	2644	.9044	-.67 (.34)	.07822 (.00051)	2248 (236)	59	M
96. Eating, Drinking Places	3037	.8426	1.50 (1.45)	.10226 (.00091)	-4482 (1153)	59	M
97. Drug and Proprietary Stores	2896	.7879	-.12 (.48)	.09825 (.00106)	509 (377)	59	M
98. Other Retail Stores	2998	.6805	-1.18 (.68)	.07983 (.00112)	4045 (558)	59	M
99. Nonstore Retailers	1758	.9191	.56 (.48)	.09781 (.00094)	-1164 (326)	59	151 (94)

Symbols:

NS = not significant
NS* = forced another variable to be insignificant
M   = multicollinearity

Table 5-7
Equations Explaining 1966 Employment by Sector

Industry Number and Name	No. Obsv.	R^2	Constant	1966 Output	1965 Equipment	No.
1. Livestock	2939	.1570	.00021 (.00001)	.36718 (.01570)	NS	1
2. Crops	2933	.2685	.00017 (.00001)	.46770 (.01714)	.03429 (.02279)	1
3. Forestry and Fishery Products	519	.9443	.00060 (.00006)	.65995 (.00705)	NS	1
4. Agricultural Services	2218	.9492	.00009 (.00001)	.71633 (.00396)	.07386 (.00974)	1
5. Iron Ore Mining	157	.9868	−.00000 (.00025)	.99516 (.00923)	NS	2
6. Nonferrous Ore Mining	422	.9325	.00018 (.00011)	.91310 (.01199)	M	2
7. Coal Mining	427	.9137	.00015 (.00009)	.93274 (.01808)	−.08023 (.05183)	2
8. Petroleum Mining	644	.3591	.00066 (.00015)	.57630 (.03039)	M	3
9. Minerals Mining	1512	.6654	.00024 (.00002)	.58954 (.01251)	.04879 (.01139)	2
10. Chemical Mining	90	.8813	−.00013 (.00129)	.84241 (.05734)	.81764 (.53831)	2
11. New Construction	2966	.9628	.00007 (.00000)	.79394 (.00287)	M	4
12. Maintenance Construction	2680	.9792	.00003 (.00001)	.60109 (.00319)	.32452 (.00633)	4
13. Ordnance	799	.9693	−.00026 (.00007)	1.30564 (.00871)	−.10029 (.00880)	5
14. Meat Packing	1332	.9108	.00018 (.00002)	.72609 (.00755)	.03765 (.00680)	6
15. Dairy Products	1488	.9275	.00011 (.00001)	.82559 (.00684)	.01403 (.00451)	62
16. Canned and Frozen Food	911	.9478	.00018 (.00002)	.83104 (.00808)	.00900 (.00689)	63
17. Grain Mill Products	1176	.9416	.00014 (.00002)	.85254 (.00701)	−.01453 (.00548)	64
18. Bakery Products	933	.9316	.0021 (.00003)	.82167 (.01305)	−.01400 (.01223)	65
19. Sugar	160	.8616	.00021 (.00041)	.90200 (.04153)	.05257 (.03538)	66
20. Candy	459	.9420	.00053 (.00011)	.71222 (.00827)	M	67
21. Beverages	1307	.9594	.00014 (.00002)	.81002 (.00535)	.01097 (.00580)	68
22. Misc. Food Products	1067	.9617	.00016 (.00002)	.83060 (.00508)	NS	69
23. Tobacco	178	.8220	.00252 (.00050)	.51039 (.01790)	M	7

Table 5-7 (cont.)

Industry Number and Name	No. Obsv.	R^2	Constant	1966 Output	1965 Equipment	No.
24. Fabrics and Yarn	665	.9470	.00016 (.00004)	.87164 (.00801)	NS	8
25. Rugs, Tire Cord, Misc. Textiles	438	.7226	.00078 (.00012)	.57924 (.02414)	.07800 (.01851)	9
26. Apparel	1546	.9795	.00006 (.00001)	.90744 (.00334)	NS	10
27. Household Textiles and Upholstery	546	.9082	−.00006 (.00011)	1.07882 (.01502)	−.04827 (.01206)	11
28. Lumber and Prod. Exc. Containers	1983	.9630	.00013 (.00001)	.74200 (.00327)	NS	12
29. Wooden Containers	684	.9214	.00017 (.00004)	.88662 (.00992)	NS	13
30. Household Furniture	828	.9581	.00015 (.00002)	.88197 (.00792)	−.01029 (.00601)	14
31. Office Furniture	510	.7592	.00032 (.00012)	.93126 (.02488)	−.11330 (.02070)	15
32. Paper and Prod. Exc. Containers	873	.8962	.00012 (.00003)	.86796 (.01129)	.03038 (.00652)	16
33. Paper Containers	464	.9541	−.00002 (.00006)	.95250 (.01226)	.05130 (.00937)	17
34. Printing and Publishing	2079	.9876	.00005 (.00001)	.86868 (.00233)	.01923 (.00253)	18
35. Basic Chemicals	1194	.9081	.00008 (.00002)	.87947 (.00925)	.02065 (.00579)	19
36. Plastics and Synthetics	656	.9047	.00016 (.00005)	.86293 (.01343)	.03191 (.00573)	20
37. Drugs, Cleaning and Toilet Items	494	.7723	.00054 (.00013)	.63385) (.02753)	.10578 (.02854)	21
38. Paint and Allied Products	253	.9724	.00029 (.00012)	.89288 (.01516)	.03725 (.01742)	22
39. Petroleum Refining	433	.8383	.00028 (.00015)	.88975 (.02227)	−.06545 (.01649)	23
40. Rubber and Plastic Products	870	.9686	.00005 (.00003)	.88711 (.00664)	.07188 (.00716)	24
41. Leather Tanning	172	.9511	.00096 (.00025)	.77828 (.01567)	.04612 (.01577)	25
42. Shoes and Other Leather Products	521	.9009	.00000 (.00007)	.92632 (.01751)	.06174 (.01278)	26
43. Glass and Glass Products	541	.9488	.00017 (.00005)	.88269 (.00984)	.01065 (.00396)	27
44. Stone and Clay Products	1671	.9611	.00004 (.00001)	.91954 (.00503)	.00690 (.00283)	28
45. Iron and Steel	981	.9526	.00011 (.00003)	.89787 (.00686)	−.01828 (.00449)	29

Table 5-7 (cont.)

Industry Number and Name	No. Obsv.	R^2	Constant	1966 Output	1965 Equipment	No.
46. Copper	264	.8171	.00068 (.00026)	.69517 (.02364)	.17543 (.03963)	30
47. Aluminum	504	.9050	.00012 (.00007)	.82164 (.01364)	.09318 (.01211)	30
48. Other Nonferrous Metals	431	.8844	.00042 (.00009)	.76097 (.01596)	.03018 (.01718)	30
49. Metal Containers	216	.9082	.00052 (.00027)	.87053 (.01892)	NS	31
50. Heating, Plumbing, Structural Metal	923	.9880	.00005 (.00001)	.95469 (.00347)	NS	32
51. Stamping, Screw Machine Products	527	.9817	.00011 (.00004)	.94326 (.00562)	M	33
52. Hardware, Plating, Wire Products	841	.9855	.00001 (.00002)	.96662 (.00574)	.02191 (.00476)	34
53. Engines and Turbines	346	.9639	.00022 (.00008)	.92219 (.00962)	NS	35
54. Farm Machinery and Equipment	703	.9820	.00024 (.00003)	.83024 (.00424)	NS	36
55. Construction and Mining Machinery	553	.9779	.00010 (.00004)	.95212 (.00665)	−.01619 (.00552)	37
56. Material Handling Equipment	347	.9823	.00027 (.00006)	.86770 (.00938)	.03993 (.00867)	37
57. Metal Working Mach. and Equipment	562	.9917	.00004 (.00003)	.97588 (.00376)	NS	38
58. Special Industrial Machinery	479	.9782	.00012 (.00003)	.94895 (.00812)	−.01331 (.00643)	39
59. General Industrial Machinery	545	.9814	.00003 (.00003)	.97839 (.00784)	.00767 (.00617)	40
60. Machine Shops and Misc. Mach.	787	.9909	.00006 (.00002)	.94343 (.00593)	.01096 (.00514)	41
61. Office and Computing Machines	500	.9572	.00015 (.00006)	.94382 (.01014)	−.01788 (.00633)	42
62. Service Industry Machinery	373	.9670	.00017 (.00006)	.90119 (.00864)	NS	43
63. Electric Apparatus and Motors	589	.9854	.00004 (.00002)	.96960 (.00486)	NS	44
64. Household Appliances	424	.9645	.00026 (.00007)	.86252 (.01057)	.02871 (.00864)	45
65. Electric Light and Wiring Equipment	362	.9740	.00003 (.00006)	.98840 (.00851)	NS	46
66. Communication Equipment	758	.9844	.00005 (.00003)	.92183 (.00633)	.04311 (.00659)	47
67. Electronic Components	690	.9736	−.00001 (.00003)	1.03266 (.00729)	−.02548 (.00585)	48

Table 5-7 (cont.)

Industry Number and Name	No. Obsv.	R^2	Constant	1966 Output	1965 Equipment	No.
68. Batteries and Engine Elec. Equipment	371	.9400	.00029 (.00007)	.86103 (.01334)	.03328 (.00574)	49
69. Motor Vehicles	892	.9795	.00006 (.00003)	.81992 (.00825)	.13072 (.00685)	50
70. Aircraft and Parts	980	.9331	.00006 (.00006)	.82203 (.00959)	.09224 (.01051)	51
71. Ships, Trains, Trailers, Cycles	860	.9083	.00022 (.00004)	.81978 (.00955)	−.01318 (.00569)	52
72. Instruments and Clocks	433	.9804	.00001 (.00005)	.97661 (.00665)	NS	53
73. Optical and Photographic Equipment	301	.9732	.00074 (.00017)	.76595 (.00735)	M	54
74. Misc. Manufactured Products	1018	.9801	.00004 (.00002)	1.01309 (.00548)	−.05375 (.00741)	55
75. Transportation	2926	.9680	.00008 (.00001)	.75362 (.00254)	M	56
76. Communication	2747	.9427	−.00003 (.00001)	1.08671 (.00511)	M	57
77. Radio, TV Broadcasting	1220	.9523	.00002 (.00003)	.62361 (.00707)	.41150 (.01754)	57
78. Electric Utility	2464	.9322	.00002 (.00001)	.95358 (.00518)	M	58
79. Gas Utility	1489	.7930	.00015 (.00003)	.77859 (.01032)	M	58
80. Water Utility	431	.9840	.00019 (.00004)	.86554 (.00886)	.07590 (.01625)	58
81. Wholesale Trade	2985	.9153	.00011 (.00001)	.66513 (.00370)	M	59
82. Finance and Insurance	3014	.9932	.00005 (.00000)	.84672 (.00128)	M	60
83. Real Estate and Rental	2575	.9920	.00005 (.00001)	.88060 (.00156)	M	60
84. Hotels, Personal and Repair Service	3009	.9596	.00007 (.00001)	.80367 (.00301)	M	61
85. Business Services	2746	.9762	.00008 (.00001)	.77233 (.00230)	M	61
86. Automobile Repair Service	2422	.9609	.00001 (.00001)	.97583 (.00400)	M	61
87. Amusements and Recreation	2533	.9870	.00008 (.00001)	.80579 (.00183)	M	61
88. Medical, Educational Institutions	3021	.9571	.00007 (.00001)	.78466 (.00303)	M	61
89. Lumber, Houseware, Farm Equip. Stores	2950	.9302	.00007 (.00000)	.81324 (.00520)	−.02192 (.00150)	59

Table 5-7 (cont.)

Industry Number and Name	No. Obsv.	R^2	Constant	1966 Output	1965 Equipment	No.
90. General Merchandise Stores	3009	.9166	.00010 (.00001)	.70640 (.00388)	M	59
91. Food Stores	3018	.9680	.00005 (.00000)	.92440 (.00429)	−.08631 (.00221)	59
92. Automotive Dealers	2950	.9632	.00007 (.00000)	.80922 (.00362)	−.02218 (.00164)	59
93. Gas Service Stations	2976	.9702	.00006 (.00000)	.83822 (.00332)	−.02325 (.00154)	59
94. Apparel, Accessory Stores	2841	.9076	.00013 (.00001)	.63188 (.00378)	M	59
95. Furniture Stores	2627	.9317	.00009 (.00001)	.75272 (.00398)	M	59
96. Eating, Drinking Places	3037	.9136	.00010 (.00001)	.68998 (.00385)	M	59
97. Drug and Proprietary Stores	2893	.9664	.00006 (.00000)	.88664 (.00430)	−.06651 (.00224)	59
98. Other Retail Stores	2992	.9440	.00008 (.00001)	.74853 (.00334)	M	59
99. Nonstore Retailers	1751	.9918	.00012 (.00001)	.86614 (.00225)	−.08072 (.00426)	59

Equation (2-15)

Sector	No. Obsv.	R^2	Constant	1966 Fed. Govt. Expenditures
100. Federal Government	3088	.5029	.00000 (.00003)	.99532 (.01781)

Equation (2-16)

Sector	No. Obsv.	R^2	Constant	1966 State and Local Govt. Expenditures
101. State and Local	3109	.9739	.00006 (.00000)	.81384 (.00239)

Equation (2-17)

Sector	No. Obsv.	R^2	Constant	1965 Personal Income
102. Household	3069	.7263	.00014 (.00001)	.55910 (.00620)

Symbols:

NS = not significant
M = multicollinearity

Table 5-7 also includes the equations for three nonindustrial labor sectors that explain the level of employment in federal government, state and local government, and households.

The Population and Labor Force Equations

Population is forecast with equations that explain population migration, births, and deaths. As given in Equation (2-29), population by race-age group in period t is equal to population in period $t-1$ plus births, minus deaths, plus net civilian migration, plus change in military employment.

Births by race are explained by relating them to population by race in the 15-34 age group. The parameters of Equation (2-22) are given in the first part of Table 5-8, where the variables were entered as relative regional shares. The results of the Equation (2-23) explaining deaths by race-age group are given in the second part of Table 5-8. The relative regional shares of deaths in 1966 are explained by the relative region shares of 1965 population in the corresponding race-age group.

Three different equations were set up to explain population migration by the 8 race-age groups. Civilian migration in the 4 working age groups 15-64 was hypothesized to migrate in response to economic factors as given in Equation (2-26). The independent variables were (1) the 1965 population associated with surplus (or deficient) labor, (2) the 1965-66 population associated with the change in civilian persons employed, (3) the 1965-66 change in military personnel, and (4) the 1965 average wage rate. The results of Equation (2-26) are reported in the third section of Table 5-8.

The fifth section of the table reports on Equation (2-27) explaining migration in the two 14 and under groups. Migration in the youth groups is hypothesized as a function of migration in the working-age groups. Migration in the retirement groups (65 and over) is a function of the prior level of population in these groups. Equation (2-28) is reported in the last section of Table 5-8.

The overall results of 6 of the 8 migration equations were not encouraging. Not only were the R^2s low, but the population forecasts were poor when the equations were used in the model. Consequently, 6 substitute equations were estimated and used in the model. In the 4 working age groups two independent variables were changed: the 1965 population associated with labor surplus was changed to just labor surplus, and the 1965-66 population associated with the change in civilian persons employed (expected population change) was changed to the change in civilian persons employed. In other words, independent variables (1) and (2) as listed above were divided by the labor force participation rate. These new equations are reported in the fourth section of Table 5-8.

The original equations for the two youth groups showed that their migration was inversely related to the migration in the 15-64 groups, which is not the expected relationship. Therefore, instead of using population migration, the level of population in the 15-34 group was used to explain the level of population in the 14 and under group. The substitute equation for Equation (2-27) is:

$$POP^t_{1rj} = g_{r27} (POP^t_{2rj}) \qquad\qquad (r = 1, 2),$$
$$(j = 1, \ldots, NR)$$

The results of the new equations are given in the sixth section of Table 5-8.

One of the reasons for the poor migration equations is that net migration as defined in Chapter 4 is not a pure migration figure, but includes the aging of people from lower to higher age groups. The components of change of the 14 and under age group between two years are births, deaths, net migrants, and the 14-year-olds which move into the 15-34 age group. The migration in the 15-34 age group, as we define it, includes the 14-year-olds turning 15 and excludes the 34-year-olds turning 35. Since the birth rate in 1966 was lower than it was in 1952, the migration of a region as we compute it can easily be negative in the 14 and under group at the same time that migration in the 15-34 age group is positive.

Labor force is estimated by relating it to population in the working age groups and to the population associated with labor force surplus or deficit. Equation (2-30) is

$$CLF^t = -.00004 + 1.134 \sum_{a=2}^{3} \sum_{r=1}^{2} POP^t_{ar} - .000000134\, PLS^{t-1}$$

The Income Equations

There are 101 function relationships explaining components of income, as given by Equations (2-32), (2-36), and (2-37). Earnings by place of work are estimated for 99 industry sectors and in addition there are estimates for transfer payments and property income. Personal income for a region is the sum of total earnings by place of residence, transfer payments, and property income less contributions for social insurance.

The results of the earnings Equation (2-32) for the 99 industry sectors are given in Table 5-9. The relative regional share of 1966 earnings by sector is explained by the relative regional shares of 1966 employment and 1965 equipment. The table shows the equipment purchasing sector number that is used in each of the industry equations. The coefficient on the equipment variable entered with a positive sign in 42 industry sectors, indicating that investment, with employment held constant, leads to higher payrolls and higher average wage rates. On the other hand, there were 22 industry sectors for which

Table 5-8
Equations Explaining 1966 Births, 1966 Deaths and 1965-1966 Population Migration

Equation (2-22)

Sector	No. Obsv.	R^2	Constant	1965 Pop.
White Births	3111	.9883	-.00000 (.00000)	1.00388 (.00196)
Nonwhite Births	2325	.9776	.00002 (.00001)	.94522 (.00297)

Equation (2-23)

Sector	No. Obsv.	R^2	Constant	1965 Pop.
White Deaths 0-14	2983	.9839	.00001 (.00000)	.96539 (.00226)
White Deaths 15-34	2916	.9783	.00003 (.00000)	.90274 (.00249)
White Deaths 35-64	3106	.9776	-.00002 (.00000)	1.04993 (.00285)
White Deaths 65 and Over	3110	.9893	-.00000 (.00000)	1.00070 (.00187)
Nonwhite Deaths 0-14	1586	.9648	.00001 (.00001)	1.00598 (.00483)
Nonwhite Deaths 15-34	1402	.9455	.00006 (.00002)	.94458 (.00606)
Nonwhite Deaths 35-64	1906	.9475	.00002 (.00001)	.95882 (.00517)
Nonwhite Deaths 65 and Over	2085	.9840	-.00001 (.00001)	1.01530 (.00284)

Equation (2-26)

Sector	No. Obsv.	R^2	Constant	1965 Pop. Surplus	1965-1966 Expected Pop. Change	1965-1966 Change in Military	1965 Average Wage Rate
White Migration 15-34	3112	.0812	−133 (111)	−.00797 (.00751)	.04637 (.00307)	WS	1291100 (343148)
White Migration 35-64	3112	.0498	32 (110)	−.06645 (.00742)	.03402 (.00303)	.13082 (.07132)	783279 (338899)
Nonwhite Migration 15-34	3112	.0422	−136 (48)	−.01490 (.00323)	.01402 (.00132)	WS	619152 (147578)
Nonwhite Migration 35-64	3112	.1465	−81 (29)	WS	.01655 (.0074)	WS	376983 (88830)

Substitute Equation (2-26)

Sector	No. Obsv.	R^2	Constant	1965 Labor Surplus	1965-1966 Employment Change	1965-1966 Change in Military	1965 Average Wage Rate
White Migration 15-34	3112	.1195	−186 (109)	−.05058 (.01791)	.09072 (.00509)	WS	1500696 (335262)
White Migration 35-64	3112	.2603	41 (97)	−.14843 (.01595)	.14134 (.00453)	.12277 (.06288)	748479 (298440)
Nonwhite Migration 15-34	3112	.0552	−150 (47)	−.05263 (.00782)	.02786 (.00222)	WS	670083 (146297)
Nonwhite Migration 35-64	3112	.1441	−105 (29)	WS	.02452 (.00111)	WS	467227 (88778)

Table 5-8 (cont.)

Equation (2-27)

Sector	No. Obsv.	R^2	Constant	1965-1966 Migration 15-64
White Migration 0-14	3112	.1144	-740 (64)	-.42893 (.02140)
Nonwhite Migration 0-14	3112	.1732	-126 (15)	-.32791 (.01285)

Substitute Equation (2-27)

Sector	No. Obsv.	R^2	Constant	1965-1966 Population 15-64
White Population 0-14	3112	.9848	.00001 (.00000)	.96950 (.00216)
Nonwhite Population 0-14	3022	.9753	.00005 (.00000)	.85905 (.00249)

Equation (2-28)

Sector	No. Obsv.	R^2	Constant	1965 Population 65 and Over
White Migration 65 and Over	3112	.8524	43 (10)	1134009 (8463)
Nonwhite Migration 65 and Over	3112	.8987	-6 (1)	138721 (835)

Symbol: WS = wrong sign

the coefficient was negative indicating that investment leads to lower average wage rates, which could be explained by a shift from high to low-wage employees. In the remaining 35 sectors the equipment variable was either collinear with employment or its coefficient was insignificant.

Earnings in the government and household sectors are estimated by applying last year's wage rate to this year's employment. By definition there can be no real change in wage rates in these sectors.

Transfer payments were hypothesized to be a function of population and unemployment as given by Equation (2-36). Population and unemployment, however, are collinear and therefore both are not allowed in the equation. It was decided that it would be desirable to have both in the equation for forecasting; therefore, the following equation is used in the model.

$$TR_j^t = .000006 + .7 \sum_{k=1}^{8} POP_{kj}^t + .297CUE_j^t \quad (j = 1, \ldots, NR)$$

This equation was derived by taking the results of a regression equation with only unemployment as an independent variable, giving this result a weight of 30 percent and giving population a weight of 70 percent.

Property income is estimated by relating it to earnings by place of residence. The Equation (2-37) is

$$PR_j^t = -.000027 + 1.08246ERN_j^t. \quad (j = 1, \ldots, NR)$$

Other Equations

Other functional relationships in the model as given in Chapter 2 include personal consumption expenditures, exports and imports, value of land, and marginal transport costs (shadow prices). The parameters of the personal consumption expenditure Equation (2-40) are given in Table 5-10. The 1966 relative regional shares of consumer expenditures are explained by the 1966 relative regional shares of personal income. No equations are given for the trade sectors (81, 88-99) since the sale to consumers from the trade sectors is assumed to have the same regional distribution as the total sales. This assumption was also necessary in estimating the basic data.

Equations were estimated for explaining the U.S. port distribution of foreign exports and imports as specified in Equations (2-42) and (2-43), but they proved unsatisfactory. It seems that it would be necessary to obtain data on port facilities themselves in order to explain the port activity. Marginal transport costs are inadequate to do the job. Instead of using functional relationships, the forecast regional distribution of foreign exports and imports by industry sector was assumed to be the same as the base year.

Table 5-9
Equation (2-32) Explaining 1966 Earnings by Industry Sector

Industry	No. Obsv.	R^2	Constant	1966 Employ.	1965 Equip.	Equip. No.
1. Livestock	2939	.3515	.00012 (.00001)	.34946 (.01456)	.33337 (.01226)	1
2. Crops	2933	.4736	.00002 (.00001)	.46656 (.01406)	.48605 (.01737)	1
3. Forestry and Fishery Products	519	.8484	−.00029 (.00013)	1.20104 (.02233)	NS	1
4. Agricultural Services	2218	.9332	−.00002 (.00001)	1.04235 (.00593)	NS	1
5. Iron Ore Mining	157	.9835	−.00027 (.00030)	1.04718 (.01091)	NS	2
6. Nonferrous Ore Mining	422	.9513	−.00011 (.00010)	1.05724 (.01168)	M	2
7. Coal Mining	427	.9065	−.00002 (.00010)	.90993 (.01942)	.32834 (.05329)	2
8. Petroleum Mining	644	.8961	−.00024 (.00008)	1.23985 (.02237)	−.08657 (.02520)	3
9. Minerals Mining	1512	.7015	−.0007 (.00002)	1.11485 (.02077)	.01624 (.01427)	2
10. Chemical Mining	90	.9331	.00064 (.00091)	.85735 (.04060)	.60227 (.37031)	2
11. New Construction	2966	.9419	−.00003 (.00001)	1.09262 (.00499)	M	4
12. Maintenance Construction	2680	.9738	−.00004 (.00001)	1.10643 (.00351)	M	4
13. Ordnance	799	.9939	−.00018 (.00004)	1.13992 (.00317)	NS	5
14. Meat Packing	1332	.9550	−.00012 (.00001)	1.13598 (.00817)	.02492 (.00577)	6

123

Industry						
15. Dairy Products	1488	.9748	−.00012 (.00001)	1.17453 (.00553)	−.00321 (.00316)	62
16. Canned and Frozen Foods	911	.9293	−.00009 (.00003)	1.01610 (.01209)	.06869 (.00886)	63
17. Grain Mill Products	1176	.9773	−.00013 (.00001)	1.14804 (.00575)	.00581 (.00391)	64
18. Bakery Products	933	.9823	−.00013 (.00002)	1.10274 (.00823)	.01825 (.00647)	65
19. Sugar	160	.9140	.00053 (.00031)	.89891 (.03070)	.04425 (.02663)	66
20. Candy	459	.9832	−.00024 (.00007)	1.16276 (.00711)	M	67
21. Beverages	1307	.9815	−.00013 (.00001)	1.19648 (.00518)	−.02306 (.00467)	68
22. Other Food	1067	.9813	−.00013 (.00002)	1.13383 (.00567)	.00681 (.00335)	69
23. Tobacco	178	.9601	−.00069 (.00031)	1.08972 (.02776)	.08175 (.01414)	7
24. Fabrics and Yarn	665	.9518	−.00006 (.00004)	1.06583 (.00932)	NS	8
25. Rugs, Tire Cord, Misc.	438	.8473	−.00001 (.00010)	1.01184 (.02057)	NS	9
26. Apparel	1546	.9802	−.00019 (.00002)	1.33487 (.00485)	−.04789 (.00456)	10
27. Household Tex. and Upholst.	546	.9820	−.00015 (.00005)	1.07424 (.00636)	.07764 (.00572)	11
28. Lumber and Prod. Exc. Containers	1983	.9580	−.00013 (.00001)	1.25422 (.00649)	.00673 (.00235)	12
29. Wooden Containers	684	.9237	−.00003 (.00004)	.99908 (.01225)	.03351 (.00636)	13
30. Household Furniture	828	.9664	−.00009 (.00002)	1.13630 (.00861)	−.06093 (.00583)	14

Table 5-9 (cont.)

Industry	No. Obsv.	R^2	Constant	1966 Employ.	1965 Equip.	Equip. No.
31. Office Furniture	510	.9703	-.00023 (.00005)	1.12810 (.00917)	-.01241 (.00766)	15
32. Paper and Prod. Exc. Containers	873	.9800	.00000 (.00001)	.98959 (.00537)	.01135 (.00292)	16
33. Paper Containers	464	.9817	-.00002 (.00004)	1.02835 (.00807)	-.00867 (.00626)	17
34. Printing and Publishing	2079	.9903	-.00009 (.00001)	1.23976 (.00289)	-.05451 (.00276)	18
35. Basic Chemicals	1194	.9627	-.00003 (.00001)	1.05078 (.00668)	-.01277 (.00393)	19
36. Plastics and Synthetics	656	.9618	-.00007 (.00003)	1.04075 (.00980)	.00655 (.00397)	20
37. Drugs, Cleaning and Toilet Items	494	.9012	-.00006 (.00009)	.97394 (.02234)	.06239 (.01885)	21
38. Paint and Allied Products	253	.9947	-.00007 (.00006)	1.02679 (.00736)	-.01010 (.00787)	22
39. Petroleum Refining	433	.9903	-.00012 (.00004)	1.09779 (.00525)	NS	23
40. Rubber and Plastic Products	870	.9754	-.00012 (.00003)	1.15996 (.00739)	-.05673 (.00748)	24
41. Leather Tanning	172	.9787	-.00008 (.00017)	.98130 (.01314)	.05047 (.01085)	25
42. Shoes and Other Leather Products	521	.9823	-.00013 (.00003)	1.05682 (.00802)	.03036 (.00603)	26
43. Glass and Glass Products	541	.9670	-.00007 (.00004)	1.06156 (.00931)	-.00473 (.00344)	27
44. Stone and Clay Products	1671	.9730	-.00004 (.00001)	1.07789 (.00439)	NS	28

125

45. Iron and Steel	981	.9904	−.00004 (.00002)	1.05285 (.00355)	.00524 (.00211)	29
46. Copper	264	1.0000	.00000 (.00000)	1.00000 (.00000)	NS	30
47. Aluminum	504	.9764	−.00012 (.00004)	1.13632 (.00881)	−.02454 (.00714)	30
48. Other Nonferrous Metals	431	.9783	−.00012 (.00004)	1.08948 (.00784)	NS	30
49. Metal Containers	216	.9330	−.00040 (.00027)	.98176 (.03176)	.12614 (.02710)	31
50. Heating, Plumbing, Struc. Metal	923	.9872	−.00008 (.00001)	1.07411 (.00485)	.00590 (.00382)	32
51. Stampings, Screw Mach. Products	527	.9893	−.00015 (.00004)	1.08148 (.00491)	M	33
52. Hardware, Plating, Wire Products	841	.9936	−.00006 (.00001)	1.06222 (.00411)	−.00800 (.00338)	34
53. Engines and Turbines	346	.9742	−.00003 (.00007)	.96871 (.01024)	.04502 (.00880)	35
54. Farm Machinery and Equipment	703	.9825	−.00031 (.00004)	1.17743 (.00917)	.04980 (.00866)	36
55. Construction and Mining Mach.	553	.9828	−.00007 (.00003)	1.01699 (.00635)	.03160 (.00502)	37
56. Material Handling Equip.	347	.9899	−.00027 (.00005)	1.12053 (.00883)	−.02591 (.00740)	37
57. Metal Working Mach.	562	.9830	−.00021 (.00004)	1.14655 (.01005)	−.03125 (.00944)	38
58. Special Industrial Machinery	479	.9864	−.00010 (.00003)	1.04426 (.00704)	.01101 (.00530)	39
59. General Industrial Machinery	545	.9905	−.00009 (.00002)	1.05417 (.00594)	−.00652 (.00465)	40
60. Machine Shops and Misc. Mach.	787	.9934	−.00014 (.00002)	1.09954 (.00589)	.01310 (.00489)	41

Table 5-9 (cont.)

Industry	No. Obsv.	R^2	Constant	1966 Employ.	1965 Equip.	Equip. No.
61. Office and Computing Machines	500	.9787	-.00015 (.00005)	1.08124 (.00802)	-.00638 (.00476)	42
62. Service Industry Machines	373	.9781	-.00013 (.00005)	1.07766 (.01013)	.01049 (.00660)	43
63. Electric Apparatus and Motors	589	.9835	-.00011 (.00003)	1.06396 (.00770)	.00951 (.00476)	44
64. Household Appliances	424	.9774	-.00025 (.00006)	1.11511 (.01061)	-.01033 (.00781)	45
65. Electric Light and Wiring	362	.9878	-.00013 (.00005)	1.03053 (.00732)	.01594 (.00557)	46
66. Communication Equipment	758	.9760	.00001 (.00004)	.99517 (.00568)	NS	47
67. Electronic Components	690	.9840	-.00005 (.00003)	1.00163 (.00557)	.03594 (.00461)	48
68. Batteries and Engine Equipment	371	.9478	.00000 (.00007)	.99954 (.01221)	NS	49
69. Motor Vehicles	892	.9970	-.00006 (.00001)	1.05417 (.00193)	M	50
70. Aircraft and Parts	980	.9817	-.00005 (.00004)	1.12153 (.00635)	-.03850 (.00631)	51
71. Ships, Trains, Trailers, Cycles	860	.9636	-.00018 (.00003)	1.14529 (.00815)	.00863 (.00413)	52
72. Instruments and Clocks	433	.9846	-.00009 (.00004)	1.06087 (.00639)	NS	53
73. Optical and Photographic Equip.	301	.9847	-.00067 (.00016)	1.21650 (.00877)	M	54
74. Misc. Manufactured Products	1018	.9906	-.00005 (.00002)	1.03105 (.00384)	.02498 (.00520)	55

75. Transportation	2926	.9823	-.00007 (.00001)	1.20185 (.00298)	M	56
76. Communication	2747	.9791	.00002 (.00000)	.93964 (.00262)	M	57
77. Radio, TV Broadcasting	1220	.9376	.00000 (.00004)	1.18848 (.01365)	-.22501 (.02615)	57
78. Electric Utility	2464	.9781	-.00000 (.00000)	1.00913 (.00304)	M	58
79. Gas Utility	1489	.9750	-.00002 (.00001)	1.02267 (.00425)	NS	58
80. Water Utility	431	.9675	-.00004 (.00006)	1.05810 (.01493)	-.06261 (.02480)	58
81. Wholesale Trade	2985	.9951	-.00004 (.00000)	1.13010 (.00145)	M	59
82. Finance and Insurance	3014	.9952	-.00005 (.00000)	1.15697 (.00146)	M	60
83. Real Estate and Rental	2575	.9890	-.00004 (.00001)	1.10741 (.00230)	M	60
84. Hotels, Personal and Repair Svc.	3009	.9593	-.00003 (.00001)	1.08433 (.00407)	M	61
85. Business Services	2746	.9824	-.00005 (.00001)	1.13265 (.00289)	M	61
86. Automobile Repair Services	2422	.9483	-.00001 (.00001)	1.01982 (.00484)	M	61
87. Amusements and Recreation	2533	.9429	-.00030 (.00002)	1.76253 (.00862)	M	61
88. Medical and Educational Instit.	3021	.9562	-.00002 (.00001)	1.05702 (.00412)	M	61
89. Lumber, Houseware, Farm Equip.	2950	.9700	-.00004 (.00000)	1.11680 (.00455)	.00550 (.00104)	59
90. General Merchandise Stores	3009	.9925	-.00001 (.00000)	.96740 (.00281)	.06852 (.00147)	59

Table 5-9 (cont.)

Industry	No. Obsv.	R^2	Constant	1966 Employ.	1965 Equip.	Equip. No.
91. Food Stores	3018	.9537	-.00006 (.00001)	1.16498 (.00650)	.00657 (.00273)	59
92. Automotive Dealers	2950	.9819	-.00006 (.00000)	1.18160 (.00368)	.00915 (.00132)	59
93. Gasoline Service Stations	2976	.9852	-.00004 (.00000)	1.09120 (.00310)	.02254 (.00118)	59
94. Apparel Accessory Stores	2841	.9880	-.00006 (.00000)	1.17116 (.00242)	M	59
95. Furniture Stores	2627	.9898	-.00005 (.00000)	1.10634 (.00350)	.02674 (.00152)	59
96. Eating, Drinking Places	3037	.9760	-.00008 (.00001)	1.24955 (.00356)	M	59
97. Drug and Proprietary Stores	2893	.9395	-.00004 (.00001)	1.08819 (.00743)	.03266 (.00312)	59
98. Other Retail Stores	2992	.9735	-.00004 (.00000)	1.12587 (.00340)	M	59
99. Nonstore Retailers	1751	.9962	-.00009 (.00001)	1.11391 (.00200)	.04571 (.00319)	59

Symbols:
NS = not significant
M = multicollinearity

Table 5-10

Equation (2-40) Explaining the 1966 Personal Consumption Expenditures by Industry Sector

Industry	No. Obsv.	R^2	Constant	1966 Personal Income
1. Livestock	3093	.9398	.00002 (.00001)	.94804 (.00432)
2. Crops	3096	.9452	.00001 (.00001)	.95709 (.00414)
3. Forestry and Fishery Products	2998	.5985	.00012 (.00002)	.65471 (.00980)
7. Coal Mining	2702	.5628	.00008 (.00002)	.86062 (.01460)
9. Minerals Mining	2175	.8022	.00015 (.00001)	.68846 (.00733)
13. Ordnance	3004	.7993	.00009 (.00001)	.72706 (.00665)
14. Meat Packing	3100	.9597	.00001 (.00001)	.97910 (.00360)
15. Dairy Products	3100	.9595	.00001 (.00001)	.97653 (.00360)
16. Canned and Frozen Foods	3100	.9597	.00001 (.00001)	.97912 (.00361)
17. Grain Mill Products	3096	.9595	.00001 (.00001)	.96873 (.00358)
18. Bakery Products	3100	.9597	.00001 (.00001)	.97943 (.00361)
19. Sugar	3078	.9597	.00001 (.00001)	.97551 (.00361)
20. Candy	3096	.9597	.00001 (.00001)	.97931 (.00361)
21. Beverages	3100	.9597	.00001 (.00001)	.97887 (.00360)
22. Misc. Food Products	3099	.9597	.00001 (.00001)	.97534 (.00359)
23. Tobacco	3098	.9124	.00004 (.00001)	.87204 (.00486)
24. Fabrics and Yarn	3031	.9564	−.00003 (.00001)	1.10082 (.00427)
25. Rugs, Tire Cord, Misc. Textiles	3041	.8962	.00005 (.00001)	.83498 (.00515)
26. Apparel	3071	.9662	−.00006 (.00001)	1.17316 (.00396)
27. Household Textiles and Upholst.	3077	.9268	.00001 (.00001)	.95541 (.00484)
28. Lumber and Prod. Exc. Containers	2881	.5869	.00014 (.00002)	.59869 (.00936)

Table 5-10 (cont.)

Industry	No. Obsv.	R^2	Constant	1966 Personal Income
30. Household Furniture	3041	.9562	−.00004 (.00001)	1.11073 (.00431)
31. Office Furniture	2891	.9268	−.00003 (.00001)	1.08405 (.00567)
32. Paper and Prod. Exc. Containers	3069	.7785	.00010 (.00001)	.70189 (.00676)
33. Paper Containers	2046	.7664	.00001 (.00003)	1.21809 (.01488)
34. Printing and Publishing	3078	.9369	−.00011 (.00001)	1.32559 (.00620)
35. Basic Chemicals	3024	.7823	.00011 (.00001)	.65509 (.00629)
36. Plastics and Synthetics	1625	.9275	−.00002 (.00002)	1.08313 (.00752)
37. Drugs, Cleaning and Toilet Items	3081	.8730	.00006 (.00001)	.80202 (.00551)
38. Paint and Allied Products	1877	.6483	.00014 (.00003)	.76362 (.01299)
39. Petroleum Refining	3090	.8701	.00008 (.00001)	.74563 (.00518)
40. Rubber and Plastic Products	3080	.7370	.00012 (.00001)	.62725 (.00675)
42. Shoes and Other Leather Products	3055	.9600	−.00003 (.00001)	1.07939 (.00399)
43. Glass and Glass Products	2932	.6197	.00013 (.00001)	.62840 (.00909)
44. Stone and Clay Products	2983	.6632	.00012 (.00001)	.65606 (.00856)
45. Iron and Steel	2328	.8975	.00002 (.00001)	.96346 (.00675)
47. Aluminum	1340	.9461	.00003 (.00002)	.99729 (.00651)
48. Other Nonferrous Metals	1223	.9460	.00004 (.00002)	.99751 (.00682)
50. Heating, Plumbing, Struc. Metal	2835	.7858	.00014 (.00001)	.60440 (.00593)
51. Stampings, Screw Mach. Prod.	2997	.9398	−.00001 (.00001)	1.03952 (.00481)
52. Hardware, Plating, Wire Prod.	3041	.8972	.00008 (.00001)	.76119 (.00467)
53. Engines and Turbines	2982	.7574	.00010 (.00001)	.71632 (.00743)
54. Farm Machinery and Equipment	1590	.8019	.00010 (.00002)	.89000 (.01110)
57. Metalworking Machinery and Equipment	2459	.7870	.00010 (.00001)	.76944 (.00808)

Table 5-10 (cont.)

Industry	No. Obsv.	R^2	Constant	1966 Personal Income
58. Special Industrial Machinery	1995	.9281	−.00003 (.00001)	1.08345 (.00675)
61. Office and Computing Machines	2806	.8781	.00001 (.00001)	.96704 (.00681)
62. Service Industry Machines	3015	.9172	.00004 (.00001)	.89441 (.00489)
63. Electric Apparatus and Motors	2104	.9349	.00005 (.00001)	.90826 (.00523)
64. Household Appliances	3079	.9280	.00001 (.00001)	.98318 (.00494)
65. Electric Light and Wiring Equipment	3039	.8970	.00007 (.00001)	.79540 (.00489)
66. Communication Equipment	3071	.9224	.00003 (.00001)	.90982 (.00476)
67. Electronic Components	2848	.9246	.00002 (.00001)	.95767 (.00513)
68. Batteries and Engine Elec. Equipment	3018	.6973	.00013 (.00001)	.59808 (.00718)
69. Motor Vehicles	3010	.7860	.00006 (.00001)	.82611 (.00786)
70. Aircraft and Parts	2339	.7551	.00013 (.00002)	.71225 (.00839)
71. Ships, Trains, Trailers, Cycles	3051	.8302	.00007 (.00001)	.79454 (.00651)
72. Instruments and Clocks	3048	.9162	.00001 (.00001)	.96084 (.00527)
73. Optical and Photographic Equip.	3071	.8152	.00008 (.00001)	.75088 (.00645)
74. Misc. Manufactured Products	3084	.8998	.00004 (.00001)	.86981 (.00523)
75. Transportation	3099	.9414	.00004 (.00001)	.88736 (.00398)
76. Communication	3032	.8203	.00005 (.00001)	.84776 (.00721)
78. Electric Utility	2845	.8594	.00007 (.00001)	.82833 (.00628)
79. Gas Utility	2387	.5908	.00005 (.00003)	1.03378 (.01762)
80. Water Utility	1222	.5171	.00003 (.00009)	1.25285 (.03466)
81. Wholesale Trade	3053	.9677	−.00005 (.00001)	1.15574 (.00382)
82. Finance and Insurance	3045	.7233	−.00019 (.00003)	1.58073 (.01772)
83. Real Estate and Rental	3018	.7685	−.00024 (.00003)	1.74148 (.01740)

Table 5-10 (cont.)

Industry	No. Obsv.	R^2	Constant	1966 Personal Income
84. Hotels, Personal and Repair Svc.	3096	.8326	.00003 (.00001)	.90705 (.00731)
85. Business Services	2761	.7392	−.00037 (.00004)	2.04710 (.02315)
86. Automobile Repair Services	2729	.9164	.00000 (.00001)	1.01116 (.00585)
87. Amusements and Recreation	2721	.7874	−.00023 (.00003)	1.64430 (.01639)
88. Medical and Educational Instit.	3069	.8864	−.00009 (.00001)	1.26489 (.00817)

The value of land per acre is estimated by relating it to property income as given in Equation (2-48). The parameters in the equation are:

$$VL_j^t = .00008 + .74416 PR_j^t \qquad (j = 1, \ldots, NR)$$

The variables were entered on a relative regional share basis.

As described earlier, the marginal transport costs for each industry are computed using the linear programming transportation algorithm, given the industry's total demand, total supply, and transport cost of shipping its product between each pair of regions. When counties are used as observations the computer costs of these computations are very high. Therefore, in this application the shadow prices were not recomputed in forecast years using the linear programming algorithm. Instead, regression equations are used where the regional variation in the relative regional shares of the output shadow prices is explained by the regional varieties in the export status. The equation is

$$TQ_{ij}^t = g_{i47} \, (EXS_{ij}^t) \qquad \begin{array}{l} (j = 1, \ldots, NR) \\ (i = 1, \ldots, 74) \\ (i \neq 4, 11, 12) \end{array}$$

where the export status is defined as

$$EXS_{ij}^t = Q_{ij}^t - Q_j^t \cdot Q_i^t / Q^t, \qquad \begin{array}{l} (j = 1, \ldots, NR) \\ (i = 1, \ldots, 74) \\ (i \neq 4, 11, 12) \end{array}$$

The export status is the difference between actual output in industry i and what the output would have been if the region had the same share of the industry i's output as the nation. The parameters of these regressions are given in Table 5-11. As measured by the overall fit, these equations appear to be poor substitutes for computing the shadow price with the linear programming algorithm.

Once the output shadow prices are estimated, the input shadow prices are computed using the following relationship

Table 5-11
Substitute Equations for Forecasting Marginal Transportation Costs (Shadow Prices)

Industry Sector	No. Obsv.	R^2	Constant	"Export Status"
1. Livestock	155	.0504	$.2807 \times 10^{-3}$	$-.2430 \times 10^{-9}$
2. Crops	175	.0290	$.2959 \times 10^{-3}$	$-.1186 \times 10^{-9}$
3. Forestry and Fishery Products	184	.0263	$.3229 \times 10^{-3}$	$-.1114 \times 10^{-8}$
5. Iron Ore Mining	137	.0336	$.3169 \times 10^{-3}$	$-.2062 \times 10^{-8}$
6. Nonferrous Ore Mining	144	.0451	$.3440 \times 10^{-3}$	$-.2296 \times 10^{-8}$
7. Coal Mining	158	.0395	$.3780 \times 10^{-3}$	$-.3599 \times 10^{-8}$
8. Petroleum Mining	95	.0239	$.3292 \times 10^{-3}$	$-.1217 \times 10^{-9}$
9. Minerals Mining	158	.0142	$.2788 \times 10^{-3}$	$-.1403 \times 10^{-8}$
10. Chemical Mining	145	.0000	$.3323 \times 10^{-3}$	.0000
13. Ordnance	138	.0110	$.3102 \times 10^{-3}$	$-.5951 \times 10^{-10}$
14. Meat Packing	160	.1034	$.4189 \times 10^{-3}$	$-.1153 \times 10^{-8}$
15. Dairy Products	146	.0174	$.3839 \times 10^{-3}$	$-.9219 \times 10^{-9}$
16. Canned and Frozen Foods	153	.0535	$.3020 \times 10^{-3}$	$-.4596 \times 10^{-9}$
17. Grain Mill Products	159	.0926	$.4069 \times 10^{-3}$	$-.1594 \times 10^{-8}$
18. Bakery Products	135	.0130	$.3762 \times 10^{-3}$	$-.6704 \times 10^{-9}$
19. Sugar	190	.2029	$.3045 \times 10^{-3}$	$-.1686 \times 10^{-8}$
20. Candy	170	.0154	$.3779 \times 10^{-3}$	$-.5340 \times 10^{-9}$
21. Beverages	157	.0305	$.4217 \times 10^{-3}$	$-.1361 \times 10^{-8}$
22. Misc. Food Products	164	.0117	$.3312 \times 10^{-3}$	$-.6888 \times 10^{-9}$
23. Tobacco	255	.0151	$.3889 \times 10^{-3}$	$-.1115 \times 10^{-8}$
24. Fabrics and Yarn	128	.0900	$.2606 \times 10^{-3}$	$-.7606 \times 10^{-9}$
25. Rugs, Tire Cord, Misc. Textiles	165	.0499	$.3681 \times 10^{-3}$	$-.2645 \times 10^{-8}$
26. Apparel	146	.0176	$.3603 \times 10^{-3}$	$-.6866 \times 10^{-9}$
27. Household Textiles and Upholstery	181	.0183	$.3716 \times 10^{-3}$	$-.5172 \times 10^{-8}$
28. Lumber and Prod. Exc. Containers	150	.0202	$.2666 \times 10^{-3}$	$-.5329 \times 10^{-9}$
29. Wooden Containers	115	.0572	$.3584 \times 10^{-3}$	$-.1799 \times 10^{-7}$
30. Household Furniture	136	.0112	$.3944 \times 10^{-3}$	$-.2521 \times 10^{-8}$
31. Office Furniture	144	.0000	$.3982 \times 10^{-3}$	.0000
32. Paper and Prod. Esc. Containers	142	.2073	$.3428 \times 10^{-3}$	$-.1754 \times 10^{-8}$
33. Paper Containers	153	.0364	$.3508 \times 10^{-3}$	$-.5295 \times 10^{-8}$
34. Printing and Publishing	156	.0146	$.4949 \times 10^{-3}$	$-.8390 \times 10^{-9}$
35. Basic Chemicals	143	.0699	$.4138 \times 10^{-3}$	$-.9554 \times 10^{-9}$
36. Plastics and Synthetics	142	.0873	$.3137 \times 10^{-3}$	$-.1783 \times 10^{-8}$
37. Drugs, Cleaning and Toilet Items	173	.0461	$.4098 \times 10^{-3}$	$-.7784 \times 10^{-9}$
38. Paint and Allied Products	210	.0000	$.3464 \times 10^{-3}$	.0000
39. Petroleum Refining	178	.0123	$.3042 \times 10^{-3}$	$-.1009 \times 10^{-9}$
40. Rubber and Plastic Products	147	.0835	$.3654 \times 10^{-3}$	$-.2651 \times 10^{-8}$
41. Leather Tanning	78	.0000	$.2697 \times 10^{-3}$	$-.0000$
42. Shoes and Other Leather Products	117	.0379	$.3717 \times 10^{-3}$	$-.2645 \times 10^{-8}$
43. Glass and Glass Products	164	.0076	$.3468 \times 10^{-3}$	$-.8742 \times 10^{-9}$
44. Stone and Clay Products	157	.0121	$.3747 \times 10^{-3}$	$-.4507 \times 10^{-9}$

Table 5-11 (cont.)

Industry Sector	No. Obsv.	R^2	Constant	"Export Status"
45. Iron and Steel	151	.0140	$.3396 \times 10^{-3}$	$-.1238 \times 10^{-9}$
46. Copper	202	.0631	$.3263 \times 10^{-3}$	$-.5058 \times 10^{-9}$
47. Aluminum	152	.0100	$.3361 \times 10^{-3}$	$-.4334 \times 10^{-9}$
48. Other Nonferrous Metals	151	.1123	$.3251 \times 10^{-3}$	$-.1559 \times 10^{-8}$
49. Metal Containers	241	.0433	$.2910 \times 10^{-3}$	$-.1006 \times 10^{-8}$
50. Heating, Plumbing, Struc. Metal	158	.0483	$.3979 \times 10^{-3}$	$-.3924 \times 10^{-8}$
51. Stampings, Screw Mach. Prod.	164	.0382	$.3292 \times 10^{-3}$	$-.9015 \times 10^{-9}$
52. Hardware, Plating, Wire Prod.	147	.0162	$.3392 \times 10^{-3}$	$-.3345 \times 10^{-9}$
53. Engines and Turbines	174	.0326	$.3194 \times 10^{-3}$	$-.2774 \times 10^{-8}$
54. Farm Machinery and Equipment	175	.0454	$.3856 \times 10^{-3}$	$-.1566 \times 10^{-8}$
55. Construction and Mining Mach.	156	.1784	$.3366 \times 10^{-3}$	$-.3844 \times 10^{-8}$
56. Material Handling Equipment	193	.0190	$.3829 \times 10^{-3}$	$-.4009 \times 10^{-8}$
57. Metalworking Mach. and Equipment	152	.0827	$.3254 \times 10^{-3}$	$-.8136 \times 10^{-9}$
58. Special Industrial Machinery	142	.0967	$.3548 \times 10^{-3}$	$-.4537 \times 10^{-8}$
59. General Industrial Machinery	142	.0748	$.3349 \times 10^{-3}$	$-.2010 \times 10^{-8}$
60. Machine Shops and Misc. Mach.	133	.0000	$.3297 \times 10^{-3}$	.0000
61. Office and Computing Machines	141	.0000	$.3581 \times 10^{-3}$	.0000
62. Service Industry Machines	172	.1317	$.4056 \times 10^{-3}$	$-.1147 \times 10^{-7}$
63. Electric Apparatus and Motors	156	.0474	$.3968 \times 10^{-3}$	$-.3563 \times 10^{-8}$
64. Household Appliances	171	.0868	$.4085 \times 10^{-3}$	$-.4233 \times 10^{-8}$
65. Electric Wiring Equipment	162	.0000	$.3323 \times 10^{-3}$	.0000
66. Communication Equipment	172	.0000	$.3436 \times 10^{-3}$	.0000
67. Electronic Components	147	.0187	$.3205 \times 10^{-3}$	$-.2322 \times 10^{-9}$
68. Batteries and Engine Elec. Equipment	184	.1213	$.3670 \times 10^{-3}$	$-.8511 \times 10^{-8}$
69. Motor Vehicles	169	.0000	$.3791 \times 10^{-3}$	$-.0000$
70. Aircraft and Parts	181	.0085	$.3443 \times 10^{-3}$	$-.5714 \times 10^{-10}$
71. Ships, Trains, Trailers, Cycles	141	.0549	$.3610 \times 10^{-3}$	$-.1064 \times 10^{-8}$
72. Instruments and Clocks	176	.0287	$.3548 \times 10^{-3}$	$-.1526 \times 10^{-8}$
73. Optic and Photographic Equip.	237	.0095	$.3689 \times 10^{-3}$	$-.1695 \times 10^{-8}$
74. Misc. Manufactured Products	153	.0260	$.3888 \times 10^{-3}$	$-.1842 \times 10^{-8}$

$$TI_{ij}^t = T_{ijj}^{t-1} - TQ_{ij}^t$$

$$(j = 1, \ldots, NR)$$
$$(i = 1, \ldots, 74)$$
$$(i \neq 4, 11, 12)$$

where T_{ijj} is the intratransport cost of shipping the product from industry i within region j. In the base year all the superscripts are the same and this relationship is an identity. We assume that the future totals of TI and TQ remain the same as in the base year.

6

The Forecasts

Economic and population projections by major Standard Metropolitan Statistical Areas (SMSAs) are presented in this chapter. The first two sections reveal the major assumptions made in the national and regional models respectively. The third section reports on the use of some 1970 data, and the use of residuals is discussed in the fifth section. The sixth section analyzes the results and shows the results in summary form. The seventh section reports on the geographic redistribution of economic activity resulting from reduced defense expenditures. The last section makes suggestions for future research. The appendix gives the results in more detail for major SMSAs.

Assumptions in the National Model

As mentioned before, the national projections that are used as control totals for the regional projections were derived from Professor Clopper Almon's Inter-industry Forecasting Project. In this section, the national model and its assumptions are described briefly.

The national model is a 185 sector input-output model that is solved using a dynamic iterative procedure. Initially, final demand projections are made, then output is derived using the input-output coefficients. Next, employment is derived from the output projections. For any given year, the model is iterated to make sure that (1) the investment expenditures are consistent with the output levels as specified by production functions, and (2) the total employment is consistent with a predetermined labor force and an assumed unemployment rate. The model recursively takes forecasts for year $t+1$ and uses them as data for making forecasts for year $t+2$.

Government expenditures are exogenously derived. The assumed annual increases in government expenditures between 1975 and 1985 are: federal government approximately 3 percent, defense expenditures approximately 1.4 percent, and state and local government expenditures approximately 1.3 percent. NASA expenditures are held constant throughout the projection period.

The independent variables in equations for private equipment and industrial construction expenditures include the interest rate and the existence of the investment tax credit. It is assumed that the investment tax credit of 7 percent will remain in effect throughout the projection period, and that the real interest rates expressed in 1969 dollars will adjust downward until about 1978 and then

135

will remain fairly constant. The real short term interest rate after 1978 is assumed to be 1.5 percent and the long term interest rate is assumed to be 2.2 percent.

Exports by industry sector are either predetermined or related to output. Imports are related to the total demand for goods and the relative prices between domestic goods and imports. It is assumed overall that import prices increase relative to U.S. prices so that by 1975 the index of the ratio of import to domestic prices is 8 percent over the 1970 ratio. The relative prices are then held constant between 1975 and 1985.

National population forecasts are the series "C" projections published by the Census Bureau. The labor force projections are derived by the Bureau of Labor Statistics and are consistent with the series "C" population projections. In order to derive the total persons employed it is assumed that the civilian unemployment rate will gradually decline reaching 3.8 percent in 1980, after which it is assumed to increase slightly to 4.1 percent by 1985.

The national forecasting model allows input-output coefficients to change over time. Some of the changes are predetermined and based on specific knowledge of the rate of adoption of technology in the industry. Other coefficients are allowed to change in order to produce a balanced input-output matrix in which the coefficients allow the final demand sectors to be consistent with the output levels.

Most of the national numbers as produced by the Almon model are used directly as controls in the regional model. Exceptions are employment and population. Since the historical data on employment used in the regional model came from a different source than that used in the national model, the percent change in employment by industry sector from the national model is applied to the base year employment sums from the regional model. The employment figures in the regional model were derived for March of each year from *County Business Patterns* whereas in the national model employment figures are annual averages from the Bureau of Labor Statistics. Since the data are from two different sources there are some differences in the industry classifications.

The population in the regional model is the resident population of the U.S. whereas in the national model the population includes persons residing overseas; therefore, an adjustment was made of approximately 1 percent to subtract out the overseas population.

Assumptions in the Regional Model

The projections given in the fifth section of this chapter were made with an overall general assumption that there would be no abrupt changes in the economy of any particular region. The changes that do take place over time are a result of gradual adjustment to the forces of change. The behavior of all variables is given by the equations discussed previously.

The regional forecasting model allows for the location of new plants into regions which previously did not have the industry in question. If a region is in a favorable position with regard to the location of a particular industry, the model will try to locate output there. If the forecast potential output for a given year exceeds a given threshold level then the output is allowed to remain in the region. If the output is below the threshold level, the new output is not allowed. The only exceptions to this procedure were the agriculture and mining industry sectors, since the location of these industries depends on the availability of natural resources. Agricultural and mining outputs in new regions were not allowed; however, they could have been accounted for if special knowledge were available of the potential startup of these activities.

The threshold levels are defined in terms of value of output. They were determined from the plant size data given in *County Business Patterns*, which gives national data on the number of reporting units by eight employment size categories. For each industry, the plant size having the greatest number of reporting units was selected to compute the threshold level, provided that this plant size was below the average plant size. The average number of employees in the selected plant size was multiplied by the appropriate output-employment ratio. For the manufacturing industries the ratio was computed from the 1967 Census of Manufacturers, which was available by plant size. For the other industries, average output employment ratios were computed from the data estimated for use in the model. Table 6-1 shows the threshold level of output for each of the industries.

In keeping with the overall assumption of no abrupt regional changes, certain limits in forecast values were placed on changes in output, employment, earnings, and labor force. The arbitrary limits discussed here were selected after experimenting with alternative values, and could be changed if the model were run under different assumptions.

In order to determine the limit on output change, the ratio of output between 1965 and 1966 for each industry in each county was compared to the appropriate national output ratio for the same period. The county ratios were separated according to whether or not they were positive or negative and the average positive and negative deviations from the national ratios were computed for each industry. These deviations were added to the national ratios in order to establish the upper and lower limits on the annual percent change in county output. Superimposed on these deviations was an overall restriction that the percent change in county output could not exceed 110 percent of the national percent change nor go below 95 percent on the national percent change.

Once the employment forecasts were made using the equations, the productivity rates were examined. Limits were put on the annual employment change in order to keep the forecast productivity rate in line with the previous year's productivity rate. The county productivity rate relative to the national rate was not allowed to decrease more than 2 percent from one year to the next and the relative rate was not allowed to increase more than 110 percent.

Table 6-1

Threshold Level of Output for New Firms by Industry Sector

Industry Sectors	Threshold (000)
11. New Construction	0
12. Maintenance Construction	0
13. Ordnance	26240
14. Meat Packing	160
15. Dairy Products	670
16. Canned and Frozen Foods	520
17. Grain Mill Products	1120
18. Bakery Products	310
19. Sugar	4920
20. Candy	60
21. Beverages	760
22. Miscellaneous Food Products	880
23. Tobacco	3490
24. Fabrics and Yarn	2470
25. Rugs, Tire Cord, Miscellaneous Textiles	420
26. Apparel	510
27. Household Textiles and Upholstery	40
28. Lumber and Products Except Containers	100
29. Wooden Containers	200
30. Household Furniture	30
31. Office Furniture	40
32. Paper and Products Except Containers	1150
33. Paper Containers	880
34. Printing and Publishing	30
35. Basic Chemicals	620
36. Plastics and Synthetics	1410
37. Drugs, Cleaning and Toilet Items	100
38. Paint and Allied Products	550
39. Petroleum Refining	1870
40. Rubber and Plastic Products	320
41. Leather Tanning	350
42. Shoes and Other Leather Products	170
43. Glass and Glass Products	3920
44. Stone and Clay Products	270
45. Iron and Steel	860
46. Copper	2900
47. Aluminum	2870
48. Other Nonferrous Metals	3380
49. Metal Containers	1930

Table 6-1 (cont.)

Industry Sectors	Threshold (000)
50. Heating, Plumbing, Struc. Metal	280
51. Stampings, Screw Machine Products	300
52. Hardware, Plating, Wire Products	230
53. Engines and Turbines	950
54. Farm Machinery and Equipment	360
55. Construction and Mining Machinery	800
56. Material Handling Equipment	1140
57. Metalworking Machinery and Equipment	290
58. Special Industrial Machinery	280
59. General Industrial Machinery	290
60. Machine Shops and Miscellaneous Machinery	200
61. Office and Computing Machines	1250
62. Service Industry Machines	410
63. Electric Apparatus and Motors	730
64. Household Appliances	360
65. Electric Light and Wiring Equipment	270
66. Communication Equipment	680
67. Electronic Components	720
68. Batteries and Engine Elec. Equipment	310
69. Motor Vehicles	1940
70. Aircraft and Parts	720
71. Ships, Trains, Trailers, Cycles	280
72. Instruments and Clocks	140
73. Optical and Photographic Equipment	110
74. Misc. Manufactured Products	30
75. Transportation	40
76. Communication	110
77. Radio, TV Broadcasting	320
78. Electric Utility	1430
79. Gas Utility	1710
80. Water Utility	130
81. Wholesale Trade	30
82. Finance and Insurance	30
83. Real Estate and Rental	340
84. Motels, Personal and Repair Services	20
85. Business Services	80
86. Automobile Repair Services	90
87. Amusements and Recreation	230
88. Medical and Educational Institutions	20
89. Lumber, Houseware, Farm Equipment Stores	20
90. General Merchandise Stores	20

Table 6-1 (cont.)

Industry Sectors	Threshold (000)
91. Food Stores	20
92. Automotive Dealers	30
93. Gasoline Service Stations	20
94. Apparel, Accessory Stores	20
95. Furniture Stores	30
96. Eating, Drinking Places	10
97. Drug and Proprietary Stores	50
98. Other Retail Stores	20
99. Nonstore Retailers	160

Restrictions were also put on the earnings by industry. The forecast real wage rate (earnings per unit of employment) relative to the national rate was not allowed to exceed the prior year's relative rate by more than 105 percent and it was not allowed to go below 98 percent of the relative rate. The national projections indicate that real wages will increase approximately 3 percent a year.

The forecast of labor force in any one region depends on the population forecasts which are made with the population migration equations. Labor force is matched with the employment forecasts to derive unemployment. The unemployment rate was computed and restrictions were placed on its change. The forecast unemployment rate relative to the national unemployment rate was computed and compared with the relative that existed in the prior year. The forecast relative was restricted so that it did not exceed 110 percent of the prior year's unemployment relative and did not go below 90 percent of the prior year's relative. This procedure allows the regional unemployment rates to adjust as the national unemployment rate changes but does not allow abrupt changes in the regional unemployment rate. If the forecast relative unemployment rate had exceeded the limit set, then the labor force was adjusted to make it consistent with the unemployment rate.

If it was necessary to adjust the labor force, then the population was adjusted with some flexibility in the labor force participation rate. If the change in labor force did not change the forecast county labor force participation rate relative to the national rate by more than 0.5 percent of the prior year's relative, then the population forecasts were left unchanged. However, if the change in labor force resulted in a change of the labor force participation relative to the national rate by more than 0.5 percent, then the population forecasts in all age-race groups were adjusted to make them consistent with the restricted labor force participation rate.

The Use of 1970 Data

As described before, a complete set of data were estimated for the years 1965 and 1966; they were used to estimate the parameters in the equations. However, because of the desirability of having a more recent take-off year, a limited amount of 1970 data were made ready for use in the model. These include employment by the 104 industry-labor sectors, population by the 8 age-race groups, and personal income by four main components—earnings, property income, transfer payments, and social insurance payments.

The 1970 employment estimates were derived in approximately the same way as the 1965 and 1966 estimates. The main source is the *County Business Patterns*. However, the 1970 estimates of employment not covered by the *County Business Patterns* are not as reliable as those in 1966. The county estimates were made by first adjusting state data to national controls and then adjusting county data to the appropriate state controls. Table 6-2 shows the 1970 national controls and Table 6-3 lists the sources of the state data for sections not covered by *County Business Patterns*. Since 1970 county employment data in the non-CBP sectors were not available, they were estimated by using county data from other years to distribute the 1970 state controls to counties. Table 6-4 summarizes the procedure used for each sector.

The 1970 population data by age and race were obtained from the 1970 Population Census. The 1970 personal income was available for each state, and estimates of county data within each state were made by first assuming that the per capita income in 1970 was the same as it was in 1966 and then adjusting these approximations proportionally to sum to the state totals. This procedure assumes that the relative per capita income of counties within each state has remained constant over time.

The full set of the 1970 estimates is a combination of the actual data described above and forecasts. The model was used to forecast the numbers from 1966 to 1970, then the forecasts were related to the actual 1970 data and adjusted. The procedures are as follows:

1. Output by industry sector is estimated by applying the output-employment ratio of the 1970 forecasts to the actual 1970 employment.
2. The earnings by labor sector were estimated by applying the forecast earnings-employment ratio to actual 1970 employment figures. The earnings by industry sector were adjusted proportionally to sum to each county's total earnings that were derived as described above.
3. Personal consumption expenditures by industry sector were derived by applying the forecast consumption-personal income ratio to the 1970 personal income.
4. The equipment purchasing sectors were matched to industry sectors and

Table 6-2
National Employment and Unemployment, 1970 (Numbers in Thousands)

Job Sector	March 1970
Employees under Social Security[a]	57,265
Agriculture[b]	3,292
Household Service[c]	2,048
Railroads[d]	623
Federal Civilian Government[e]	2,758
State and Local Civilian Government[e]	9,922
Non-Agricultural Self-Employed[f]	5,271
Military[g]	(1,755)
Total Civilian Jobs	81,179
Multijob Holders[i]	3,222
Net Workers Commuting	–
Total Civilians Employed[h]	77,957
Civilian Unemployment[h]	3,732
Civilian Labor Force[h]	81,689

[a]U.S. Department of Commerce, Bureau of the Census COUNTY BUSINESS PATTERNS, U.S. Summary 1970.
[b]U.S. Department of Labor, Bureau of Labor Statistics, EMPLOYMENT AND EARNINGS, Vol. 17, No. 10, April, 1971, Table A.1, and Vol. 16, No. 10, April, 1970, Table A.28.
[c]Ibid., Vol. 17, No. 10, April, 1971, Table A.18, and Vol. 16, No. 10, April, 1970, Table A.28.
[d]Ibid., Vol. 17, No. 10, April, 1971, Table B.2.
[e]Ibid., Vol. 17, No. 10, April , 1971, Table B.1.
[f]Ibid., Vol. 16, No. 10, April, 1970, Table A.20 and Table A.28.
[g]Military stationed in U.S. only as of June 30, 1970. Directorate for Information Operations, Office of the Secretary of Defense, U.S. Department of Defense.
[h]U.S. Department of Labor, Bureau of Labor Statistics, EMPLOYMENT AND EARNINGS, Vol. 17, No. 10, April, 1971, Table A.1.
[i]Residual: Total Civilian jobs less total civilians employed.

the 1970 equipment was estimated by applying the forecast equipment-employment ratio to the actual 1970 employment.

5. The 1970 construction expenditures by type of construction, was estimated by applying the forecast construction expenditures-construction employment ratio to the 1970 construction employment.

6. The regional distributions of defense expenditures by industry and NASA expenditures in 1970 were assumed to be the same as it was in 1966 with adjustments that made sure that defense expenditures by industry did not exceed output by industry.

7. The 1970 general government expenditures were estimated by applying

Table 6-3

Sources of State Employment, 1970, Not Covered by *County Business Patterns*

Agriculture:

U.S. Department of Agriculture, *Agricultural Statistics*, Table 649, p. 453 (Farm Employment). Hawaii and Alaska from 1970 Census *General Social and Economic Characteristics*, Table 54 (Employment by Occupation) from respective state volumes.

Household Service:

Obtained by letting 1966 employment grow at the national rate.

Railroads:

Office of Director of Research, U.S. Railroad Retirement Board.

Federal Civilian Government

U.S. Bureau of Census, Department of Commerce, *Public Employment in 1970*, Series GE70, No. 1, Table 5, p. 11.

State and Local Government

U.S. Bureau of Census, Department of Commerce, *Public Employment* in 1970, Series GE70, No. 1, Table 5, p. 11.

Non-agricultural Self-employed:

Data for 1969. Social Security Administration, U.S. Department of Health, Education and Welfare, *Social Security Bulletin*, Annual Statistical Supplement, 1969, Table 45 (Workers with Taxable Earnings) p. 60.

Military:

U.S. Department of Defense, Directorate for Information Operations. The figures for the Virginia and Maryland counties adjacent to the District of Columbia were included in the D.C. figure; therefore the totals for Maryland, Virginia, and D.C. were reallocated according to 1966 weights.

---

the forecast government expenditures-personal income ratio to the 1970 personal income.

8. The 1970 deaths by age and race groups were estimated by applying the forecast death-population ratio to the actual 1970 population.

9. The 1970 births by race were estimated by applying the forecast birth-population ratio to the actual 1970 population in the 15-34 age group.

10. The 1970 value of land was estimated by applying the forecast value of land-earnings ratio to the actual 1970 earnings.

11. The 1970 multijob holders were estimated by applying the national ratio of multijob holders to employment in nonagricultural and nongovernmental sectors to the corresponding employment in each county.

12. The 1970 commuters were estimated by applying the forecast commuter rate to the actual 1970 employment in the nonagricultural sector.

13. The 1970 estimate of labor force was derived by applying the forecast labor force-population ratio to the actual 1970 population.

Table 6-4
Procedures Used to Obtain 1970 County Employment in Sectors Not Covered by *County Business Patterns*

Agriculture
The 1966 county numbers were used to distribute 1970 state controls within each state. The 1970 ratio between livestock and crops was assumed to be the same as the 1966 ratio.

Household Service
The 1966 county employment per capita was applied to the 1970 population and then these approximations were adjusted proportionally to the 1970 state control within each state.

Railroads
The 1970 ratio of railroad to other transportation employment was assumed to be the same as the 1966 ratio.

Federal Civilian Government
The 1970 county estimates were made by using 1969 numbers to distribute 1970 state controls within each state. The 1969 employment was obtained from the Bureau of Management Services, U.S. Civil Service Commission, *Annual Report of Federal Civilian Employment in the United States by Geographic Area (December 31, 1969).*

State and Local Government
Separate state and local county figures were obtained from the Census Bureau, U.S. Department of Commerce *1967 Census of Governments*, Vol. 3, No. 2, Table 20. These figures were put on a per capita basis and applied to the 1970 county population, and then these approximations were adjusted proportionally to sum to 1970 state controls.

Non-Agricultural Self-Employed
National self-employed-employee ratios by industry sector were obtained from the Office of Business Economics, U.S. Department of Commerce *Survey of Current Business*, Vol. 51, No. 7, July 1971. These ratios were applied to the county employee estimates by industry sector, and the county sums were derived and adjusted proportionally to sum to the appropriate state controls. The county self-employed by industry were readjusted to the county totals before they were added to the other industry employment.

Military
It is assumed that the 1970 county distribution within each state is the same as it was in 1966.

14. The 1970 regional distributions of foreign exports and imports by industry sector were assumed to be the same as they were in 1966.

The success of the model in forecasting 1970 employment varied by industry, but overall there was a strong correlation between the 1970 forecast values and the actual values. The major coefficients of determination (R^2) between the forecast and actual values are as follows:

Total Jobs	.9961
Population	.9956
Personal Income	.9547

The Use of Residuals

Forecasters have long been plagued with the fact that they cannot explain 100 percent of the variation in the variables being forecast. The problem is illustrated in Figure 6-1, where Y is the dependent variable and X is the independent variable. The dots represent observations, and the line $Y = a + bX$ is a regression line that minimizes the sum of the squared vertical distances between the observations and the line. Assume that X increases from year to year and that the observations represent time series data. The most recent observation, illustrated with the circle around the dot, is not on the regression line. If a forecast were made of Y given next year's value of X, the forecast figure would be on the regression line. Thus, the next year forecast value would differ greatly from the base year value. The difference occurs not only because X

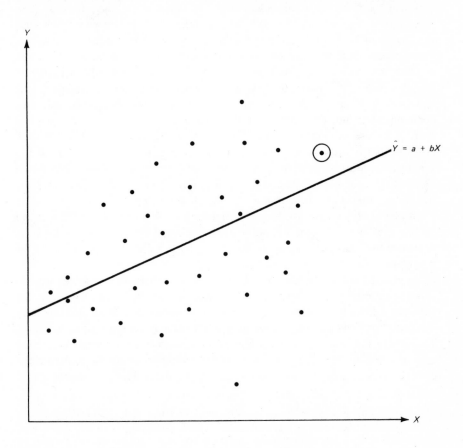

Figure 6-1. A Hypothetical Regression Line

is different, but also because of the adjustment from the actual value to the regression line.

If the deviations from the regression line (residuals) were purely random, then the next year's observation could just as easily be below the line as above it, and the use of the regression line itself would be the best way to forecast. Recognizing that the residuals are not always purely random, but may be autocorrelated, forecasters have devised means to adjust the predicted value of Y as given by the regression equation. One simple procedure is to assume a parallel shift in the regression line so that it goes through the most recent observation. Other more elaborate schemes try to predict the residual itself from the pattern of the residuals from year to year.

The same type of problem exists using cross section data instead of time series data. In the application in this study, the circled observation would represent the value for a particular county. If forecasts are made for next year, the county's forecast would show a large change from the base year figure since the change in Y not only incorporates the change in X but also the movement to the regression line. With county data there is probably less reason to believe that residuals are purely random. There is probably some reason why a particular county's value is higher (or lower) than what would be indicated by the regression line, and if there is, the model is not completely specified. One common procedure to account for the uniqueness of certain regional observations is to use dummy variables. For example, it may be observed that all counties that border the Atlantic Ocean have similar residuals, and if a dummy variable is entered as a constant, then the coastal counties' regression line would be parallel to the one illustrated in the diagram. There would be one regression line for coastal counties and another for the other counties.

In this study the use of dummy variables is carried to its limit. That is, we assume that there is some unique constant in every county that has not been explained by a particular equation. Therefore, there are separate parallel lines for predicting Y for each of the counties.[1]

As pointed out in the previous chapter, the use of residuals also allows us to allocate national totals to the region. In making forecasts in any one year, the forecasts of some variables rely on some variables that have already been forecast. For example, the employment forecasts rely on the output forecasts. To allocate national figures with regression equations, it is necessary that the sum of the county output figures total the national output figure before the county output figures are used to forecast employment. Thus, it is essential that

---

[1]Experimental 1970 projections were made from the 1966 base with various assumptions as to the value of the residuals. Comparison of forecast employment and population with actual 1970 employment and population indicated that adding the full value of the residual to the predicted values gave the best results. Other runs assumed that the value of the residuals approached zero at varying rates of decline and one run did not add in the residuals at all.

a procedure be developed to forecast output so that the output figure will not be severely readjusted proportionally at a later stage to sum to national totals.[2] By adding each county's residuals to the predicted value as given by the regression equation and the use of the regional shares as explained in the previous chapter, we are assured that forecasts of the output and other variables will sum to the national totals. The predicted county values may not sum to the national totals without the use of residuals because, as discussed in the previous chapter, not all counties were used as observations when estimating the parameters in the equations.

Summary of Results

There are 438 counties classified as being members of 219 Standard Metropolitan Statistical Areas (SMSA).[3] The forecasting model was run with these counties and with the other counties grouped into a rest-of-the-nation category. This section summarizes the results. The Appendix Table includes more detailed projections for SMSAs that had more than one million in population in 1970.

SMSA counties are expected to grow faster than non-SMSA counties, although the non-SMSA growth rate picks up as 1985 is approached and the SMSA growth rate levels off. The matching annual growth rate in population can be seen at the bottom of Table 6-5. Along with population, the growth rates of the economic variables such as jobs, per capita income, and gross regional product[4] are also expected to be higher in SMSAs than in the rest-of-the-nation. Manufacturing jobs are expected to grow faster in SMSAs, but jobs in finance, insurance, and real estate are expected to grow faster in non-SMSAs.

Among the fastest growing SMSAs are Hartford, Connecticut, which is stimulated by the rapid growth in the insurance industry; Midland, Texas, where a rapid growth in machinery manufacturing is expected; Lafayette, Indiana, which is stiumlated by a rapid growth in the lumber and fabricated metals industries; and Ann Arbor, Michigan, where a surge in business and personal services is expected. The SMSAs that show population declines between 1970 and 1985 are: Binghamton, New York; Lake Charles, Louisiana; Anderson, Indiana; Kanoska, Wisconsin; Peoria, Illinois; Charleston, West Virginia; Wheeling, West Virginia; and Beaumont-Port Arthur, Texas. A number of other SMSAs show positive but slow growth.

Both rapid growth and slow growth or declining areas are scattered through-

---

[2]Minor proportional adjustments have to be made because of the constraints discussed in the second section of this chapter.

[3]As defined by Bureau of the Budget January 1, 1967 and reported in U.S. Department of Commerce, Bureau of Census, POPULATION ESTIMATES Current Population Reports Series P–25, No. 371 August 14, 1967.

[4]Gross regional product is the sum of value added by industry with regional value added derived by applying national value-added coefficients to output by sector.

Table 6-5

Population Data and Projections by Standard Metropolitan Statistical Area (Thousands)

SMSA	1960	1970	1975	1980	1985	AVERAGE ANNUAL RATE OF GROWTH				
						1960-1970	1970-1975	1975-1980	1980-1985	1970-1985
ABILENE, TEX.	120.	114.	115.	122.	130.	-.5	.2	1.1	1.3	.9
AKRON, OHIO	605.	679.	730.	785.	846.	1.2	1.4	1.5	1.5	1.5
ALBANY, GA.	76.	90.	95.	104.	116.	1.7	1.2	1.9	2.0	1.7
ALBANY-SCHENECTADY-TROY, N.Y.	658.	721.	764.	814.	868.	.9	1.2	1.3	1.3	1.2
ALBUQUERQUE, N. MEX.	262.	316.	336.	361.	397.	1.9	1.3	1.5	1.9	1.5
ALLENTOWN-BETHLEHEM-EASTON, PA.-N.J.	492.	544.	578.	613.	648.	1.0	1.2	1.2	1.1	1.2
ALTOONA, PA.	137.	135.	150.	167.	186.	-.1	2.0	2.1	2.3	2.1
AMARILLO, TEX.	149.	144.	156.	176.	197.	-.3	1.6	2.4	2.7	2.1
ANAHEIM-SANTA ANA-GARDEN GROVE, CALIF.	704.	1420.	1634.	1893.	2170.	7.0	2.8	2.9	2.7	2.8
ANDERSON, IND.	126.	138.	136.	130.	127.	.9	-.4	-.8	-.5	-.6
ANN ARBOR, MICH.	172.	234.	284.	335.	378.	3.1	3.8	3.3	2.4	3.2
ASHEVILLE, N.C.	130.	145.	164.	186.	210.	1.1	2.4	2.6	2.4	2.5
ATLANTA, GA.	1017.	1390.	1466.	1595.	1753.	3.1	1.1	1.7	1.9	1.5
ATLANTIC CITY, N.J.	161.	175.	176.	187.	196.	.8	.2	1.2	1.0	.8
AUGUSTA, GA.-S.C.	217.	253.	269.	297.	332.	1.6	1.2	2.0	2.0	1.8
AUSTIN, TEX.	212.	296.	339.	398.	461.	3.3	2.8	3.2	2.9	3.0
BAKERSFIELD, CALIF.	292.	329.	326.	340.	358.	1.2	-.2	.8	1.4	.6
BALTIMORE, MD.	1727.	1955.	2072.	2238.	2402.	1.2	1.2	1.5	1.4	1.4
BATON ROUGE, LA.	230.	285.	319.	363.	419.	2.1	2.2	2.6	2.9	2.6
BAY CITY, MICH.	107.	117.	124.	130.	135.	.9	1.1	.9	.8	.9
BEAUMONT-PORT ARTHUR, TEX.	306.	316.	314.	312.	312.	.3	-.1	-.1	-.0	-.1
BILLINGS, MONT.	79.	87.	97.	109.	122.	1.0	2.1	2.3	2.2	2.2
BINGHAMTON, N.Y.-PA.	284.	303.	280.	266.	257.	.7	-1.6	-1.0	-.7	-1.1
BIRMINGHAM, ALA.	635.	645.	679.	733.	809.	.2	1.0	1.5	2.0	1.5
BLOOMINGTON-NORMAL, ILL.	84.	104.	112.	121.	128.	2.2	1.3	1.7	1.1	1.4
BOISE CITY, IDAHO	93.	112.	117.	124.	131.	1.8	.8	1.3	1.0	1.0
BOSTON, LAWRENCE-HAVERHILL, LOWELL, MASS.	3109.	3375.	3613.	3913.	4226.	.8	1.4	1.6	1.5	1.5
BRIDGEPORT, STAMFORD, NORWALK, CONN.	654.	793.	829.	885.	925.	1.9	.9	1.3	1.0	1.0
BROCKTON, MASS.	248.	333.	356.	381.	397.	2.9	1.3	1.3	.8	1.2
BROWNSVILLE-HARLINGEN-SAN BENITO, TEX.	151.	140.	152.	168.	188.	-.7	1.6	2.0	2.2	1.9
BUFFALO, N.Y.	1307.	1349.	1439.	1540.	1644.	.3	1.3	1.4	1.3	1.3
CANTON, OHIO	340.	372.	407.	433.	453.	.9	1.8	1.2	.9	1.3
CEDAR RAPIDS, IOWA	137.	163.	178.	193.	207.	1.8	1.8	1.3	1.4	1.6
CHAMPAIGN-URBANA, ILL.	132.	163.	168.	179.	191.	2.1	.5	1.3	1.3	1.6
CHARLESTON, S.C.	255.	304.	307.	325.	352.	1.8	.2	1.2	1.2	1.0
CHARLESTON, W. VA.	253.	230.	220.	218.	219.	-1.0	-.8	-.2	.0	-.3
CHARLOTTE, N.C.	317.	409.	444.	479.	501.	2.6	1.6	1.5	.9	1.3
CHATTANOOGA, TENN.-GA.	283.	305.	335.	366.	392.	.7	1.9	1.8	1.4	1.7

City										
CHICAGO, ILL.	6221.	6979.	7399.	7896.	8447.	1.1	1.2	1.3	1.3	1.3
CINCINNATI, OHIO-KY.-IND.	1268.	1385.	1504.	1662.	1842.	.9	1.7	2.0	2.1	1.9
CLEVELAND, OHIO	1909.	2064.	2217.	2372.	2505.	.8	1.4	1.4	1.1	1.3
COLORADO SPRINGS, COLO.	144.	236.	249.	269.	285.	5.0	1.1	1.5	1.1	1.2
COLUMBIA, S.C.	261.	323.	328.	343.	362.	2.1	1.0	.9	1.0	.8
COLUMBUS, GA.-ALA.	218.	239.	251.	269.	282.	.9	1.0	1.4	1.0	1.1
COLUMBUS, OHIO	755.	916.	965.	1022.	1061.	1.9	1.0	1.2	.8	1.0
CORPUS CHRISTI, TEX.	267.	285.	289.	304.	325.	.7	.3	1.0	1.3	.9
DALLAS, TEX.	1084.	1517.	1609.	1738.	1898.	3.4	1.3	1.5	1.8	1.5
DAVENPORT-ROCK ISLAND-MOLINE, IOWA-ILL.	319.	363.	387.	410.	439.	1.3	1.3	1.2	1.4	1.3
DAYTON, OHIO	727.	850.	913.	984.	1047.	1.6	1.6	1.5	1.2	1.4
DECATUR, ILL.	118.	125.	136.	145.	153.	.6	1.4	1.3	1.6	1.6
DENVER, COLO.	929.	1228.	1320.	1438.	1561.	2.8	1.4	1.7	2.0	2.4
DES MOINES, IOWA	266.	286.	327.	371.	409.	.7	2.7	2.5	1.3	1.7
DETROIT, MICH.	3762.	4200.	4675.	5087.	5431.	1.1	2.1	1.7	1.5	1.5
DUBUQUE, IOWA	80.	91.	96.	105.	113.	1.2	1.3	1.6	1.0	1.0
DULUTH-SUPERIOR, MINN.-WIS.	277.	265.	274.	292.	307.	.4	.7	1.3	1.3	.8
DURHAM, N.C.	112.	133.	136.	141.	149.	1.7	.5	.6	1.2	1.2
EL PASO, TEX.	314.	359.	407.	466.	522.	.5	2.5	2.7	2.3	2.5
ERIE, PA.	251.	264.	308.	349.	392.	1.3	3.1	2.5	2.0	2.6
EUGENE, OREG.	163.	213.	230.	249.	275.	2.7	1.5	1.6	.8	1.7
EVANSVILLE, IND.-KY.	223.	233.	237.	244.	254.	1.3	.3	.6	1.1	.6
FARGO-MOORHEAD, N. DAK.-MINN.	106.	120.	123.	129.	136.	.4	.4	1.0	3.4	.8
FAYETTEVILLE, N.C.	148.	212.	226.	270.	320.	3.6	1.3	3.5	2.7	2.7
FLINT, MICH.	416.	497.	573.	640.	671.	2.9	2.9	2.2	2.4	2.0
FORT LAUDERDALE-HOLLYWOOD, FLA.	334.	620.	711.	809.	925.	6.2	2.7	2.6	3.0	2.7
FORT SMITH, ARK.-OKLA.	135.	160.	171.	186.	206.	1.7	1.3	1.6	2.0	2.7
FORT WAYNE, IND.	232.	280.	327.	374.	420.	1.9	3.1	2.7	3.3	2.6
FORT WORTH, TEX.	573.	762.	838.	966.	1121.	2.8	1.9	2.8	.4	2.0
FRESNO, CALIF.	366.	413.	435.	460.	497.	1.2	1.0	1.1	1.9	2.0
GADSDEN, ALA.	97.	94.	103.	115.	127.	-.3	1.7	2.2	2.3	2.8
GALVESTON-TEXAS CITY, TEX.	140.	170.	188.	219.	258.	1.0	2.1	3.0	2.4	3.3
GARY-HAMMOND-EAST CHICAGO, IND.	574.	633.	637.	646.	661.	1.0	.1	.3	1.6	.3
GRAND RAPIDS, MICH.	462.	539.	612.	682.	752.	1.5	2.5	2.2	1.7	2.4
GREAT FALLS, MONT.	73.	82.	93.	104.	117.	1.1	2.3	2.3	1.9	2.4
GREEN BAY, WIS.	125.	158.	177.	199.	225.	2.4	2.5	2.4	2.3	2.3
GREENSBORO-HIGH POINT, N.C.	247.	289.	320.	351.	379.	1.6	2.2	1.8	2.4	1.8
GREENVILLE, S.C.	256.	300.	325.	354.	385.	1.6	2.0	1.7	1.7	1.7
HAMILTON-MIDDLETOWN, OHIO	199.	226.	241.	248.	264.	1.3	1.6	.6	1.2	1.0
HARRISBURG, PA.	372.	411.	435.	476.	518.	1.2	1.3	1.8	1.8	1.5
HARTFORD-NEW BRITAIN, CONN.	690.	817.	975.	1199.	1459.	1.7	1.2	4.1	3.9	3.9
HONOLULU, HAWAII	500.	629.	686.	755.	828.	2.3	3.5	1.9	1.9	1.8
HOUSTON, TEX.	1418.	1985.	2313.	2681.	3068.	3.4	3.1	3.0	2.7	2.9
HUNTINGTON-ASHLAND, W. VA.-KY.-OHIO	255.	254.	266.	283.	299.	-.0	1.0	1.2	1.1	1.1
HUNTSVILLE, ALA.	154.	228.	238.	260.	287.	3.9	.9	1.8	1.6	1.5
INDIANAPOLIS, IND.	917.	1079.	1162.	1257.	1364.	1.6	1.5	1.6	1.6	1.6
JACKSON, MICH.	132.	143.	159.	172.	186.	.8	2.1	1.5	1.6	1.8

Table 6-5 (cont.)

SMSA	1960	1970	1975	1980	1985	AVERAGE ANNUAL RATE OF GROWTH 1960-1970	1970-1975	1975-1980	1980-1985	1970-1985
JACKSON, MISS.	221.	259.	297.	345.	397.	1.6	2.7	3.0	2.8	2.9
JACKSONVILLE, FLA.	455.	529.	593.	665.	742.	1.5	2.3	2.3	2.2	2.3
JERSEY CITY, N.J.	611.	609.	656.	704.	756.	-.0	1.5	1.4	1.4	1.4
JOHNSTOWN, PA.	281.	263.	254.	258.	266.	-.7	-.7	.3	.6	.1
KALAMAZOO, MICH.	170.	202.	223.	245.	268.	1.7	2.1	1.9	1.7	1.9
KANSAS CITY, MO.-KANS.	1093.	1254.	1360.	1490.	1641.	1.4	1.6	1.8	1.9	1.8
KENOSHA, WIS.	101.	118.	118.	114.	108.	1.6	.1	-.8	-1.1	-.6
KNOXVILLE, TENN.	368.	400.	443.	492.	537.	.8	2.0	2.1	1.8	2.0
LAFAYETTE, LA.	85.	110.	121.	139.	161.	2.6	2.0	2.7	3.0	2.6
LAFAYETTE-WEST LAFAYETTE, IND.	89.	109.	129.	151.	177.	2.0	3.3	3.2	3.1	3.2
LAKE CHARLES, LA.	145.	145.	135.	130.	126.	-.0	-1.5	-.8	-.6	-1.0
LANCASTER, PA.	278.	320.	343.	376.	412.	1.4	1.4	1.8	1.8	1.7
LANSING, MICH.	299.	378.	438.	504.	559.	2.4	2.9	2.8	2.1	2.6
LAREDO, TEX.	65.	73.	80.	90.	104.	1.2	1.8	2.3	2.8	2.3
LAS VEGAS, NEV.	127.	273.	295.	339.	388.	7.7	1.5	2.8	2.7	2.3
LAWTON, OKLA.	91.	108.	112.	126.	144.	1.7	.7	2.3	2.7	1.9
LEWISTON-AUBURN, MAINE	86.	91.	97.	105.	113.	.6	1.2	1.6	1.5	1.5
LEXINGTON, KY.	132.	174.	202.	232.	254.	2.8	2.9	2.8	1.9	2.5
LIMA, OHIO	104.	111.	121.	131.	140.	.7	1.6	1.6	1.4	1.6
LINCOLN, NEBR.	155.	168.	170.	175.	175.	.8	.3	.6	-.0	.3
LITTLE ROCK-NORTH LITTLE ROCK, ARK.	243.	287.	333.	386.	449.	1.7	2.9	3.0	3.0	3.0
LORAIN-ELYRIA, OHIO	217.	257.	278.	296.	317.	1.7	1.6	1.3	1.4	1.4
LOS ANGELES-LONG BEACH, CALIF.	6039.	7032.	7481.	8183.	8905.	1.5	1.2	1.8	1.7	1.6
LOUISVILLE, KY.-IND.	725.	827.	889.	952.	1012.	1.3	1.4	1.4	1.2	1.4
LUBBOCK, TEX.	156.	179.	199.	223.	251.	1.4	2.1	2.3	2.3	2.1
LYNCHBURG, VA.	111.	123.	136.	153.	170.	1.1	2.0	2.3	2.1	2.1
MCALLEN-PHARR-EDINBURG, TEX.	181.	182.	196.	221.	264.	.0	1.6	2.3	2.6	2.2
MACON, GA.	180.	206.	217.	238.	261.	1.3	1.0	1.9	2.0	1.6
MADISON, WIS.	222.	290.	321.	365.	407.	2.7	2.0	2.5	2.2	2.3
MANCHESTER, N.H.	178.	224.	241.	262.	282.	2.3	1.5	1.6	1.5	1.5
MANSFIELD, OHIO	118.	130.	150.	170.	190.	1.0	2.8	2.5	2.3	2.5
MEMPHIS, TENN.-ARK.	675.	770.	824.	891.	967.	1.3	1.4	1.6	1.6	1.5
MIAMI, FLA.	935.	1268.	1458.	1692.	1897.	3.0	2.8	3.0	2.3	2.7
MIDLAND, TEX.	68.	65.	77.	93.	114.	-.3	3.3	3.8	4.0	3.7
MILWAUKEE, WIS.	1233.	1340.	1470.	1613.	1748.	.8	1.9	1.9	1.6	1.8
MINNEAPOLIS-ST. PAUL, MINN.	1482.	1814.	1951.	2104.	2235.	2.0	1.5	1.5	1.2	1.4
MOBILE, ALA.	363.	377.	420.	466.	527.	.4	2.2	2.1	2.5	2.2
MONROE, LA.	102.	115.	126.	142.	158.	1.3	1.8	2.4	2.1	2.1
MONTGOMERY, ALA.	200.	201.	217.	243.	273.	.1	1.5	2.2	2.4	2.0
MUNCIE, IND.	111.	129.	130.	133.	137.	1.5	.3	.3	.6	.4
MUSKEGON-MUSKEGON HEIGHTS, MICH.	150.	157.	167.	172.	180.	.5	1.2	.5	1.0	.9

151

City										
NASHVILLE, TENN.	464.	541.	584.	650.	708.	1.5	1.5	2.2	1.7	1.8
NEW BEDFORD, FALL RIVER, MASS.	398.	444.	490.	540.	589.	1.1	1.9	2.0	1.7	1.9
NEW HAVEN, WATERBURY, MERIDEN, CONN.	660.	745.	766.	781.	783.	1.2	.6	.4	.1	.3
NEW LONDON-GROTON-NORWICH, CONN.	186.	230.	241.	238.	238.	2.2	.9	-.3	.0	.2
NEW ORLEANS, LA.	907.	1046.	1119.	1213.	1326.	1.8	1.3	1.6	1.8	1.6
NEW YORK, N.Y.	10695.	11529.	12060.	12620.	13180.	.9	1.0	.9	.8	.9
NEWARK, N.J.	1689.	1857.	1952.	2061.	2190.	.9	1.6	1.1	1.2	1.1
NEWPORT NEWS-HAMPTON, VA.	225.	292.	317.	355.	396.	2.6	1.6	2.7	2.2	2.0
NORFOLK-PORTSMOUTH, VA.	579.	681.	725.	787.	862.	1.6	1.3	1.7	1.8	1.6
ODESSA, TEX.	91.	92.	96.	103.	115.	.1	.9	1.4	2.2	1.5
OGDEN, UTAH	111.	126.	127.	140.	156.	1.3	1.7	1.9	2.3	1.4
OKLAHOMA, CITY, OKLA.	512.	641.	697.	772.	872.	2.2	.7	2.0	2.4	2.1
OMAHA, NEBR.-IOWA	458.	540.	558.	589.	629.	1.7	.7	1.1	1.3	1.0
ORLANDO, FLA.	318.	428.	448.	481.	520.	3.0	.9	1.4	1.6	1.3
OXNARD-VENTURA, CALIF.	199.	376.	399.	451.	524.	6.4	1.2	2.4	3.0	2.2
PATERSON-CLIFTON-PASSAIC, N.J.	1187.	1359.	1500.	1679.	1863.	1.4	2.0	2.3	2.1	2.1
PENSACOLA, FLA.	203.	243.	246.	254.	266.	1.8	.3	.6	1.0	.6
PEORIA, ILL.	313.	342.	330.	321.	321.	.9	-.7	-.5	-.0	-.4
PHILADELPHIA, PA.-N.J.	4343.	4818.	5128.	5530.	5940.	1.0	1.2	1.5	1.4	2.0
PHOENIX, ARIZ.	664.	968.	1074.	1198.	1314.	3.8	2.1	2.1	2.0	1.1
PINE BLUFF, ARK.	81.	85.	86.	91.	100.	-.0	.5	.1	.1	.5
PITTSBURGH, PA.	2405.	2401.	2447.	2463.	2476.	.5	.1	.0	.1	1.1
PITTSFIELD, MASS.	142.	149.	150.	150.	162.	.5	-.0	1.0	.5	1.4
PORTLAND, MAINE	183.	193.	200.	215.	227.	2.1	.8	1.4	1.1	1.2
PORTLAND, OREG.-WASH.	822.	1009.	1081.	1167.	1242.	2.7	1.4	1.5	1.2	1.2
PROVIDENCE-PAWTUCKET-WARWICK, R.I.	719.	769.	818.	872.	924.	2.5	1.2	1.3	1.3	1.5
PROVO-OREM, UTAH	107.	138.	134.	139.	148.	-1.0	-.5	.7	-.5	.8
PUEBLO, COLO.	119.	118.	119.	126.	134.	.0	1.0	1.0	1.3	.8
RACINE, WIS.	142.	171.	188.	202.	218.	1.9	1.5	1.4	1.5	1.6
RALEIGH, N.C.	169.	228.	247.	271.	290.	3.0	-.2	1.8	1.4	1.6
READING, PA.	275.	296.	331.	365.	397.	3.7	1.5	2.0	1.7	2.0
RENO, NEV.	85.	121.	121.	134.	148.	.7	2.0	2.6	2.0	2.3
RICHMOND, VA.	436.	518.	581.	661.	750.	1.7	-.2	2.2	2.5	2.5
ROANOKE, VA.	159.	181.	203.	227.	249.	1.3	2.3	2.6	1.8	2.1
ROCHESTER, N.Y.	733.	883.	1024.	1181.	1322.	1.9	2.2	2.2	2.3	2.7
ROCKFORD, ILL.	230.	272.	298.	319.	340.	1.7	2.9	2.9	1.3	1.5
SACRAMENTO, CALIF.	626.	801.	810.	875.	974.	2.5	1.8	1.3	2.1	1.3
SAGINAW, MICH.	191.	220.	255.	285.	315.	1.4	2.5	1.5	1.4	2.1
SALEM, OREG.	147.	187.	190.	200.	214.	2.3	1.4	2.2	2.0	2.0
SALINAS-MONTEREY, CALIF.	198.	250.	270.	305.	346.	-.4	3.0	1.0	2.5	2.4
ST. JOSEPH, MO.	91.	87.	91.	96.	103.	-1.2	.3	2.0	1.4	.9
ST. LOUIS, MO.-ILL.	2105.	2363.	2445.	2560.	2695.	1.2	1.5	1.0	2.5	2.2
SALT LAKE CITY, UTAH	448.	558.	554.	566.	579.	2.2	.8	.9	1.2	1.1
SAN ANGELO, TEX.	65.	71.	81.	94.	108.	2.9	.7	-.4	1.0	.9
SAN ANTONIO, TEX.	716.	864.	938.	1061.	1202.	1.9	2.5	3.1	2.7	2.8
SAN BERNARDINO-RIVERSIDE-ONTARIO, CALIF.	810.	1143.	1226.	1341.	1496.	3.4	1.4	1.8	2.2	2.2

Table 6-5 (cont.)

SMSA	1960	1970	1975	1980	1985	AVERAGE ANNUAL RATE OF GROWTH				
						1960-1970	1970-1975	1975-1980	1980-1985	1970-1985
SAN DIEGO, CALIF.	1033.	1358.	1376.	1481.	1615.	2.7	.3	1.5	1.7	1.2
SAN FRANCISCO-OAKLAND, CALIF.	2649.	3110.	3211.	3350.	3513.	1.6	.6	.9	.9	.8
SAN JOSE, CALIF.	642.	1065.	1146.	1267.	1409.	5.1	1.5	2.0	2.1	1.9
SANTA BARBARA, CALIF.	169.	264.	273.	299.	331.	4.5	.7	1.8	2.0	1.5
SAVANNAH, GA.	188.	188.	202.	223.	247.	-.0	1.4	2.0	2.1	1.8
SCRANTON, PA.	235.	234.	255.	284.	316.	-.0	1.7	2.2	2.7	2.0
SEATTLE-EVERETT, WASH.	1107.	1422.	1631.	1864.	2130.	2.5	2.7	2.7	2.7	2.7
SHREVEPORT, LA.	281.	295.	313.	341.	377.	.5	1.2	1.7	2.0	1.6
SIOUX CITY, IOWA-NEBR.	120.	116.	122.	130.	136.	-.3	1.0	1.2	.9	1.1
SIOUX FALLS, S. DAK.	87.	95.	103.	112.	118.	1.0	1.7	1.7	1.1	1.5
SOUTH BEND, IND.	271.	280.	291.	310.	330.	.3	.8	1.2	1.2	1.1
SPOKANE, WASH.	278.	287.	298.	316.	337.	.3	.7	1.1	1.3	1.1
SPRINGFIELD, ILL.	147.	161.	166.	176.	189.	1.0	.6	1.2	1.5	1.1
SPRINGFIELD, MO.	126.	153.	171.	191.	210.	1.9	2.2	2.3	1.9	2.1
SPRINGFIELD, OHIO	131.	157.	166.	177.	185.	1.8	1.0	1.3	.9	1.1
SPRINGFIELD-CHICOPEE-HOLYOKE, MASS.	533.	583.	643.	703.	773.	.9	2.0	1.8	1.9	1.9
STEUBENVILLE-WEIRTON, OHIO-W. VA.	168.	166.	196.	220.	238.	-.1	3.4	2.3	1.6	2.4
STOCKTON, CALIF.	250.	290.	306.	327.	353.	1.5	1.0	1.4	1.5	1.3
SYRACUSE, N.Y.	564.	636.	691.	759.	827.	1.2	1.7	1.9	1.7	1.8
TACOMA, WASH.	322.	411.	446.	484.	520.	2.5	1.6	1.6	1.5	1.6
TALLAHASSEE, FLA.	74.	103.	112.	124.	140.	3.3	1.6	2.1	2.4	2.1
TAMPA-ST. PETERSBURG, FLA.	772.	1013.	1151.	1303.	1473.	2.7	2.6	2.5	2.4	2.5
TERRE HAUTE, IND.	172.	175.	189.	208.	229.	.2	1.6	1.9	2.0	1.8
TEXARKANA, TEX.-ARK.	92.	101.	97.	101.	111.	.9	-.9	1.0	1.9	.6
TOLEDO, OHIO-MICH.	631.	693.	742.	781.	813.	.9	1.4	1.0	.8	1.0
TOPEKA, KANS.	141.	155.	158.	168.	180.	.9	.3	1.3	1.4	1.0
TRENTON, N.J.	266.	304.	343.	398.	458.	1.3	2.4	3.0	2.8	2.7
TUCSON, ARIZ.	266.	352.	386.	429.	474.	2.8	1.8	2.1	2.0	2.0
TULSA, OKLA.	419.	477.	509.	553.	601.	1.3	1.3	1.7	1.7	1.5
TUSCALOOSA, ALA.	109.	116.	124.	135.	147.	.6	1.3	1.7	1.6	1.6
TYLER, TEX.	86.	97.	111.	127.	145.	1.2	2.7	2.5	2.6	2.7
UTICA-ROME, N.Y.	331.	340.	360.	389.	418.	.3	1.1	1.6	1.4	1.4
VALLEJO-NAPA, CALIF.	200.	249.	250.	271.	298.	2.2	.1	2.0	1.9	1.8
WACO, TEX.	150.	148.	159.	175.	194.	-.2	1.4	2.4	2.0	1.8
WASHINGTON, D.C.-MD.-VA.	2002.	2713.	2961.	3334.	3722.	3.0	1.8	1.6	2.2	2.1
WATERLOO, IOWA	122.	133.	145.	157.	171.	.8	1.7	1.6	1.7	1.7
WEST PALM BEACH, FLA.	228.	349.	378.	415.	450.	4.2	1.6	1.8	1.6	1.7
WHEELING, W. VA.-OHIO	190.	183.	180.	178.	177.	-.4	-.3	-.2	-.1	-.2
WICHITA, KANS.	382.	389.	393.	408.	428.	.2	.2	.8	1.0	.6

WICHITA FALLS, TEX.	130.	128.	125.	130.	134.	-.2	-.3	.7	.7	.3
WILKES-BARRE-HAZLETON, PA.	347.	342.	355.	363.	373.	-.1	.7	.4	.5	.6
WILMINGTON, DEL.-N.J.-MD.	415.	500.	543.	595.	651.	1.9	1.7	1.8	1.8	1.8
WILMINGTON, N.C.	92.	107.	111.	120.	131.	1.5	.8	1.5	1.8	1.3
WINSTON-SALEM, N.C.	189.	214.	250.	288.	325.	1.2	3.1	2.8	2.4	2.8
WORCESTER, FITCHBURG-LEOMINSTER, MASS.	583.	638.	671.	699.	710.	.9	1.0	.8	.3	.7
YORK, PA.	290.	330.	369.	410.	455.	1.3	2.2	2.2	2.1	2.2
YOUNGSTOWN-WARREN, OHIO	509.	536.	552.	546.	550.	.5	.6	-.2	.2	.2
SMSA TOTAL	118390.	137841.	147805.	160323.	173583.	1.5	1.4	1.6	1.6	1.5
NON-SMSA COUNTIES	60933.	65327.	67652.	71211.	75981.	.7	.7	1.0	1.3	1.0
UNITED STATES	179323.	203168.	215458.	231534.	249564.	1.2	1.2	1.4	1.5	1.4

out the nation with rapid growth of one SMSA in a major region often being offset by slow growth or decline in another SMSA in the same region. Some examples of differential growths within states are: (1) Lafayette, Indiana, expected to grow 3.2 percent a year between 1970 and 1985, while Anderson, Indiana is expected to have a decline of 0.6 percent a year; (2) a growth of 3.7 percent a year for Midland, Texas is contrasted by a 0.1 percent decline rate for Beaumont-Port Arthur, Texas; (3) a 2.8 percent growth rate for Anaheim, California is offset by a 0.6 percent growth rate in Bakersfield, California; (4) Rochester, N.Y. is expected to grow 2.7 percent a year while Binghamton, N.Y. is expected to decline 1.1 percent a year; and (5) a growth rate of 2.6 percent for Erie, Pennsylvania is offset by a 0.1 percent rate in Johnstown, Pennsylvania. The annual rates of growth in population for each of the SMSAs are given in Table 6-5.

Population by State and Region

Table 6-6 summarizes the urban county population forecasts by state and region. The 1970-1985 growth rate is forecast to be faster than the 1960-1970 growth rate in New England, the Mideast, and the Great Lakes regions. The growth rates in the Southwest, Rocky Mountains, and Far West are expected to slow down. The largest changes in the growth rates occur in the Rocky Mountain and Far West regions.

States that show a forecast growth rate substantially greater than the growth rate during the 1960s are the District of Columbia, Mississippi, Montana, Oklahoma, and Arkansas. A substantially slower growth rate is shown for Nevada, Utah, and Arizona. Growth in the District of Columbia and North Dakota starts out slowly and then picks up in later years. Michigan's growth rate starts out fast but then slows down in later years. Most of the states in the Southwest, Far West, and Rocky Mountain states have slower growth rates in the 1970-1975 period compared to 1960-70, but their growth rates pick up after 1975. It appears that the 1970-71 recession is having considerable effect on the forecast growth in the previous fast-growth areas. After time for adjustment, however, some of these previous fast-growth states recover back to their 1960s growth rates, but in general the states in the Rocky Mountain and the Far West regions do not. States that are particularly hard hit, when measured by population growth rates, are Nevada and Utah.

Table 6-7 compares our 1970-85 annual growth rates with forecast growth rates in other studies. They include forecasts made by the Bureau of Economic Analysis (BEA)[5] and the National Planning Association (NPA)[6] The other

[5]U.S. Department of Commerce, Office of Business Economics, SURVEY OF CURRENT BUSINESS, April 1972.

[6]REGIONAL DEMOGRAPHIC PROJECTIONS 1960–85, Report No. 72–R–1.

forecasts are for all counties within each state whereas our forecasts are only for the SMSA counties. As a consequence, the other growth rates are lower on the average since urban areas are expected to grow faster than nonurban areas.

The BEA projections are remarkably similar to ours although made with completely different methodology. The growth rates in the northeastern part of the United States are approximately the same under both forecasts. The growth rates produced by the forecasting model are higher in the Plains, Southeast, and Southwest, whereas the growth in the Far West is faster with the BEA forecast. The growth in the Far West under the BEA forecasts is being offset by slower growth in the south. The NPA projections assume a lower national growth rate, and compared with the forecasting model they are lower in the eastern and southern areas and higher in the western areas of the United States.

Economic Variables by State and Region

The forecasts of jobs are similar to the population forecasts; however, since the high unemployment rates in 1970 are expected to be reduced in the forecast years, the rate of growth in jobs is faster at the beginning of the forecast period than at the end. The 1970-85 growth rate in jobs is faster than the growth rate in population in SMSAs and slower in the non-SMSA counties. The job growth rate is much faster than population in Idaho, West Virginia, South Dakota, North Dakota, and Utah. Table 6-8 shows the total job forecasts by state and region.

Manufacturing jobs are forecast to grow the fastest in the Southwest, the Southeast, and the Rocky Mountain regions. Jobs in the public utilities are expected to decline in New England. The finance, insurance, and real estate industries are expected to grow the fastest in the Southeast and New England regions.

Per capita income grows rapidly in all regions in the first years of the forecast but then slows down as the national economy adjusts to full employment. The Mideast and New England regions are expected to experience the most rapid growth in per capita income. The growth in per capita income in the Far West is expected to be slower than the average for all SMSAs.

Table 6-9 shows the per capita income of SMSA counties averaged by states and regions relative to the per capita income for all SMSA counties. The income relative is forecast to be greater in 1985 than it was in 1970 in New England, the Mideast, and the Southeast regions. The relative is expected to decline in the other regions.

Table 6-10 shows the forecast unemployment rates summarized by states and regions. Both overall SMSA unemployment rate and the non-SMSA rate is expected to follow the national pattern throughout the forecast period, going down until 1980 then picking up again. There is a large improvement between 1970 and 1975 in the non-SMSA counties. In all years the SMSA unemployment

Table 6-6
Population Data and Projections of SMSA Counties Summarized by State and Region (Thousands)

STATE AND REGION	1960	1970	1975	1980	1985	AVERAGE ANNUAL RATE OF GROWTH				
						1960–1970	1970–1975	1975–1980	1980–1985	1970–1985
CONNECTICUT	2189.	2585.	2811.	3103.	3406.	1.7	1.7	2.0	1.9	1.8
MAINE	269.	284.	297.	320.	340.	.5	.9	1.5	1.4	1.2
MASSACHUSETTS	5014.	5524.	5923.	6386.	6856.	1.0	1.4	1.5	1.4	1.4
NEW HAMPSHIRE	178.	224.	241.	262.	282.	2.3	1.5	1.6	1.5	1.5
RHODE ISLAND	719.	769.	818.	872.	924.	.7	1.2	1.3	1.5	1.5
NEW ENGLAND	8369.	9385.	10090.	10942.	11808.	1.1	1.4	1.6	1.5	1.5
DELAWARE	307.	386.	418.	456.	497.	2.3	1.6	1.7	1.7	1.7
DISTRICT OF COLUMBIA	764.	757.	761.	843.	937.	-.1	.1	2.1	2.1	1.4
MARYLAND	2474.	3192.	3449.	3776.	4104.	2.5	1.5	1.8	1.7	1.7
NEW JERSEY	4788.	5390.	5806.	6313.	6852.	1.2	1.5	1.7	1.6	1.6
NEW YORK	14537.	15726.	16580.	17530.	18474.	.8	1.1	1.1	1.0	1.1
PENNSYLVANIA	8925.	9366.	9882.	10497.	11134.	.5	1.1	1.2	1.2	1.2
MIDEAST	31794.	34816.	36897.	39414.	41998.	.9	1.2	1.3	1.3	1.3
ILLINOIS	7933.	8903.	9407.	9995.	10656.	1.2	1.1	1.2	1.3	1.2
INDIANA	2824.	3183.	3358.	3574.	3827.	1.2	1.1	1.4	1.4	1.3
MICHIGAN	5962.	6806.	7637.	8384.	9013.	1.3	2.3	1.9	1.6	1.9
OHIO	7394.	8212.	8828.	9451.	10060.	1.0	1.4	1.4	1.2	1.4
WISCONSIN	1867.	2122.	2318.	2538.	2752.	1.3	1.8	1.8	1.6	1.7
GREAT LAKES	25981.	29226.	31548.	33942.	36309.	1.2	1.5	1.5	1.3	1.4
IOWA	916.	1006.	1100.	1203.	1302.	.9	1.8	1.8	1.6	1.7
KANSAS	852.	949.	998.	1070.	1157.	1.1	1.0	1.4	1.6	1.3
MINNESOTA	1753.	2081.	2230.	2404.	2552.	1.7	1.4	1.5	1.2	1.4
MISSOURI	2598.	2916.	3050.	3243.	3462.	1.2	.9	1.1	1.3	1.1
NEBRASKA	542.	634.	654.	690.	729.	1.6	.6	1.1	1.1	.9
NORTH DAKOTA	67.	74.	74.	77.	81.	1.0	.0	.9	.8	.6
SOUTH DAKOTA	87.	95.	103.	112.	118.	1.0	1.7	1.7	1.1	1.5
PLAINS	6814.	7755.	8211.	8799.	9402.	1.3	1.1	1.4	1.3	1.3

ALABAMA	1604.	1707.	1828.	2002.	2225.	1.8	2.1	1.8	1.4	.6
ARKANSAS	492.	559.	619.	694.	788.	2.3	2.5	2.3	2.0	1.3
FLORIDA	3321.	4552.	5098.	5742.	6414.	2.3	2.2	2.4	2.3	3.2
GEORGIA	1814.	2280.	2410.	2631.	2889.	1.6	1.9	1.6	1.1	2.3
KENTUCKY	1058.	1209.	1314.	1422.	1511.	1.5	1.2	1.6	1.7	1.3
LOUISIANA	1750.	1996.	2132.	2327.	2567.	1.7	2.0	1.8	1.3	1.3
MISSISSIPPI	221.	259.	297.	345.	397.	2.9	2.8	3.0	2.7	1.6
NORTH CAROLINA	1404.	1738.	1898.	2105.	2305.	1.9	1.8	2.1	1.8	2.1
SOUTH CAROLINA	852.	1017.	1062.	1138.	1230.	1.3	1.5	1.4	.9	1.8
TENNESSEE	1697.	1918.	2076.	2275.	2466.	1.7	1.6	1.8	1.6	1.2
VIRGINIA	2048.	2569.	2837.	3190.	3565.	2.2	2.2	2.3	2.0	2.3
WEST VIRGINIA	575.	545.	549.	563.	575.	.3	.4	.5	.1	-.5
SOUTHEAST	16837.	20349.	22118.	24433.	26931.	1.9	1.9	2.0	1.7	1.9
ARIZONA	929.	1319.	1459.	1628.	1788.	2.0	1.9	2.2	2.0	3.5
NEW MEXICO	262.	316.	336.	361.	397.	1.5	1.9	1.5	1.3	1.9
OKLAHOMA	1069.	1282.	1375.	1511.	1683.	1.8	2.2	1.9	1.4	1.8
TEXAS	6503.	8054.	8841.	9927.	11162.	2.2	2.3	2.3	1.9	2.1
SOUTHWEST	8763.	10970.	12011.	13427.	15031.	2.1	2.3	2.2	1.8	2.2
COLORADO	1192.	1582.	1689.	1833.	1980.	1.5	1.5	1.6	1.3	2.8
IDAHO	93.	112.	117.	124.	131.	1.0	1.0	1.3	.8	1.8
MONTANA	152.	169.	190.	213.	239.	2.3	2.2	2.3	2.3	1.0
UTAH	666.	822.	815.	845.	884.	.5	.9	.7	-.2	2.1
ROCKY MOUNTAIN	2103.	2685.	2811.	3016.	3233.	1.2	1.4	1.4	.9	2.4
CALIFORNIA	14177.	18101.	19144.	20842.	22789.	1.5	1.8	1.7	1.1	2.4
HAWAII	500.	629.	686.	755.	828.	1.8	1.9	1.9	1.7	2.3
NEVADA	212.	394.	416.	474.	536.	2.0	2.5	2.6	1.1	6.2
OREGON	1038.	1281.	1365.	1475.	1583.	1.4	1.4	1.5	1.3	2.1
WASHINGTON	1801.	2249.	2510.	2805.	3136.	2.2	2.2	2.2	2.2	2.2
FAR WEST	17728.	22654.	24121.	26350.	28872.	1.6	1.8	1.8	1.3	2.5
SMSA TOTAL	118390.	137841.	147805.	160323.	173583.	1.5	1.6	1.6	1.4	1.5
NON-SMSA COUNTIES	60933.	65327.	67652.	71211.	75981.	1.0	1.3	1.0	.7	.7
UNITED STATES	179323.	203169.	215458.	231534.	249564.	1.4	1.5	1.4	1.2	1.2

Table 6-7

Population Projections by State and Region from Alternative Sources (Average Annual Rate of Growth)

State and Region	MMFM[a] 1970-1985	BEA[b] 1969-1990	NPA[c] 1970-1985
Connecticut	1.8	1.7	1.5
Maine	1.2	1.3	0.6
Massachusetts	1.4	1.5	1.0
New Hampshire	1.5	1.5	1.7
Rhode Island	1.2	1.3	1.3
Vermont	–	1.4	1.5
New England	1.5	1.5	1.2
Delaware	1.7	1.7	1.8
District of Columbia	1.4	0.0	1.4
Maryland	1.7	1.7	1.8
New Jersey	1.6	1.3	1.4
New York	1.1	1.3	1.0
Pennsylvania	1.2	1.1	0.6
Mideast	1.3	1.3	1.0
Illinois	1.2	1.2	1.1
Indiana	1.2	1.5	1.2
Michigan	1.9	1.5	1.3
Ohio	1.4	1.5	1.2
Wisconsin	1.7	1.2	1.1
Great Lakes	1.4	1.4	1.2
Iowa	1.7	0.8	0.6
Kansas	1.3	0.8	0.7
Minnesota	1.4	1.3	1.1
Missouri	1.1	1.4	0.9
Nebraska	0.9	0.8	0.8
North Dakota	0.6	0.2	0.3
South Dakota	1.5	0.2	0.5
Plains	1.3	1.1	0.8
Alabama	1.8	0.9	0.7
Arkansas	2.3	0.8	0.5
Florida	2.3	1.9	2.4
Georgia	1.6	1.5	1.3
Kentucky	1.5	1.0	0.8
Louisiana	1.7	1.0	1.3
Mississippi	2.9	0.7	0.6
North Carolina	1.9	1.1	1.5
South Carolina	1.3	1.1	1.1

Table 6-7 (cont.)

State and Region	MMFM[a] 1970-1985	BEA[b] 1969-1990	NPA[c] 1970-1985
Tennessee	1.7	1.4	0.8
Virginia	2.2	1.6	1.4
West Virginia	0.3	0.7	0.3
Southeast	1.9	1.3	1.3
Arizona	2.0	1.8	2.4
New Mexico	1.5	0.9	1.2
Oklahoma	1.8	1.1	0.8
Texas	2.2	1.4	1.4
Southwest	2.1	1.4	1.4
Colorado	1.5	1.6	2.0
Idaho	1.0	0.5	1.0
Montana	2.3	0.4	0.8
Utah	0.5	1.4	1.6
Wyoming	–	0.9	0.9
Rocky Mountain	1.2	1.4	1.6
Alaska	–	1.6	2.9
California	1.5	1.9	1.6
Hawaii	1.8	1.6	1.9
Nevada	2.0	3.0	2.8
Oregon	1.4	1.4	1.3
Washington	2.2	1.4	1.8
Far West	1.6	1.8	1.7
United States	1.4	1.4	1.2

[a]Multiregional, Multi-industry Forecasting Model, Table 6.6. Urban Counties only.
[b]Bureau of Economic Analysis, SURVEY OF CURRENT BUSINESS, April 1972.
[c]National Planning Association, REGIONAL DEMOGRAPHIC PROJECTIONS, 1960-1985, Report No. 72-R-1.

rate is lower than the non-SMSA unemployment rate. Twelve states have a higher unemployment rate in 1985 than they had in 1970.

Projections of other economic variables are summarized by region in Table 6-11. Gross regional product and most of its components are expected to grow most rapidly in the Southeast and Southwest regions, although government expenditures are expected to grow more rapidly in New England, the Plains, and the Great Lakes regions.

Central City Versus Suburban Forecast

Population and jobs are expected to grow faster in suburban counties than they are in central city counties. Table 6-12 summarizes the central city versus suburban growth for SMSAs over one million in each of the major regions.

Table 6-8
Job Projections of SMSA Counties Summarized by State and Region (Thousands)

STATE AND REGION	1970	1975	1980	1985	AVERAGE ANNUAL RATE OF GROWTH			
					1970–1975	1975–1980	1980–1985	1970–1985
CONNECTICUT	1157.	1309.	1485.	1634.	2.5	2.5	1.9	2.3
MAINE	134.	147.	162.	172.	2.0	1.9	1.2	1.7
MASSACHUSETTS	2396.	2661.	2927.	3080.	2.1	1.9	1.0	1.7
NEW HAMPSHIRE	100.	113.	126.	137.	2.3	2.3	1.6	2.1
RHODE ISLAND	326.	369.	409.	431.	2.4	2.1	1.1	1.9
NEW ENGLAND	4114.	4599.	5109.	5454.	2.2	2.1	1.3	1.9
DELAWARE	172.	194.	215.	232.	2.3	2.1	1.5	2.0
DISTRICT OF COLUMBIA	656.	683.	775.	855.	.8	2.5	2.0	1.8
MARYLAND	1267.	1443.	1635.	1785.	2.6	2.5	1.7	2.3
NEW JERSEY	2248.	2529.	2813.	3026.	2.3	2.1	1.5	2.0
NEW YORK	7234.	8078.	8870.	9375.	2.2	1.9	1.1	1.7
PENNSYLVANIA	3983.	4402.	4811.	5070.	2.0	1.8	1.0	1.6
MIDEAST	15561.	17328.	19119.	20343.	2.2	2.0	1.2	1.8
ILLINOIS	4098.	4540.	4892.	5064.	2.0	1.5	.7	1.4
INDIANA	1367.	1520.	1643.	1712.	2.1	1.6	.8	1.5
MICHIGAN	2691.	3211.	3647.	3894.	3.5	2.5	1.3	2.5
OHIO	3425.	3809.	4122.	4278.	2.1	1.6	.7	1.5
WISCONSIN	949.	1091.	1220.	1315.	2.8	2.2	1.5	2.2
GREAT LAKES	12531.	14170.	15524.	16264.	2.5	1.8	.9	1.7
IOWA	499.	565.	621.	657.	2.5	1.9	1.1	1.8
KANSAS	412.	445.	483.	510.	1.5	1.6	1.1	1.4
MINNESOTA	1014.	1149.	1275.	1344.	2.5	2.1	1.0	1.9
MISSOURI	1447.	1578.	1726.	1809.	1.7	1.8	.9	1.5
NEBRASKA	347.	371.	399.	416.	1.4	1.4	.8	1.2
NORTH DAKOTA	45.	48.	52.	55.	1.4	1.7	1.1	1.4
SOUTH DAKOTA	50.	59.	68.	74.	3.2	2.7	1.7	2.5
PLAINS	3815.	4215.	4625.	4865.	2.0	1.9	1.0	1.6

ALABAMA	688.	765.	857.	935.	2.1	2.3	1.7	2.0
ARKANSAS	250.	287.	331.	367.	2.8	2.8	2.0	2.6
FLORIDA	1862.	2150.	2469.	2723.	2.9	2.8	2.0	2.5
GEORGIA	1161.	1286.	1471.	1620.	2.0	2.7	1.9	2.2
KENTUCKY	540.	610.	669.	700.	2.5	1.8	.9	1.7
LOUISIANA	762.	852.	959.	1054.	2.2	2.4	1.9	2.2
MISSISSIPPI	123.	144.	167.	187.	3.1	3.0	2.2	2.8
NORTH CAROLINA	925.	1042.	1172.	1267.	2.4	2.4	1.6	2.1
SOUTH CAROLINA	453.	486.	535.	572.	1.4	1.9	1.3	1.6
TENNESSEE	887.	1022.	1171.	1290.	2.8	2.7	1.9	2.5
VIRGINIA	1068.	1191.	1364.	1511.	2.2	2.7	2.0	2.3
WEST VIRGINIA	229.	249.	268.	278.	1.6	1.5	.7	1.3
SOUTHEAST	8948.	10084.	11434.	12504.	2.4	2.5	1.8	2.2
ARIZONA	510.	596.	694.	770.	3.1	3.1	2.1	2.8
NEW MEXICO	128.	133.	142.	148.	.8	1.4	.8	1.0
OKLAHOMA	593.	645.	713.	771.	1.7	2.0	1.6	1.8
TEXAS	3442.	3895.	4447.	4877.	2.5	2.7	1.8	2.3
SOUTHWEST	4672.	5269.	5997.	6567.	2.4	2.6	1.8	2.3
COLORADO	696.	761.	844.	899.	1.8	2.1	1.3	1.7
IDAHO	53.	59.	67.	73.	2.3	2.4	1.7	2.2
MONTANA	71.	80.	89.	96.	2.4	2.3	1.4	2.0
UTAH	312.	332.	359.	380.	1.3	1.6	1.1	1.3
ROCKY MOUNTAIN	1131.	1232.	1360.	1447.	1.7	2.0	1.3	1.6
CALIFORNIA	7358.	8061.	8900.	9426.	1.8	2.0	1.1	1.7
HAWAII	289.	310.	343.	367.	1.4	2.0	1.4	1.6
NEVADA	212.	223.	255.	277.	1.1	2.6	1.7	1.8
OREGON	532.	597.	665.	716.	2.3	2.1	1.5	2.0
WASHINGTON	912.	1049.	1206.	1331.	2.8	2.8	2.0	2.5
FAR WEST	9303.	10241.	11369.	12116.	1.9	2.1	1.3	1.8
SMSA TOTAL	60076.	67139.	74536.	79560.	2.2	2.1	1.3	1.9
NON-SMSA COUNTIES	22858.	24363.	25635.	26278.	1.3	1.0	.5	.9
UNITED STATES	82933.	91502.	100170.	105838.	2.0	1.8	1.1	1.6

Table 6-9

Per Capita Income of SMSA Counties Averaged by State and Region Relative to per Capita Income of All SMSA Counties

STATE AND REGION	1970	1975	1980	1985
CONNECTICUT	1.11	1.12	1.13	1.15
MAINE	.80	.81	.82	.83
MASSACHUSETTS	1.00	1.00	1.00	1.00
NEW HAMPSHIRE	.90	.91	.93	.95
RHODE ISLAND	.92	.93	.93	.94
NEW ENGLAND	1.02	1.02	1.03	1.03
DELAWARE	1.15	1.15	1.13	1.13
DISTRICT OF COLUMBIA	1.33	1.36	1.38	1.41
MARYLAND	1.04	1.00	.99	.98
NEW JERSEY	1.11	1.10	1.09	1.09
NEW YORK	1.08	1.13	1.18	1.22
PENNSYLVANIA	.96	.96	.97	.97
MIDEAST	1.06	1.07	1.09	1.11
ILLINOIS	1.12	1.12	1.10	1.09
INDIANA	.93	.93	.92	.90
MICHIGAN	1.02	1.04	1.04	1.04
OHIO	.96	.97	.96	.94
WISCONSIN	.98	.99	.98	.99
GREAT LAKES	1.02	1.03	1.02	1.01

IOWA	.99	.99	.97	.96
KANSAS	.95	.91	.89	.87
MINNESOTA	1.07	1.09	1.09	1.09
MISSOURI	1.01	1.02	1.02	1.01
NEBRASKA	.96	.94	.93	.92
NORTH DAKOTA	.87	.88	.89	.91
SOUTH DAKOTA	.79	.84	.89	.95
PLAINS	1.01	1.01	1.01	1.00
ALABAMA	.80	.80	.80	.81
ARKANSAS	.78	.79	.80	.81
FLORIDA	.94	.93	.93	.93
GEORGIA	.97	.97	.99	1.01
KENTUCKY	.94	.94	.93	.93
LOUISIANA	.74	.74	.75	.76
MISSISSIPPI	.83	.84	.83	.83
NORTH CAROLINA	.80	.82	.83	.84
SOUTH CAROLINA	.81	.79	.79	.79
TENNESSEE	.87	.90	.93	.97
VIRGINIA	1.02	.95	.93	.92
WEST VIRGINIA	.93	.95	.98	1.00
SOUTHEAST	.89	.88	.89	.90
ARIZONA	.92	.93	.94	.95
NEW MEXICO	.86	.79	.74	.71
OKLAHOMA	.88	.85	.83	.82
TEXAS	.87	.87	.87	.86
SOUTHWEST	.88	.87	.87	.86

Table 6-9 (cont.)

STATE AND REGION	1970	1975	1980	1985
COLORADO	.95	.93	.92	.91
IDAHO	.83	.87	.91	.97
MONTANA	.86	.83	.80	.78
UTAH	.80	.79	.78	.78
ROCKY MOUNTAIN	.90	.88	.87	.87
CALIFORNIA	1.06	1.04	1.02	1.00
HAWAII	1.15	1.05	1.01	.99
NEVADA	1.04	1.03	1.03	1.03
OREGON	.92	.93	.94	.96
WASHINGTON	.99	.97	.96	.96
FAR WEST	1.04	1.02	1.01	.99
SMSA TOTAL	1.00	1.00	1.00	1.00
NON-SMSA COUNTIES	.71	.69	.67	.65
UNITED STATES	.91	.90	.90	.89

Overall, suburban population growth in large SMSAs between 1970 and 1985 is expected to grow 1.8 percent a year whereas the central city counties are expected to grow 1.3 percent a year. The forecasts for central cities counties show greater improvement in the unemployment rate; and the per capita income is higher in the central city counties and is expected to grow at a faster rate. The summary of jobs by industry shows little shift in manufacturing jobs but that many of the service industries, which are usually considered central city functions, are expected to shift to the suburban counties. Service industries are expected to grow 4.0 percent a year in suburban counties versus 2.5 percent in central city counties. Finance, insurance, and real estate also are expected to grow more rapidly in the suburban counties.

When the central city versus suburban forecasts in large SMSAs are compared by major regions, some of the conclusions are different. The population in the central city counties of the New England region is expected to decline 0.7 percent a year whereas the suburban counties are expected to increase 2.0 percent a year. The central city county population growth in the Southeast and Southwest regions is expected to be faster than suburban county growth. Jobs in the service industries are expected to grow faster in suburban counties in all regions except the Southwest. Unemployment rates in 1985 are expected to be higher in suburban counties in the New England, Rocky Mountain, and Far West regions.

**Regional Effects of Reduced
Defense Expenditures**

In order to illustrate the usefulness of the model for impact analysis, projections were made assuming large cuts in defense expenditures. The objective was not to measure the short-run hardships that could be caused by large immediate cuts in the defense expenditures, but to trace out the long-run regional shifts that would take place after the economy has had ample time for adjustment. Defense expenditure cuts in real dollars are assumed to take place between 1973 and 1980, and then the defense budget is assumed constant until 1985. Although the cuts are large, they are assumed to occur gradually over time and it is assumed there will be appropriate fiscal action to compensate for the employment losses due to the defense expenditure cuts. The national unemployment rates under the low defense budget are assumed to be approximately the same as under the "normal" defense budget.

The low defense budget is similar (although not exactly equal) to the

Table 6-10
Average Unemployment Rate Projections of SMSA Counties Summarized by State and Region

STATE AND REGION	1970	1975	1980	1985
CONNECTICUT	3.3	3.5	2.8	3.3
MAINE	4.8	4.4	4.0	4.3
MASSACHUSETTS	4.9	4.7	3.7	4.4
NEW HAMPSHIRE	3.3	3.7	2.8	3.1
RHODE ISLAND	5.2	4.9	3.9	4.1
NEW ENGLAND	4.5	4.4	3.5	4.1
DELAWARE	3.1	3.4	2.6	2.9
DISTRICT OF COLUMBIA	3.3	3.7	2.8	3.1
MARYLAND	3.1	3.3	2.8	3.1
NEW JERSEY	4.9	4.6	4.0	4.5
NEW YORK	4.7	4.4	3.5	3.6
PENNSYLVANIA	4.6	4.4	3.6	3.9
MIDEAST	4.5	4.3	3.5	3.7
ILLINOIS	3.2	3.5	2.8	3.4
INDIANA	3.1	3.2	2.8	3.3
MICHIGAN	3.5	3.7	3.1	3.2
OHIO	3.7	3.9	3.3	3.8
WISCONSIN	3.4	3.3	3.0	3.3
GREAT LAKES	3.4	3.6	3.0	3.4

IOWA	2.7	2.4	2.6	2.2
KANSAS	3.7	3.4	4.0	3.6
MINNESOTA	3.0	2.6	3.2	3.1
MISSOURI	3.2	2.9	3.6	3.3
NEBRASKA	3.0	2.9	3.2	3.0
NORTH DAKOTA	2.7	3.0	3.2	3.5
SOUTH DAKOTA	2.6	2.5	3.0	3.3
PLAINS	3.1	2.8	3.3	3.1
ALABAMA	4.5	4.0	4.9	4.9
ARKANSAS	5.0	4.1	5.5	5.5
FLORIDA	3.7	3.2	3.7	3.4
GEORGIA	3.2	3.0	3.8	3.5
KENTUCKY	3.2	2.8	3.1	2.9
LOUISIANA	4.3	3.8	4.8	4.8
MISSISSIPPI	4.4	3.5	3.8	3.4
NORTH CAROLINA	3.4	3.1	3.5	3.4
SOUTH CAROLINA	4.4	4.0	5.1	5.2
TENNESSEE	3.3	3.1	3.5	3.7
VIRGINIA	2.9	2.6	2.9	2.0
WEST VIRGINIA	4.5	4.4	5.3	6.5
SOUTHEAST	3.6	3.3	3.9	3.7
ARIZONA	4.1	3.7	4.9	5.3
NEW MEXICO	6.3	4.7	6.1	5.5
OKLAHOMA	4.4	3.5	4.5	4.1
TEXAS	4.5	3.9	4.8	4.7
SOUTHWEST	4.5	3.8	4.8	4.7

Table 6-10 (cont.)

STATE AND REGION	1970	1975	1980	1985
COLORADO	3.9	4.0	3.4	3.9
IDAHO	4.4	4.0	3.1	3.1
MONTANA	5.2	5.5	4.5	5.4
UTAH	6.1	5.4	4.3	4.2
ROCKY MOUNTAIN	4.7	4.5	3.7	4.0
CALIFORNIA	6.1	5.5	4.8	5.5
HAWAII	3.5	4.8	3.6	4.2
NEVADA	5.7	6.1	4.6	6.0
OREGON	4.8	4.6	4.0	4.1
WASHINGTON	5.0	5.1	4.0	4.5
FAR WEST	5.8	5.4	4.7	5.2
SMSA TOTAL	4.3	4.2	3.5	3.9
NON-SMSA COUNTIES	5.3	4.8	4.4	4.8
UNITED STATES	4.6	4.4	3.8	4.1

minimum deterrence budget developed by Kaufmann.[7] The basic assumptions of this alternative are as follows:[8]

a. Strategic nuclear deterrence is based solely on the Polaris-Poseidon force; Minuteman, bombers, and CONUS active defenses are phased out;
b. Theater nuclear forces are phased out of the inventory;
c. 6 division forces and 6 tactical air wings are dropped from the force structure, and General Purpose Force planning is based on the assumption of the capability simultaneously to cope with one major and one minor contingency;
d. Proportionate reduction in other programs associated with the General Purpose Forces (categories 4, 5, 7, 8, and 9), and a cut in military assistance;
e. A reduction in the pay raise to reflect the reduction in manpower;
f. The armed forces are assumed to number 2.3 million.

Under these assumptions the total defense expenditures are cut approximately 47 percent with procurement down 69 percent. The major breakdown of defense expenditures assumed for 1985 (expressed in millions (1969 prices)) under both the normal and minimum deterrence budgets is as follows:

Defense Budget	Normal	Minimum Deterrence	Percent Change
Total Procurement	41189.	12474.	− 69.1
Civilian Employee Compensation	8169.	8169.	.0
Military Compensation	18860.	14998.	− 20.5
Military Construction	950.	950.	.0
Total Expenditures	69167.	36864.	− 46.7

As seen by the table, defense expenditures are cut approximately 32 billion dollars. In order to compensate for this cut, nondefense federal expenditures are increased approximately by 13 billion dollars. It was not necessary to fully compensate for the drop in defense expenditures in order to achieve approximately the same level of employment. The shifts in federal spending cause a shift in industry outputs from manufacturing with high productivity rates to services with low productivity rates. A summary of these output shifts is given in Table

[7]William W. Kaufmann, "Alternative Post-Vietnam Defense Budgets," U.S. Congress, 91st Congress, 1st Session, Joint Economic Committee, Subcommittee on Economy in Government, THE MILITARY BUDGET AND NATIONAL ECONOMIC PRIORITIES, PART 1 (Washington: Government Printing Office, 1969), pp. 163-181; as reported in ADJUSTMENTS OF THE U.S. ECONOMY TO REDUCTIONS IN MILITARY SPENDING edited by Bernard Udis, United States Arms Control and Disarmament Agency, ACDA/E−156, December 1970.
[8]ADJUSTMENTS OF THE U.S. ECONOMY TO REDUCTIONS IN MILITARY SPENDING, p. 11.

Table 6-11

Selected Projections of SMSA Counties Summarized by Region

NEW ENGLAND

JOBS BY INDUSTRY	1970	1975	1980	1985	AVERAGE ANNUAL RATE OF GROWTH			
					1970-1975	1975-1980	1980-1985	1970-1985
1 NATURAL RESOURCES (1-10)	35.	32.	27.	22.	-1.8	-3.3	-3.5	-2.9
2 CONSTRUCTION (11,12)	162.	187.	207.	224.	2.9	2.0	1.6	2.2
3 MANUFACTURING (13-74)	1307.	1420.	1490.	1487.	1.7	1.0	-.0	.9
4 PUBLIC UTILITIES (75-80)	198.	199.	197.	191.	.1	-.2	-.6	-.2
5 WHOLESALE TRADE (81)	211.	254.	288.	314.	3.7	2.5	1.7	2.6
6 RETAIL TRADE (86,89-99)	690.	787.	885.	954.	2.6	2.3	1.5	2.2
7 FINANCE, INS. & REAL ESTATE (82,83)	236.	300.	372.	438.	4.8	4.3	3.2	4.1
8 SERVICES (84,85,87,88,102)	745.	890.	1070.	1212.	3.6	3.7	2.5	3.2
9 STATE & LOCAL GOVT. (101)	415.	426.	460.	494.	.5	1.5	1.4	1.2
10 FEDERAL GOVERNMENT (100)	92.	85.	93.	98.	-1.7	1.8	1.2	.4
11 MILITARY (103)	24.	20.	20.	20.	-4.3	.0	-.0	-1.4
TOTAL JOBS	4114.	4599.	5109.	5454.	2.2	2.1	1.3	1.9
CIVILIAN UNEMPLOYMENT RATE	4.5	4.4	3.5	4.1				
POPULATION	9385.	10090.	10942.	11808.	1.4	1.6	1.5	1.5
PERCENT NON-WHITE	4.5	4.6	4.9	5.1				
PER CAPITA INCOME	4215.	5093.	5905.	6545.	3.8	3.0	2.1	2.9
GROSS REGIONAL PRODUCT	44062.	55002.	67946.	78825.	4.4	4.2	3.0	3.9
PERSONAL CONSUMPTION EXPENDITURES	32167.	40338.	51797.	61408.	4.5	5.0	3.4	4.3
PRIVATE INVESTMENT	6382.	8341.	9956.	11081.	5.4	3.5	2.1	3.7
GOVERNMENT EXPENDITURES	10119.	10867.	12239.	13552.	1.4	2.4	2.0	1.9

MIDEAST

JOBS BY INDUSTRY	1970	1975	1980	1985	AVERAGE ANNUAL RATE OF GROWTH			
					1970-1975	1975-1980	1980-1985	1970-1985
1 NATURAL RESOURCES (1-10)	143.	134.	116.	100.	-1.4	-2.9	-3.1	-2.4
2 CONSTRUCTION (11,12)	612.	701.	769.	831.	2.7	1.9	1.5	2.0
3 MANUFACTURING (13-74)	3971.	4343.	4573.	4573.	1.8	1.0	-.0	.9
4 PUBLIC UTILITIES (75-80)	1016.	1080.	1135.	1158.	1.2	1.0	.4	.9
5 WHOLESALE TRADE (81)	951.	1132.	1277.	1382.	3.5	2.4	1.6	2.5
6 RETAIL TRADE (86,89-99)	2369.	2660.	2966.	3173.	2.3	2.2	1.4	1.9

JOBS BY INDUSTRY	1970	1975	1980	1985	AVERAGE ANNUAL RATE OF GROWTH 1970–1975	1975–1980	1980–1985	1970–1985
7 FINANCE, INS. & REAL ESTATE (82,83)	1015.	1284.	1561.	1788.	4.7	3.9	2.7	3.8
8 SERVICES (84,85,87,88,102)	2910.	3394.	3984.	4439.	3.1	3.2	2.2	2.8
9 STATE & LOCAL GOVT. (101)	1781.	1867.	1967.	2082.	.9	1.0	1.1	1.0
10 FEDERAL GOVERNMENT (100)	657.	624.	661.	708.	-1.0	1.1	1.4	.5
11 MILITARY (103)	136.	110.	110.	110.	-4.3	.0	.0	-1.4
TOTAL JOBS	15561.	17328.	19119.	20343.	2.2	2.0	1.2	1.8
CIVILIAN UNEMPLOYMENT RATE	4.5	4.3	3.5	3.7				
POPULATION	34816.	36897.	39414.	41998.	1.2	1.3	1.3	1.3
PERCENT NON-WHITE	15.2	15.7	16.4	17.1				
PER CAPITA INCOME	4374.	5347.	6287.	7034.	4.0	3.2	2.2	3.2
GROSS REGIONAL PRODUCT	196069.	240241.	293079.	336260.	4.1	4.0	2.7	3.6
PERSONAL CONSUMPTION EXPENDITURES	117872.	147196.	189570.	224190.	4.4	5.1	3.4	4.3
PRIVATE INVESTMENT	22634.	30430.	37254.	42312.	5.9	4.0	2.5	4.2
GOVERNMENT EXPENDITURES	37694.	40981.	44949.	49302.	1.7	1.8	1.8	1.8

GREAT LAKES

JOBS BY INDUSTRY	1970	1975	1980	1985	AVERAGE ANNUAL RATE OF GROWTH 1970–1975	1975–1980	1980–1985	1970–1985
1 NATURAL RESOURCES (1-10)	176.	163.	138.	117.	-1.5	-3.2	-3.3	-2.7
2 CONSTRUCTION (11,12)	527.	626.	684.	733.	3.4	1.8	1.4	2.2
3 MANUFACTURING (13-74)	4044.	4539.	4800.	4805.	2.3	1.1	1.0	1.1
4 PUBLIC UTILITIES (75-80)	702.	765.	811.	828.	1.7	1.2	.4	1.1
5 WHOLESALE TRADE (81)	743.	902.	1018.	1098.	3.9	2.4	1.5	2.6
6 RETAIL TRADE (86,89-99)	2131.	2442.	2716.	2880.	2.7	2.1	1.2	2.0
7 FINANCE, INS. & REAL ESTATE (82,83)	590.	755.	925.	1064.	4.9	4.1	2.8	3.9
8 SERVICES (84,85,87,88,102)	1948.	2239.	2580.	2796.	2.8	2.8	1.6	2.4
9 STATE & LOCAL GOVT. (101)	1317.	1407.	1503.	1584.	1.3	1.3	1.1	1.2
10 FEDERAL GOVERNMENT (100)	274.	268.	285.	294.	-.5	1.2	.6	.5
11 MILITARY (103)	80.	64.	64.	64.	-4.3	.0	-.0	-1.4
TOTAL JOBS	12531.	14170.	15524.	16264.	2.5	1.8	.9	1.7
CIVILIAN UNEMPLOYMENT RATE	3.4	3.6	3.0	3.4				
POPULATION	29226.	31548.	33942.	36309.	1.5	1.5	1.3	1.4
PERCENT NON-WHITE	13.2	14.0	14.8	15.5				
PER CAPITA INCOME	4237.	5125.	5869.	6385.	3.8	2.7	1.7	2.7
GROSS REGIONAL PRODUCT	154976.	196786.	241857.	277485.	4.8	4.1	2.7	3.9
PERSONAL CONSUMPTION EXPENDITURES	92010.	116719.	147580.	170409.	4.8	4.7	2.9	4.1
PRIVATE INVESTMENT	21917.	30821.	37261.	42526.	6.8	3.8	2.6	4.4
GOVERNMENT EXPENDITURES	23536.	26585.	29336.	31652.	2.4	2.0	1.5	2.0

Table 6-11(cont.)

172

PLAINS

JOBS BY INDUSTRY	1970	1975	1980	1985	AVERAGE ANNUAL RATE OF GROWTH			
					1970-1975	1975-1980	1980-1985	1970-1985
1 NATURAL RESOURCES (1-10)	74.	68.	59.	51.	-1.5	-2.9	-3.1	-2.5
2 CONSTRUCTION (11,12)	193.	225.	248.	268.	3.1	1.9	1.6	2.2
3 MANUFACTURING (13-74)	873.	963.	1026.	1042.	2.0	1.3	.3	1.2
4 PUBLIC UTILITIES (75-80)	252.	276.	294.	302.	1.8	1.3	.6	1.2
5 WHOLESALE TRADE (81)	268.	321.	363.	394.	3.6	2.4	1.6	2.6
6 RETAIL TRADE (86,89-99)	718.	816.	914.	982.	2.5	2.3	1.4	2.1
7 FINANCE, INS. & REAL ESTATE (82,83)	223.	268.	307.	331.	3.7	2.7	1.5	2.6
8 SERVICES (84,85,87,88,102)	709.	788.	886.	936.	2.1	2.3	1.1	1.9
9 STATE & LOCAL GOVT. (101)	370.	378.	407.	433.	.4	1.5	1.2	1.1
10 FEDERAL GOVERNMENT (100)	106.	90.	98.	103.	-3.2	1.7	1.0	-.2
11 MILITARY (103)	29.	23.	23.	23.	-4.3	.0	.0	-1.4
TOTAL JOBS	3815.	4215.	4625.	4865.	2.0	1.9	1.0	1.6
CIVILIAN UNEMPLOYMENT RATE	3.1	3.3	2.8	3.1				
POPULATION	7755.	8211.	8799.	9402.	1.1	1.4	1.3	1.3
PERCENT NON-WHITE	8.3	8.5	8.9	9.2				
PER CAPITA INCOME	4184.	5036.	5791.	6331.	3.7	2.8	1.8	2.8
GROSS REGIONAL PRODUCT	43162.	53844.	66411.	76714.	4.4	4.2	2.9	3.8
PERSONAL CONSUMPTION EXPENDITURES	26628.	32859.	41508.	48177.	4.2	4.7	3.0	4.0
PRIVATE INVESTMENT	5750.	7886.	9757.	11247.	6.3	4.3	2.8	4.5
GOVERNMENT EXPENDITURES	7659.	8108.	9068.	9916.	1.1	2.2	1.8	1.7

SOUTHEAST

JOBS BY INDUSTRY	1970	1975	1980	1985	AVERAGE ANNUAL RATE OF GROWTH			
					1970-1975	1975-1980	1980-1985	1970-1985
1 NATURAL RESOURCES (1-10)	186.	178.	165.	154.	-.9	-1.6	-1.4	-1.3
2 CONSTRUCTION (11,12)	595.	702.	783.	864.	3.3	2.2	2.0	2.5
3 MANUFACTURING (13-74)	1663.	1873.	2032.	2100.	2.4	1.6	.7	1.6

(continued)

	1970	1975	1980	1985	AVERAGE ANNUAL RATE OF GROWTH			
					1970-1975	1975-1980	1980-1985	1970-1985
4 PUBLIC UTILITIES (75-80)	580.	620.	656.	676.	1.3	1.1	.6	1.0
5 WHOLESALE TRADE (81)	572.	700.	812.	903.	4.0	3.0	2.1	3.0
6 RETAIL TRADE (86,89-99)	1522.	1779.	2060.	2280.	3.1	2.9	2.0	2.7
7 FINANCE, INS. & REAL ESTATE (82,83)	476.	647.	839.	1018.	6.1	5.2	3.9	5.1
8 SERVICES (84,85,87,88,102)	1631.	1918.	2290.	2574.	3.2	3.5	2.3	3.0
9 STATE & LOCAL GOVT. (101)	999.	1030.	1130.	1236.	.6	1.8	1.8	1.4
10 FEDERAL GOVERNMENT (100)	385.	363.	393.	426.	-1.2	1.6	1.6	.7
11 MILITARY (103)	338.	273.	273.	273.	-4.3	.0	.0	-1.4
TOTAL JOBS	8948.	10084.	11434.	12504.	2.4	2.5	1.8	2.2
CIVILIAN UNEMPLOYMENT RATE	3.7	3.9	3.3	3.6				
POPULATION	20349.	22118.	24433.	26931.	1.7	2.0	1.9	1.9
PERCENT NON-WHITE	21.3	21.3	21.6	22.0				
PER CAPITA INCOME	3699.	4411.	5114.	5665.	3.5	3.0	2.0	2.8
GROSS REGIONAL PRODUCT	96420.	123891.	159747.	192889.	5.0	5.1	3.8	4.6
PERSONAL CONSUMPTION EXPENDITURES	66764.	84191.	110476.	133929.	4.6	5.4	3.9	4.6
PRIVATE INVESTMENT	14097.	19555.	24033.	27896.	6.5	4.1	4.6	4.6
GOVERNMENT EXPENDITURES	21048.	21955.	24426.	26989.	.8	2.1	2.0	1.7

SOUTHWEST

JOBS BY INDUSTRY

	1970	1975	1980	1985	AVERAGE ANNUAL RATE OF GROWTH			
					1970-1975	1975-1980	1980-1985	1970-1985
1 NATURAL RESOURCES (1-10)	174.	170.	165.	161.	-.4	-.6	-.5	-.5
2 CONSTRUCTION (11,12)	315.	371.	416.	464.	3.2	2.3	2.2	2.6
3 MANUFACTURING (13-74)	820.	938.	1053.	1124.	2.7	2.3	1.3	2.1
4 PUBLIC UTILITIES (75-80)	283.	307.	328.	340.	1.6	1.4	.7	1.2
5 WHOLESALE TRADE (81)	309.	378.	440.	490.	4.0	3.0	2.2	3.1
6 RETAIL TRADE (86,89-99)	830.	963.	1111.	1225.	3.0	2.9	2.0	2.6
7 FINANCE, INS. & REAL ESTATE (82,83)	253.	315.	376.	420.	4.4	3.5	2.2	3.4
8 SERVICES (84,85,87,88,102)	848.	1017.	1232.	1400.	3.6	3.8	2.5	3.3
9 STATE & LOCAL GOVT. (101)	459.	475.	525.	576.	.7	2.0	1.9	1.5
10 FEDERAL GOVERNMENT (100)	197.	186.	202.	219.	-1.2	1.7	1.6	.7
11 MILITARY (103)	184.	148.	148.	148.	-4.3	.0	-.0	-1.4
TOTAL JOBS	4672.	5269.	5997.	6567.	2.4	2.6	1.8	2.3
CIVILIAN UNEMPLOYMENT RATE	4.7	4.8	3.8	4.5				
POPULATION	10970.	12011.	13427.	15031.	1.8	2.2	2.3	2.1
PERCENT NON-WHITE	12.2	12.4	12.7	13.0				
PER CAPITA INCOME	3631.	4330.	4989.	5471.	3.5	2.8	1.8	2.7
GROSS REGIONAL PRODUCT	52330.	67447.	87282.	105656.	5.1	5.2	3.8	4.7

Table 6-11 (cont.)

					AVERAGE ANNUAL RATE OF GROWTH			
					1970-1975	1975-1980	1980-1985	1970-1985
PERSONAL CONSUMPTION EXPENDITURES	34936.	44285.	58487.	71288.	4.7	5.6	4.0	4.8
PRIVATE INVESTMENT	7399.	10041.	12446.	14517.	6.1	4.3	3.1	4.5
GOVERNMENT EXPENDITURES	12343.	12824.	14402.	16002.	.8	2.3	2.1	1.7

ROCKY MOUNTAIN

JOBS BY INDUSTRY	1970	1975	1980	1985	1970-1975	1975-1980	1980-1985	1970-1985
1 NATURAL RESOURCES (1-10)	32.	29.	25.	22.	-2.0	-3.0	-3.1	-2.7
2 CONSTRUCTION (11,12)	61.	70.	76.	82.	2.8	1.7	1.4	2.0
3 MANUFACTURING (13-74)	161.	181.	196.	201.	2.3	1.6	.5	1.5
4 PUBLIC UTILITIES (75-80)	70.	71.	72.	72.	.3	.3	-.1	.2
5 WHOLESALE TRADE (81)	72.	85.	96.	105.	3.4	2.4	1.7	2.5
6 RETAIL TRADE (86,89-99)	205.	233.	263.	285.	2.6	2.4	1.6	2.2
7 FINANCE, INS. & REAL ESTATE (82,83)	59.	71.	81.	87.	3.6	2.7	1.4	2.6
8 SERVICES (84,85,87,88,102)	200.	234.	279.	311.	3.2	3.5	2.2	3.0
9 STATE & LOCAL GOVT. (101)	143.	145.	154.	164.	.3	1.3	1.2	.9
10 FEDERAL GOVERNMENT (100)	74.	68.	72.	76.	-1.7	-1.2	1.0	.1
11 MILITARY (103)	54.	44.	44.	44.	-4.3	-.0	.0	-1.4
TOTAL JOBS	1131.	1232.	1360.	1447.	1.7	2.0	1.3	1.6
CIVILIAN UNEMPLOYMENT RATE	4.7	4.5	3.7	4.0				
POPULATION	2685.	2811.	3016.	3233.	.9	1.4	1.4	1.2
PERCENT NON-WHITE	4.0	4.2	4.5	4.7				
PER CAPITA INCOME	3717.	4392.	5034.	5513.	3.3	2.7	1.8	2.6
GROSS REGIONAL PRODUCT	12074.	14608.	17821.	20472.	3.8	4.0	2.8	3.5
PERSONAL CONSUMPTION EXPENDITURES	8582.	10345.	13056.	15228.	3.7	4.7	3.1	3.8
PRIVATE INVESTMENT	1594.	2109.	2522.	2810.	5.6	3.6	2.2	3.8
GOVERNMENT EXPENDITURES	2944.	3018.	3284.	3538.	.5	1.7	1.5	1.2

FAR WEST

JOBS BY INDUSTRY	1970	1975	1980	1985	AVERAGE ANNUAL RATE OF GROWTH			
					1970-1975	1975-1980	1980-1985	1970-1985
1 NATURAL RESOURCES (1-10)	216.	204.	182.	162.	-1.1	-2.3	-2.4	-1.9
2 CONSTRUCTION (11,12)	431.	500.	553.	601.	3.0	2.0	1.7	2.2
3 MANUFACTURING (13-74)	1878.	2044.	2187.	2223.	1.7	1.3	.3	1.1
4 PUBLIC UTILITIES (75-80)	558.	599.	634.	645.	1.4	1.1	1.1	1.0
5 WHOLESALE TRADE (81)	524.	625.	709.	768.	3.5	2.5	1.6	2.5
6 RETAIL TRADE (86,89-99)	1579.	1781.	1997.	2137.	2.4	2.3	1.4	2.0
7 FINANCE, INS. & REAL ESTATE (82,83)	499.	597.	694.	768.	3.6	3.0	2.0	2.9
8 SERVICES (84,85,87,88,102)	1690.	2025.	2436.	2729.	3.6	3.7	2.3	3.2
9 STATE & LOCAL GOVT. (101)	1206.	1237.	1324.	1411.	.5	1.4	1.3	1.0
10 FEDERAL GOVERNMENT (100)	377.	350.	374.	395.	-1.5	1.4	1.1	.3
11 MILITARY (103)	345.	278.	278.	278.	-4.3	.0	.0	-1.4
TOTAL JOBS	9303.	10241.	11369.	12116.	1.9	2.1	1.3	1.8
CIVILIAN UNEMPLOYMENT RATE	5.8	5.4	4.7	5.2				
POPULATION	22654.	24121.	26350.	28872.	1.3	1.8	1.8	1.6
PERCENT NON-WHITE	11.8	12.3	12.8	13.2				
PER CAPITA INCOME	4331.	5109.	5826.	6294.	3.3	2.6	1.5	2.5
GROSS REGIONAL PRODUCT	117753.	143879.	176976.	203877.	4.0	4.1	2.8	3.7
PERSONAL CONSUMPTION EXPENDITURES	76698.	93147.	118860.	139361.	3.9	4.9	3.2	4.0
PRIVATE INVESTMENT	15648.	20924.	25362.	28483.	5.8	3.8	2.3	4.0
GOVERNMENT EXPENDITURES	33122.	34765.	38268.	41614.	1.0	1.9	1.7	1.5

NON-SMSA COUNTIES

JOBS BY INDUSTRY	1970	1975	1980	1985	AVERAGE ANNUAL RATE OF GROWTH			
					1970-1975	1975-1980	1980-1985	1970-1985
1 NATURAL RESOURCES (1-10)	3209.	3069.	2697.	2321.	-.9	-2.6	-3.0	-2.2
2 CONSTRUCTION (11,12)	899.	1030.	1098.	1166.	2.7	1.3	1.2	1.7
3 MANUFACTURING (13-74)	5384.	5830.	6056.	5982.	1.6	.8	-.2	.7
4 PUBLIC UTILITIES (75-80)	953.	1012.	1048.	1051.	1.2	.7	.0	.7
5 WHOLESALE TRADE (81)	724.	858.	951.	1016.	3.4	2.1	1.3	2.3
6 RETAIL TRADE (86,89-99)	3557.	4002.	4418.	4681.	2.4	2.0	1.2	1.8
7 FINANCE, INS. & REAL ESTATE (82,83)	596.	807.	1039.	1250.	6.1	5.0	3.7	4.9

Table 6-11 (cont.)

	1970	1975	1980	1985	1970-1975	1975-1980	1980-1985	1970-1985
					AVERAGE ANNUAL RATE OF GROWTH			
8 SERVICES (84,85,87,88,102)	3143.	3495.	3979.	4293.	2.1	2.6	1.5	2.1
9 STATE & LOCAL GOVT. (101)	3231.	3268.	3363.	3525.	.2	.6	.9	.6
10 FEDERAL GOVERNMENT (100)	595.	535.	529.	536.	-2.1	-.3	.3	-.7
11 MILITARY (103)	566.	457.	457.	457.	-4.3	-.0	.0	-1.4
TOTAL JOBS	22858.	24363.	25635.	26278.	1.3	1.0	.5	.9
CIVILIAN UNEMPLOYMENT RATE	5.3	4.8	4.4	4.8				
POPULATION	65327.	67652.	71211.	75981.	.7	1.0	1.3	1.0
PERCENT NON-WHITE	10.5	11.1	11.8	12.3				
PER CAPITA INCOME	2931.	3425.	3853.	4104.	3.1	2.4	1.3	2.2
GROSS REGIONAL PRODUCT	201858.	244867.	292131.	330413.	3.9	3.5	2.5	3.3
PERSONAL CONSUMPTION EXPENDITURES	118570.	137355.	163504.	182811.	2.9	3.5	2.2	2.9
PRIVATE INVESTMENT	29532.	39018.	45101.	49678.	5.6	2.9	1.9	3.5
GOVERNMENT EXPENDITURES	52488.	55205.	58037.	61581.	1.0	1.0	1.2	1.1

SMSA TOTAL

JOBS BY INDUSTRY

	1970	1975	1980	1985	1970-1975	1975-1980	1980-1985	1970-1985
					AVERAGE ANNUAL RATE OF GROWTH			
1 NATURAL RESOURCES (1-10)	1036.	979.	878.	788.	-1.1	-2.2	-2.2	-1.8
2 CONSTRUCTION (11,12)	2895.	3382.	3736.	4068.	3.1	2.0	1.7	2.3
3 MANUFACTURING (13-74)	14717.	16301.	17357.	17554.	2.0	1.3	.2	1.2
4 PUBLIC UTILITIES (75-80)	3659.	3916.	4127.	4211.	1.4	1.0	.4	.9
5 WHOLESALE TRADE (81)	3652.	4398.	5004.	5455.	3.7	2.6	1.7	2.7
6 RETAIL TRADE (86,89-99)	10043.	11460.	12913.	13916.	2.6	2.4	1.5	2.2
7 FINANCE, INS., & REAL ESTATE (82,83)	3351.	4239.	5157.	5913.	4.7	3.9	2.7	3.8
8 SERVICES (84,85,87,88,102)	10680.	12506.	14757.	16396.	3.2	3.3	2.1	2.9
9 STATE & LOCAL GOVT. (101)	6691.	6965.	7470.	7979.	.8	1.4	1.3	1.2
10 FEDERAL GOVERNMENT (100)	2163.	2035.	2179.	2319.	-1.2	1.4	1.2	.5
11 MILITARY (103)	1188.	960.	960.	960.	-4.3	.0	.0	-1.4
TOTAL JOBS	60075.	67139.	74536.	79560.	2.2	2.1	1.3	1.9
CIVILIAN UNEMPLOYMENT RATE	4.3	4.2	3.5	3.9				
POPULATION	137841.	147805.	160323.	173583.	1.4	1.6	1.6	1.5
PERCENT NON-WHITE	13.5	14.0	14.5	15.0				
PER CAPITA INCOME	4145.	4985.	5758.	6327.	3.7	2.9	1.9	2.8
GROSS REGIONAL PRODUCT	716845.	895697.	1111117.	1292177.	4.5	4.3	3.0	3.9
PERSONAL CONSUMPTION EXPENDITURES	455656.	569078.	731133.	863990.	4.4	5.0	3.3	4.3

	1970	1975	1980	1985				
PRIVATE INVESTMENT	95420.	130109.	158591.	180873.	6.2	4.0	2.6	4.3
GOVERNMENT EXPENDITURES	148465.	159101.	175971.	192565.	1.4	2.0	1.8	1.7

UNITED STATES

JOBS BY INDUSTRY	1970	1975	1980	1985	AVERAGE ANNUAL RATE OF GROWTH			
					1970-1975	1975-1980	1980-1985	1970-1985
1 NATURAL RESOURCES (1-10)	4245.	4048.	3574.	3109.	-1.0	-2.5	-2.8	-2.1
2 CONSTRUCTION (11,12)	3794.	4412.	4834.	5234.	3.0	1.8	1.6	2.1
3 MANUFACTURING (13-74)	20101.	22131.	23413.	23537.	1.9	1.1	.1	1.1
4 PUBLIC UTILITIES (75-80)	4611.	4928.	5175.	5261.	1.3	1.0	.3	.9
5 WHOLESALE TRADE (81)	4375.	5255.	5956.	6471.	3.7	2.5	1.7	2.6
6 RETAIL TRADE (86,89-99)	13601.	15462.	17330.	18598.	2.6	2.3	1.4	2.1
7 FINANCE, INS. & REAL ESTATE (82,83)	3948.	5046.	6195.	7164.	4.9	4.1	2.9	4.0
8 SERVICES (84,85,87,88,102)	13823.	16000.	18736.	20689.	2.9	3.2	2.0	2.7
9 STATE & LOCAL GOVT. (101)	9922.	10233.	10833.	11504.	.6	1.1	1.2	1.0
10 FEDERAL GOVERNMENT (100)	2758.	2570.	2708.	2855.	-1.4	-1.0	1.1	.2
11 MILITARY (103)	1755.	1417.	1417.	1417.	-4.3	-.0	.0	-1.4
TOTAL JOBS	82933.	91502.	100170.	105838.	2.0	1.8	1.1	1.6
CIVILIAN UNEMPLOYMENT RATE	4.6	4.4	3.8	4.1				
POPULATION	203168.	215458.	231534.	249564.	1.2	1.4	1.5	1.4
PERCENT NON-WHITE	12.6	13.1	13.7	14.2				
PER CAPITA INCOME	3755.	4495.	5172.	5651.	3.6	2.8	1.8	2.7
GROSS REGIONAL PRODUCT	918703.	1140564.	1403247.	1622590.	4.3	4.1	2.9	3.8
PERSONAL CONSUMPTION EXPENDITURES	574226.	706433.	894837.	1046801.	4.1	4.7	3.1	4.0
PRIVATE INVESTMENT	124952.	169127.	203692.	230551.	6.1	3.7	2.5	4.1
GOVERNMENT EXPENDITURES	200953.	214306.	234008.	254146.	1.3	1.8	1.7	1.6

JOBS AND POPULATION IN THOUSANDS, GROSS REGIONAL PRODUCT IN MILLIONS (1969 PRICES)

Table 6-12

Selected Projections of Central City and Suburban Counties in SMSAs with 1970 Population Over One Million Summarized by Region

NEW ENGLAND: CENTRAL CITY COUNTIES

JOBS BY INDUSTRY	1970	1975	1980	1985	AVERAGE ANNUAL RATE OF GROWTH			
					1970–1975	1975–1980	1980–1985	1970–1985
1 NATURAL RESOURCES (1–10)	1.	1.	1.	1.	-1.2	-1.6	-1.5	-1.4
2 CONSTRUCTION (11,12)	23.	23.	25.	26.	-.2	1.8	1.1	.9
3 MANUFACTURING (13–74)	86.	87.	86.	80.	.4	-.4	-1.4	-.4
4 PUBLIC UTILITIES (75–80)	51.	47.	42.	37.	-1.6	-2.0	-2.5	-2.0
5 WHOLESALE TRADE (81)	44.	49.	53.	55.	2.4	1.5	.6	1.5
6 RETAIL TRADE (86,89–99)	83.	86.	89.	89.	.7	.7	-.1	.4
7 FINANCE, INS. & REAL ESTATE (82,83)	73.	83.	86.	80.	2.3	.7	-1.3	-.6
8 SERVICES (84,85,87,88,102)	144.	161.	181.	193.	2.3	2.4	1.3	2.0
9 STATE & LOCAL GOVT. (101)	60.	44.	47.	49.	-5.9	1.2	.6	-1.3
10 FEDERAL GOVERNMENT (100)	33.	23.	24.	23.	-6.8	1.3	-.3	-2.3
11 MILITARY (103)	2.	2.	2.	2.	-4.3	.0	.0	-1.4
TOTAL JOBS	600.	607.	636.	636.	.2	.9	-.0	.4
CIVILIAN UNEMPLOYMENT RATE	5.1	4.7	3.3	3.6				
POPULATION	735.	700.	688.	663.	-1.0	-.3	-.8	-.7
PERCENT NON-WHITE	16.0	16.9	18.3	19.5				
PER CAPITA INCOME	6017	7838	9750	11509	5.3	4.4	3.3	4.3
GROSS REGIONAL PRODUCT	7626.	8233.	9121.	9429.	1.5	2.0	.7	1.4
PERSONAL CONSUMPTION EXPENDITURES	5431.	6451.	7986.	8965.	3.4	4.3	2.3	3.3
PRIVATE INVESTMENT	870.	992.	1135.	1173.	2.6	2.7	.7	2.0
GOVERNMENT EXPENDITURES	1238.	1042.	1157.	1242.	-3.5	2.1	1.4	.0

NEW ENGLAND: SUBURBAN COUNTIES

JOBS BY INDUSTRY	1970	1975	1980	1985	AVERAGE ANNUAL RATE OF GROWTH			
					1970–1975	1975–1980	1980–1985	1970–1985
1 NATURAL RESOURCES (1–10)	7.	7.	6.	5.	-.4	-2.3	-2.8	-1.8
2 CONSTRUCTION (11,12)	39.	46.	51.	55.	3.6	1.9	1.6	2.4
3 MANUFACTURING (13–74)	326.	353.	370.	366.	1.6	.9	-.2	.8

JOBS BY INDUSTRY	1970	1975	1980	1985	AVERAGE ANNUAL RATE OF GROWTH 1970-1975	1975-1980	1980-1985	1970-1985
4 PUBLIC UTILITIES (75-80)	37.	40.	42.	44.	1.5	1.1	.6	1.1
5 WHOLESALE TRADE (81)	51.	63.	73.	81.	4.3	3.0	2.1	3.1
6 RETAIL TRADE (86,89-99)	191.	222.	253.	275.	3.0	2.6	1.7	2.5
7 FINANCE, INS. & REAL ESTATE (82,83)	31.	38.	44.	49.	4.1	3.1	2.0	3.1
8 SERVICES (84,85,87,88,102)	189.	234.	289.	334.	4.3	4.2	2.9	3.8
9 STATE & LOCAL GOVT. (101)	105.	117.	127.	137.	2.3	1.6	1.5	1.8
10 FEDERAL GOVERNMENT (100)	19.	21.	25.	27.	1.5	3.1	2.1	2.2
11 MILITARY (103)	10.	8.	8.	8.	-4.3	.0	.0	-1.4
TOTAL JOBS	1003.	1149.	1288.	1382.	2.7	2.3	1.4	2.1
CIVILIAN UNEMPLOYMENT RATE	4.1	4.3	3.5	4.3				
POPULATION	2640.	2913.	3225.	3563.	2.0	2.0	2.0	2.0
PERCENT NON-WHITE	1.5	1.6	1.7	1.8				
PER CAPITA INCOME	3931.	4682.	5331.	5786.	3.5	2.6	1.6	2.6
GROSS REGIONAL PRODUCT	11240.	14821.	18983.	22669.	5.5	5.0	3.5	4.7
PERSONAL CONSUMPTION EXPENDITURES	8205.	10460.	13518.	16127.	4.9	5.1	3.5	4.5
PRIVATE INVESTMENT	1712.	2220.	2688.	2998.	5.2	3.8	2.2	3.7
GOVERNMENT EXPENDITURES	2786.	3139.	3531.	3900.	2.4	2.4	2.0	2.2

MIDEAST: CENTRAL CITY COUNTIES

JOBS BY INDUSTRY	1970	1975	1980	1985	AVERAGE ANNUAL RATE OF GROWTH 1970-1975	1975-1980	1980-1985	1970-1985
1 NATURAL RESOURCES (1-10)	18.	19.	18.	16.	.5	-.8	-1.7	-.7
2 CONSTRUCTION (11,12)	283.	307.	336.	360.	1.7	1.8	1.4	1.6
3 MANUFACTURING (13-74)	1802.	1980.	2086.	2071.	1.9	1.0	-.1	.9
4 PUBLIC UTILITIES (75-80)	650.	671.	686.	681.	.7	.4	-.1	.3
5 WHOLESALE TRADE (81)	581.	676.	750.	796.	3.0	2.1	1.2	2.1
6 RETAIL TRADE (86,89-99)	1135.	1224.	1321.	1364.	1.5	1.5	.6	1.2
7 FINANCE, INS. & REAL ESTATE (82,83)	741.	916.	1084.	1209.	4.2	3.4	2.2	3.3
8 SERVICES (84,85,87,88,102)	1745.	1999.	2293.	2495.	2.7	2.7	1.7	2.4
9 STATE & LOCAL GOVT. (101)	849.	861.	887.	920.	.3	.6	.8	.5
10 FEDERAL GOVERNMENT (100)	446.	404.	419.	443.	-2.0	.7	1.1	-.0
11 MILITARY (103)	32.	26.	26.	26.	-4.3	.0	.0	-1.4
TOTAL JOBS	8282.	9084.	9904.	10381.	1.8	1.7	.9	1.5
CIVILIAN UNEMPLOYMENT RATE	5.4	4.9	3.8	4.0				

Table 6-12 (cont.)

	1970	1975	1980	1985	1970–1975	1975–1980	1980–1985	1970–1985
POPULATION	15588.	16118.	16788.	17473.	.7	.8	.8	.8
PERCENT NON-WHITE	26.2	27.5	29.3	30.9				
PER CAPITA INCOME	5166.	6545.	7954.	9107.	4.7	3.9	2.7	3.8
GROSS REGIONAL PRODUCT	114875.	135169.	159476.	176369.	3.3	3.3	2.0	2.9
PERSONAL CONSUMPTION EXPENDITURES	66069.	82398.	106229.	124590.	4.4	5.1	3.2	4.2
PRIVATE INVESTMENT	11216.	14497.	17812.	19921.	5.1	4.1	2.2	3.8
GOVERNMENT EXPENDITURES	18537.	19231.	20801.	22617.	.7	1.6	1.7	1.3

MIDEAST: SUBURBAN COUNTIES

AVERAGE ANNUAL RATE OF GROWTH

JOBS BY INDUSTRY

	1970	1975	1980	1985	1970–1975	1975–1980	1980–1985	1970–1985
1 NATURAL RESOURCES (1-10)	53.	50.	43.	37.	-1.3	-2.7	-3.0	-2.3
2 CONSTRUCTION (11,12)	201.	248.	272.	295.	4.2	1.8	1.7	2.6
3 MANUFACTURING (13-74)	1075.	1160.	1218.	1225.	1.5	1.0	.1	.9
4 PUBLIC UTILITIES (75-80)	187.	213.	239.	258.	2.6	2.3	1.6	2.1
5 WHOLESALE TRADE (81)	213.	263.	307.	343.	4.2	3.1	2.2	3.2
6 RETAIL TRADE (86,89-99)	748.	873.	1006.	1111.	3.1	2.8	2.0	3.2
7 FINANCE, INS. & REAL ESTATE (82,83)	152.	211.	280.	347.	6.6	5.7	4.3	5.5
8 SERVICES (84,85,87,88,102)	692.	844.	1035.	1204.	4.0	4.1	3.0	3.7
9 STATE & LOCAL GOVT. (101)	506.	573.	620.	669.	2.5	1.6	1.5	1.9
10 FEDERAL GOVERNMENT (100)	145.	157.	175.	192.	1.6	2.1	1.9	1.9
11 MILITARY (103)	91.	73.	73.	73.	-4.3	.0	.0	-1.4
TOTAL JOBS	4063.	4665.	5267.	5755.	2.8	2.4	1.8	2.3
CIVILIAN UNEMPLOYMENT RATE	3.4	3.5	3.0	3.1				
POPULATION	11620.	12564.	13671.	14807.	1.6	1.7	1.6	1.6
PERCENT NON-WHITE	6.7	7.0	7.4	7.7				
PER CAPITA INCOME	3778.	4455.	5090.	5612.	3.3	2.7	2.0	2.6
GROSS REGIONAL PRODUCT	47282.	61558.	78746.	94679.	5.3	4.9	3.7	4.6
PERSONAL CONSUMPTION EXPENDITURES	33279.	41349.	53051.	63332.	4.3	5.0	3.5	4.3
PRIVATE INVESTMENT	6926.	9760.	11853.	13612.	6.9	3.9	2.8	4.5
GOVERNMENT EXPENDITURES	11977.	13938.	15522.	17187.	3.0	2.2	2.0	2.4

GREAT LAKES: CENTRAL CITY COUNTIES

JOBS BY INDUSTRY	1970	1975	1980	1985	AVERAGE ANNUAL RATE OF GROWTH			
					1970-1975	1975-1980	1980-1985	1970-1985
1 NATURAL RESOURCES (1-10)	19.	20.	19.	17.	1.2	-1.1	-2.0	-.6
2 CONSTRUCTION (11,12)	251.	293.	320.	342.	3.1	1.8	1.3	2.1
3 MANUFACTURING (13-74)	1957.	2201.	2337.	2347.	2.4	1.2	.4	1.2
4 PUBLIC UTILITIES (75-80)	407.	440.	464.	473.	1.6	1.1	.4	1.0
5 WHOLESALE TRADE (81)	464.	553.	618.	662.	3.5	2.2	1.4	2.4
6 RETAIL TRADE (86,89-99)	1017.	1138.	1243.	1298.	2.3	1.8	.9	1.6
7 FINANCE, INS. & REAL ESTATE (82,83)	364.	444.	517.	567.	4.0	3.1	1.8	3.0
8 SERVICES (84,85,87,88,102)	1057.	1198.	1346.	1420.	2.5	2.3	1.1	2.0
9 STATE & LOCAL GOVT. (101)	564.	602.	637.	666.	1.3	1.1	.9	1.1
10 FEDERAL GOVERNMENT (100)	142.	137.	145.	145.	-.8	1.1	.0	.1
11 MILITARY (103)	8.	6.	6.	6.	-4.3	-.0	.0	-1.4
TOTAL JOBS	6250.	7032.	7654.	7943.	2.4	1.7	.7	1.6
CIVILIAN UNEMPLOYMENT RATE	3.4	3.6	3.0	3.4				
POPULATION	12651.	13563.	14515.	15413.	1.4	1.4	1.2	1.3
PERCENT NON-WHITE	21.6	23.0	24.6	25.8				
PER CAPITA INCOME	4882.	5974.	6886.	7517.	4.0	2.8	1.8	2.9
GROSS REGIONAL PRODUCT	82506.	102320.	123492.	139320.	4.3	3.8	2.4	3.5
PERSONAL CONSUMPTION EXPENDITURES	48769.	61643.	77671.	88855.	4.7	4.6	2.7	4.0
PRIVATE INVESTMENT	9603.	13240.	16045.	18229.	6.4	3.8	2.6	4.3
GOVERNMENT EXPENDITURES	9372.	10776.	11960.	12894.	2.8	2.1	1.5	2.1

GREAT LAKES: SUBURBAN COUNTIES

JOBS BY INDUSTRY	1970	1975	1980	1985	AVERAGE ANNUAL RATE OF GROWTH			
					1970-1975	1975-1980	1980-1985	1970-1985
1 NATURAL RESOURCES (1-10)	36.	33.	29.	25.	-1.4	-3.0	-3.0	-2.5
2 CONSTRUCTION (11,12)	69.	92.	101.	110.	5.7	1.9	1.7	3.1
3 MANUFACTURING (13-74)	479.	548.	590.	598.	2.7	1.5	.3	1.5
4 PUBLIC UTILITIES (75-80)	60.	70.	78.	82.	3.0	2.1	1.0	2.0
5 WHOLESALE TRADE (81)	59.	77.	92.	103.	5.3	3.4	2.3	3.7
6 RETAIL TRADE (86,89-99)	279.	336.	389.	428.	3.7	3.0	1.9	2.8
7 FINANCE, INS. & REAL ESTATE (82,83)	43.	64.	89.	115.	8.0	6.9	5.1	6.6
8 SERVICES (84,85,87,88,102)	210.	271.	351.	421.	5.2	6.2	3.6	4.6
9 STATE & LOCAL GOVT. (101)	169.	197.	225.	249.	3.2	2.6	2.0	2.6
10 FEDERAL GOVERNMENT (100)	36.	40.	44.	49.	2.3	2.2	1.8	2.1

Table 6-12 (cont.)

	1970	1975	1980	1985	1970–1975	1975–1980	1980–1985	1970–1985
11 MILITARY (103)	40.	32.	32.	32.	-4.3	.0	.0	-1.4
TOTAL JOBS	1480.	1761.	2022.	2213.	3.5	2.8	1.8	2.7
CIVILIAN UNEMPLOYMENT RATE	2.9	3.3	2.8	3.1				
POPULATION	4681.	5178.	5713.	6296.	2.0	2.0	1.9	2.0
PERCENT NON-WHITE	4.0	4.2	4.4	4.6				
PER CAPITA INCOME	3649.	4337.	4933.	5337.	3.5	2.6	1.6	2.5
GROSS REGIONAL PRODUCT	17167.	23713.	31139.	37712.	6.5	5.4	3.8	5.2
PERSONAL CONSUMPTION EXPENDITURES	10920.	14209.	18500.	22099.	5.3	5.3	3.6	4.7
PRIVATE INVESTMENT	3375.	4956.	5956.	6812.	7.7	3.7	2.7	4.7
GOVERNMENT EXPENDITURES	3395.	4136.	4713.	5223.	3.9	2.6	2.1	2.9

PLAINS: CENTRAL CITY COUNTIES

	1970	1975	1980	1985	AVERAGE ANNUAL RATE OF GROWTH 1970–1975	1975–1980	1980–1985	1970–1985
JOBS BY INDUSTRY								
1 NATURAL RESOURCES (1-10)	9.	9.	8.	8.	.2	-.9	-1.0	-.5
2 CONSTRUCTION (11,12)	78.	87.	97.	105.	2.4	2.1	1.6	2.0
3 MANUFACTURING (13-74)	438.	487.	517.	517.	2.1	1.2	-.0	1.1
4 PUBLIC UTILITIES (75-80)	135.	148.	158.	163.	1.9	1.3	.5	1.2
5 WHOLESALE TRADE (81)	144.	173.	194.	209.	3.6	2.4	1.5	2.5
6 RETAIL TRADE (86,89-99)	303.	345.	386.	412.	2.6	2.3	1.3	2.1
7 FINANCE, INS. & REAL ESTATE (82,83)	114.	136.	154.	162.	3.5	2.4	1.1	2.3
8 SERVICES (84,85,87,88,102)	346.	377.	415.	432.	1.7	1.9	.8	1.5
9 STATE & LOCAL GOVT. (101)	142.	133.	141.	148.	-1.3	1.1	1.1	.3
10 FEDERAL GOVERNMENT (100)	63.	49.	53.	54.	-4.9	1.5	.3	-1.0
11 MILITARY (103)	6.	5.	5.	5.	-4.3	.0	.0	-1.4
TOTAL JOBS	1778.	1949.	2129.	2216.	1.8	1.8	.8	1.5
CIVILIAN UNEMPLOYMENT RATE	3.6	3.6	3.0	3.4				
POPULATION	2836.	2999.	3211.	3399.	1.1	1.4	1.1	1.2
PERCENT NON-WHITE	14.9	15.3	15.9	16.6				
PER CAPITA INCOME	4903.	6062.	7085.	7814.	4.2	3.1	2.0	3.1
GROSS REGIONAL PRODUCT	21144.	26100.	31911.	36343.	4.2	4.0	2.6	3.6
PERSONAL CONSUMPTION EXPENDITURES	12877.	16171.	20651.	23866.	4.6	4.9	2.9	4.1
PRIVATE INVESTMENT	2661.	3575.	4528.	5241.	5.9	4.7	2.9	4.5
GOVERNMENT EXPENDITURES	4228.	4169.	4677.	5114.	-.3	2.3	1.8	1.3

PLAINS: SUBURBAN COUNTIES

JOBS BY INDUSTRY	1970	1975	1980	1985	AVERAGE ANNUAL RATE OF GROWTH			
					1970-1975	1975-1980	1980-1985	1970-1985
1 NATURAL RESOURCES (1-10)	16.	15.	13.	11.	-1.5	-3.2	-3.2	-2.7
2 CONSTRUCTION (11,12)	39.	51.	56.	61.	5.3	1.9	1.7	2.9
3 MANUFACTURING (13-74)	161.	172.	182.	186.	1.3	1.1	.5	.9
4 PUBLIC UTILITIES (75-80)	32.	36.	40.	42.	2.5	1.7	1.1	1.8
5 WHOLESALE TRADE (81)	31.	39.	45.	51.	4.3	3.2	2.3	3.2
6 RETAIL TRADE (86,89-99)	132.	153.	176.	192.	2.9	2.8	1.8	2.5
7 FINANCE, INS. & REAL ESTATE (82,83)	25.	32.	40.	47.	5.1	4.4	3.4	4.3
8 SERVICES (84,85,87,88,102)	95.	123.	156.	180.	5.2	4.7	2.9	4.3
9 STATE & LOCAL GOVT. (101)	80.	94.	109.	117.	3.4	2.8	1.6	2.6
10 FEDERAL GOVERNMENT (100)	11.	13.	15.	18.	2.1	3.9	3.5	3.2
11 MILITARY (103)	1.	1.	1.	1.	-4.3	.0	.0	-1.4
TOTAL JOBS	624.	729.	832.	907.	3.1	2.6	1.7	2.5
CIVILIAN UNEMPLOYMENT RATE	2.7	3.2	2.5	2.8				
POPULATION	2058.	2189.	2343.	2534.	1.2	1.4	1.6	1.4
PERCENT NON-WHITE	4.6	4.8	5.0	5.2				
PER CAPITA INCOME	3615.	4248.	4832.	5251.	3.2	2.6	1.7	2.5
GROSS REGIONAL PRODUCT	8119.	10571.	13472.	15988.	5.3	4.9	3.4	4.5
PERSONAL CONSUMPTION EXPENDITURES	4626.	5627.	7084.	8357.	3.9	4.6	3.3	3.9
PRIVATE INVESTMENT	1254.	1906.	2354.	2767.	8.4	4.2	3.2	5.3
GOVERNMENT EXPENDITURES	1084.	1429.	1653.	1827.	5.5	2.9	2.0	3.5

SOUTHEAST: CENTRAL CITY COUNTIES

JOBS BY INDUSTRY	1970	1975	1980	1985	AVERAGE ANNUAL RATE OF GROWTH			
					1970-1975	1975-1980	1980-1985	1970-1985
1 NATURAL RESOURCES (1-10)	29.	28.	27.	26.	-.3	-.8	-.5	-.6
2 CONSTRUCTION (11,12)	120.	145.	166.	186.	3.8	2.6	2.3	2.9
3 MANUFACTURING (13-74)	255.	284.	302.	304.	2.1	1.3	.1	1.2
4 PUBLIC UTILITIES (75-80)	174.	186.	196.	201.	1.3	1.0	.5	.9
5 WHOLESALE TRADE (81)	158.	197.	233.	261.	4.4	3.3	2.3	3.3

Table 6-12(cont.)

	1970	1975	1980	1985	AVERAGE ANNUAL RATE OF GROWTH 1970–1975	1975–1980	1980–1985	1970–1985
6 RETAIL TRADE (86,89–99)	355.	428.	510.	574.	3.7	3.5	2.4	3.2
7 FINANCE, INS. & REAL ESTATE (82,83)	129.	181.	240.	293.	6.8	5.6	4.0	5.5
8 SERVICES (84,85,87,88,102)	404.	492.	603.	692.	4.0	4.1	2.7	3.6
9 STATE & LOCAL GOVT. (101)	201.	211.	241.	269.	1.0	2.6	2.2	1.9
10 FEDERAL GOVERNMENT (100)	54.	53.	62.	70.	-.7	3.3	2.5	1.7
11 MILITARY (103)	22.	18.	18.	18.	-4.3	-.0	-.0	-1.4
TOTAL JOBS	1901.	2222.	2597.	2895.	3.1	3.1	2.2	2.8
CIVILIAN UNEMPLOYMENT RATE	3.5	3.7	3.0	3.2				
POPULATION	3897.	4334.	4877.	5419.	2.1	2.4	2.1	2.2
PERCENT NON-WHITE	22.5	22.4	22.7	23.2				
PER CAPITA INCOME	4121	5092	6034	6792	4.2	3.4	2.4	3.3
GROSS REGIONAL PRODUCT	22937.	31764.	43409.	54222.	6.5	6.2	4.4	5.7
PERSONAL CONSUMPTION EXPENDITURES	17057.	22364.	30305.	37306.	5.4	6.1	4.2	5.2
PRIVATE INVESTMENT	3512.	4857.	6094.	7112.	6.5	4.5	3.1	4.7
GOVERNMENT EXPENDITURES	3441.	3854.	4514.	5170.	2.3	3.2	2.7	2.7

SOUTHEAST: SUBURBAN COUNTIES

JOBS BY INDUSTRY	1970	1975	1980	1985	AVERAGE ANNUAL RATE OF GROWTH 1970–1975	1975–1980	1980–1985	1970–1985
1 NATURAL RESOURCES (1–10)	14.	15.	16.	18.	1.8	1.7	1.8	1.8
2 CONSTRUCTION (11,12)	40.	53.	60.	69.	5.4	2.6	2.8	3.6
3 MANUFACTURING (13–74)	82.	83.	85.	87.	.0	.6	.4	.4
4 PUBLIC UTILITIES (75–80)	33.	39.	45.	50.	3.2	3.0	2.2	2.8
5 WHOLESALE TRADE (81)	26.	34.	42.	49.	5.3	4.3	3.3	4.3
6 RETAIL TRADE (86,89–99)	106.	128.	156.	181.	3.8	3.9	3.0	3.6
7 FINANCE, INS. & REAL ESTATE (82,83)	22.	34.	49.	64.	8.7	7.3	5.3	7.1
8 SERVICES (84,85,87,88,102)	88.	113.	145.	172.	5.0	4.9	3.4	4.4
9 STATE & LOCAL GOVT. (101)	68.	78.	90.	100.	3.0	2.7	2.1	2.6
10 FEDERAL GOVERNMENT (100)	59.	59.	63.	68.	-.2	1.5	1.3	.9
11 MILITARY (103)	38.	31.	31.	31.	-4.3	1.0	.0	-1.4
TOTAL JOBS	577.	667.	782.	889.	2.9	3.2	2.6	2.9
CIVILIAN UNEMPLOYMENT RATE	2.6	3.1	2.5	2.8				
POPULATION	1843.	1989.	2194.	2434.	1.5	2.0	2.1	1.9
PERCENT NON-WHITE	7.1	7.1	7.2	7.3				
PER CAPITA INCOME	3611.	4163.	4762.	5275.	2.8	2.7	2.0	2.5
GROSS REGIONAL PRODUCT	6777.	9318.	12939.	16664.	6.4	6.6	5.1	6.0

	1970	1975	1980	1985	1970–1975	1975–1980	1980–1985	1970–1985
PERSONAL CONSUMPTION EXPENDITURES	5023.	6197.	8197.	10170.	4.2	5.6	4.3	4.7
PRIVATE INVESTMENT	1088.	1615.	2049.	2478.	7.9	4.8	3.8	5.5
GOVERNMENT EXPENDITURES	1906.	2120.	2377.	2620.	2.1	2.3	1.9	2.1

SOUTHWEST: CENTRAL CITY COUNTIES

JOBS BY INDUSTRY	1970	1975	1980	1985	AVERAGE ANNUAL RATE OF GROWTH			
					1970–1975	1975–1980	1980–1985	1970–1985
1 NATURAL RESOURCES (1-10)	39.	35.	31.	28.	-2.1	-2.0	-2.3	-2.1
2 CONSTRUCTION (11,12)	127.	149.	166.	181.	3.2	2.1	1.7	2.4
3 MANUFACTURING (13-74)	321.	373.	423.	458.	3.0	2.5	1.6	2.4
4 PUBLIC UTILITIES (75-80)	117.	130.	141.	147.	2.0	1.6	.8	1.5
5 WHOLESALE TRADE (81)	134.	166.	193.	214.	4.3	3.0	2.0	3.1
6 RETAIL TRADE (86,89-99)	266.	317.	369.	407.	3.5	3.0	1.9	2.8
7 FINANCE, INS. & REAL ESTATE (82,83)	104.	125.	142.	149.	3.7	2.5	1.0	2.4
8 SERVICES (84,85,87,88,102)	300.	368.	449.	515.	4.1	4.0	2.7	3.6
9 STATE & LOCAL GOVT. (101)	110.	120.	140.	157.	1.8	3.0	2.3	2.3
10 FEDERAL GOVERNMENT (100)	30.	31.	36.	40.	.3	3.4	2.2	1.9
11 MILITARY (103)	2.	2.	2.	2.	-4.3	-.0	-.0	-1.4
TOTAL JOBS	1551.	1816.	2092.	2297.	3.2	2.8	1.9	2.6
CIVILIAN UNEMPLOYMENT RATE	3.7	4.2	3.2	3.7				
POPULATION	3069.	3459.	3917.	4418.	2.4	2.5	2.4	2.4
PERCENT NON-WHITE	19.4	19.3	19.3	19.5				
PER CAPITA INCOME	4261.	5237.	6081.	6672.	4.1	3.0	1.9	3.0
GROSS REGIONAL PRODUCT	19707.	26794.	35414.	43015.	6.1	5.6	3.9	5.2
PERSONAL CONSUMPTION EXPENDITURES	12530.	16638.	22321.	27239.	5.7	5.9	4.0	5.2
PRIVATE INVESTMENT	2784.	3886.	4834.	5570.	6.7	4.4	2.8	4.6
GOVERNMENT EXPENDITURES	2707.	2979.	3451.	3884.	1.9	2.9	2.4	2.4

SOUTHWEST: SUBURBAN COUNTIES

JOBS BY INDUSTRY	1970	1975	1980	1985	AVERAGE ANNUAL RATE OF GROWTH			
					1970–1975	1975–1980	1980–1985	1970–1985
1 NATURAL RESOURCES (1-10)	15.	14.	12.	11.	-1.8	-2.8	-2.3	-2.3
2 CONSTRUCTION (11,12)	9.	11.	12.	14.	4.5	2.2	2.3	3.0

Table 6-12(cont.)

		1970	1975	1980	1985	1970–1975	1975–1980	1980–1985	1970–1985
3	MANUFACTURING (13–74)	24.	29.	33.	35.	3.2	2.6	1.6	2.5
4	PUBLIC UTILITIES (75–80)	4.	5.	6.	7.	4.1	3.8	3.0	3.6
5	WHOLESALE TRADE (81)	2.	3.	4.	5.	5.1	4.7	4.9	4.9
6	RETAIL TRADE (86,89–99)	20.	24.	29.	34.	3.4	3.6	3.1	3.4
7	FINANCE, INS. & REAL ESTATE (82,83)	3.	4.	5.	7.	6.3	5.4	3.9	5.2
8	SERVICES (84,85,87,88,102)	16.	20.	23.	26.	3.6	3.6	2.4	3.2
9	STATE & LOCAL GOVT. (101)	20.	23.	24.	26.	2.0	1.6	1.6	1.7
10	FEDERAL GOVERNMENT (100)	1.	1.	1.	2.	1.8	1.9	1.9	1.9
11	MILITARY (103)	0.	0.	0.	0.	-4.3	.0	.0	-1.4
	TOTAL JOBS	116.	133.	150.	167.	2.8	2.4	2.0	2.4
	CIVILIAN UNEMPLOYMENT RATE	3.5	3.7	3.1	3.4				
	POPULATION	432.	464.	502.	548.	1.4	1.6	1.8	1.6
	PERCENT NON-WHITE	12.6	12.8	13.1	13.4				
	PER CAPITA INCOME	2439.	2929.	3414.	3845.	3.7	3.1	2.4	3.0
	GROSS REGIONAL PRODUCT	1235.	1650.	2176.	2751.	5.8	5.5	4.7	5.3
	PERSONAL CONSUMPTION EXPENDITURES	766.	969.	1272.	1597.	4.7	5.5	4.5	4.9
	PRIVATE INVESTMENT	283.	419.	524.	633.	7.8	4.5	3.8	5.4
	GOVERNMENT EXPENDITURES	224.	273.	303.	336.	3.9	2.1	2.0	2.7

ROCKY MOUNTAIN: CENTRAL CITY COUNTIES

JOBS BY INDUSTRY

		1970	1975	1980	1985	AVERAGE ANNUAL RATE OF GROWTH			
						1970–1975	1975–1980	1980–1985	1970–1985
1	NATURAL RESOURCES (1–10)	6.	5.	4.	4.	-2.7	-3.0	-3.5	-3.1
2	CONSTRUCTION (11,12)	18.	20.	21.	22.	1.7	1.5	1.2	1.5
3	MANUFACTURING (13–74)	49.	58.	65.	69.	3.2	2.4	1.2	2.3
4	PUBLIC UTILITIES (75–80)	31.	31.	30.	29.	-.2	-.4	-.9	-.5
5	WHOLESALE TRADE (81)	34.	40.	44.	47.	3.2	2.2	1.4	2.3
6	RETAIL TRADE (86,89–99)	59.	67.	75.	81.	2.4	2.4	1.6	2.1
7	FINANCE, INS. & REAL ESTATE (82,83)	27.	32.	34.	34.	2.9	1.6	-.1	1.5
8	SERVICES (84,85,87,88,102)	68.	71.	75.	76.	.7	1.2	.1	.7
9	STATE & LOCAL GOVT. (101)	32.	27.	29.	30.	-3.4	1.4	1.2	-.3

187

	1970	1975	1980	1985	AVERAGE ANNUAL RATE OF GROWTH 1970-1975	1975-1980	1980-1985
10 FEDERAL GOVERNMENT (100)	17.	14.	14.	15.	-5.1	1.2	.7	-1.1
11 MILITARY (103)	14.	11.	11.	11.	-4.3	.0	.0	-1.4
TOTAL JOBS	355.	372.	403.	418.	1.0	1.6	.7	1.1
CIVILIAN UNEMPLOYMENT RATE	3.9	3.6	3.3	3.6				
POPULATION	515.	516.	543.	567.	.1	1.0	.9	.6
PERCENT NON-WHITE	11.0	11.8	12.8	13.6				
PER CAPITA INCOME	5370.	6677.	7928.	8879.	4.4	3.4	2.3	3.4
GROSS REGIONAL PRODUCT	4420.	5140.	6111.	6829.	3.0	3.5	2.2	2.9
PERSONAL CONSUMPTION EXPENDITURES	2860.	3435.	4354.	5026.	3.7	4.7	2.9	3.8
PRIVATE INVESTMENT	568.	697.	811.	877.	4.1	3.0	1.6	2.9
GOVERNMENT EXPENDITURES	783.	701.	768.	824.	-2.2	1.8	1.4	.3

ROCKY MOUNTAIN: SUBURBAN COUNTIES

JOBS BY INDUSTRY	1970	1975	1980	1985	AVERAGE ANNUAL RATE OF GROWTH 1970-1975	1975-1980	1980-1985
1 NATURAL RESOURCES (1-10)	5.	5.	5.	5.	.8	-.2	-.4	.0
2 CONSTRUCTION (11,12)	14.	18.	20.	22.	4.9	1.9	1.6	2.8
3 MANUFACTURING (13-74)	41.	46.	48.	48.	2.4	1.2	-.1	1.1
4 PUBLIC UTILITIES (75-80)	4.	5.	6.	7.	2.6	2.6	2.4	2.5
5 WHOLESALE TRADE (81)	5.	7.	6.	10.	2.6	4.5	4.0	4.6
6 RETAIL TRADE (86,89-99)	43.	52.	61.	68.	3.8	3.3	2.2	3.1
7 FINANCE, INS. & REAL ESTATE (82,83)	6.	7.	9.	11.	5.5	4.6	2.2	4.3
8 SERVICES (84,85,87,88,102)	34.	45.	57.	68.	5.7	5.0	3.0	4.7
9 STATE & LOCAL GOVT. (101)	34.	40.	44.	47.	3.0	1.9	3.3	2.1
10 FEDERAL GOVERNMENT (100)	9.	10.	11.	12.	2.6	2.6	1.3	2.2
11 MILITARY (103)	1.	1.	1.	1.	-4.3	.0	1.3	-1.4
TOTAL JOBS	195.	235.	271.	298.	3.7	2.9	1.9	2.8
CIVILIAN UNEMPLOYMENT RATE	3.8	4.5	3.7	4.3				
POPULATION	713.	803.	895.	995.	2.4	2.2	2.1	2.2
PERCENT NON-WHITE	1.5	1.6	1.7	1.7				
PER CAPITA INCOME	3130.	3618.	4036.	4316.	2.9	2.2	1.3	2.1
GROSS REGIONAL PRODUCT	2094.	2905.	3834.	4666.	6.5	5.6	3.9	5.3
PERSONAL CONSUMPTION EXPENDITURES	1542.	1978.	2559.	3067.	5.0	5.2	3.6	4.6
PRIVATE INVESTMENT	416.	602.	740.	836.	7.4	4.1	2.4	4.6
GOVERNMENT EXPENDITURES	553.	693.	782.	855.	4.5	2.4	1.8	2.9

Table 6-12(cont.)

FAR WEST: CENTRAL CITY COUNTIES

JOBS BY INDUSTRY	1970	1975	1980	1985	AVERAGE ANNUAL RATE OF GROWTH			
					1970-1975	1975-1980	1980-1985	1970-1985
1 NATURAL RESOURCES (1-10)	63.	57.	50.	43.	-1.9	-2.8	-3.0	-2.6
2 CONSTRUCTION (11,12)	248.	284.	315.	340.	2.7	2.1	1.6	2.1
3 MANUFACTURING (13-74)	1283.	1392.	1479.	1487.	1.6	1.2	.1	1.0
4 PUBLIC UTILITIES (75-80)	362.	386.	403.	404.	1.3	.9	.0	.7
5 WHOLESALE TRADE (81)	374.	445.	502.	541.	3.5	2.4	1.5	2.5
6 RETAIL TRADE (86,89-99)	919.	1032.	1152.	1220.	2.3	2.5	1.4	1.9
7 FINANCE, INS. & REAL ESTATE (82,83)	352.	412.	467.	501.	3.2	2.5	1.4	2.4
8 SERVICES (84,85,87,88,102)	1047.	1250.	1490.	1654.	3.5	3.5	2.1	3.0
9 STATE & LOCAL GOVT. (101)	626.	633.	680.	724.	.2	1.5	1.3	1.0
10 FEDERAL GOVERNMENT (100)	204.	186.	200.	209.	-1.9	1.5	.9	.1
11 MILITARY (103)	115.	93.	93.	93.	-4.3	.0	.0	-1.4
TOTAL JOBS	5593.	6169.	6831.	7218.	2.0	2.0	1.1	1.7
CIVILIAN UNEMPLOYMENT RATE	5.7	5.2	4.5	5.0				
POPULATION	12158.	12902.	14079.	15318.	1.2	1.7	1.7	1.5
PERCENT NON-WHITE	13.7	14.4	15.2	15.8				
PER CAPITA INCOME	4786.	5718.	6557.	7106.	3.6	2.7	1.6	2.6
GROSS REGIONAL PRODUCT	72822.	89341.	109917.	125833.	4.1	4.1	2.7	3.6
PERSONAL CONSUMPTION EXPENDITURES	47113.	57662.	73805.	86010.	4.1	4.9	3.1	4.0
PRIVATE INVESTMENT	8894.	11734.	14214.	15800.	5.5	3.8	2.1	3.8
GOVERNMENT EXPENDITURES	18463.	19254.	21360.	23260.	.8	2.1	1.7	1.5

FAR WEST: SUBURBAN COUNTIES

JOBS BY INDUSTRY	1970	1975	1980	1985	AVERAGE ANNUAL RATE OF GROWTH			
					1970-1975	1975-1980	1980-1985	1970-1985
1 NATURAL RESOURCES (1-10)	56.	53.	46.	40.	-1.1	-2.7	-2.9	-2.2
2 CONSTRUCTION (11,12)	89.	111.	123.	134.	4.4	2.0	1.7	2.7
3 MANUFACTURING (13-74)	409.	446.	484.	503.	1.7	1.6	.8	1.4
4 PUBLIC UTILITIES (75-80)	94.	105.	115.	122.	2.2	1.9	1.1	1.8
5 WHOLESALE TRADE (81)	68.	83.	96.	107.	3.9	2.9	2.1	3.0
6 RETAIL TRADE (86,89-99)	329.	377.	429.	467.	2.7	2.6	1.7	2.3

(table continued from previous page)

	1970	1975	1980	1985	AVERAGE ANNUAL RATE OF GROWTH			
					1970-1975	1975-1980	1980-1985	1970-1985
7 FINANCE, INS. & REAL ESTATE (82,83)	70.	82.	95.	105.	3.3	2.9	2.0	2.7
8 SERVICES (84,85,87,88,102)	303.	379.	469.	540.	4.4	4.3	2.8	3.9
9 STATE & LOCAL GOVT. (101)	241.	270.	291.	311.	2.3	1.5	1.3	1.7
10 FEDERAL GOVERNMENT (100)	52.	56.	61.	67.	1.4	1.8	1.8	1.6
11 MILITARY (103)	45.	37.	37.	37.	-4.3	.0	.0	-1.4
TOTAL JOBS	1757.	1999.	2247.	2433.	2.6	2.3	1.6	2.2
CIVILIAN UNEMPLOYMENT RATE	5.7	5.5	4.8	5.5				
POPULATION	5401.	5883.	6467.	7162.	1.7	1.9	2.0	1.9
PERCENT NON-WHITE	5.4	5.6	5.8	6.0				
PER CAPITA INCOME	3837.	4478.	5071.	5452.	3.1	2.5	1.4	2.3
GROSS REGIONAL PRODUCT	22916.	28898.	36056.	42258.	4.7	4.9	3.4	4.1
PERSONAL CONSUMPTION EXPENDITURES	15400.	18893.	24121.	28568.	4.6	5.0	3.4	4.6
PRIVATE INVESTMENT	3547.	5007.	6150.	7040.	6.9	4.1	2.7	4.6
GOVERNMENT EXPENDITURES	6289.	7149.	7965.	8750.	2.6	2.2	1.9	2.2

SMSA TOTAL: CENTRAL CITY COUNTIES

JOBS BY INDUSTRY

	1970	1975	1980	1985	AVERAGE ANNUAL RATE OF GROWTH			
					1970-1975	1975-1980	1980-1985	1970-1985
1 NATURAL RESOURCES (1-10)	183.	174.	159.	144.	-1.0	-1.8	-2.1	-1.6
2 CONSTRUCTION (11,12)	1147.	1307.	1445.	1563.	2.6	2.0	1.6	2.1
3 MANUFACTURING (13-74)	6192.	6862.	7294.	7334.	2.1	1.2	.1	1.1
4 PUBLIC UTILITIES (75-80)	1926.	2039.	2121.	2134.	1.1	.8	.1	.7
5 WHOLESALE TRADE (81)	1933.	2298.	2588.	2785.	3.5	2.4	1.5	2.4
6 RETAIL TRADE (86,89-99)	4137.	4638.	5146.	5445.	2.3	2.1	1.1	1.8
7 FINANCE, INS. & REAL ESTATE (82,83)	1905.	2329.	2723.	2996.	4.0	3.1	1.9	3.0
8 SERVICES (84,85,87,88,102)	5111.	5915.	6853.	7476.	2.9	2.9	1.7	2.5
9 STATE & LOCAL GOVT. (101)	2583.	2631.	2801.	2963.	.4	1.3	1.1	.9
10 FEDERAL GOVERNMENT (100)	991.	896.	953.	1003.	-2.0	1.2	1.0	.1
11 MILITARY (103)	202.	163.	163.	163.	-4.3	.0	.0	-1.4
TOTAL JOBS	26310.	29252.	32247.	34002.	2.1	1.9	1.1	1.7
CIVILIAN UNEMPLOYMENT RATE	4.6	4.4	3.6	3.9				
POPULATION	51449.	54592.	58618.	62670.	1.2	1.4	1.3	1.3
PERCENT NON-WHITE	20.5	21.4	22.5	23.4				
PER CAPITA INCOME	4873.	6001.	7043.	7808.	4.2	3.2	2.1	3.1

Table 6-12(cont.)

	1970	1975	1980	1985	AVERAGE ANNUAL RATE OF GROWTH 1970-1975	1975-1980	1980-1985	1970-1985
GROSS REGIONAL PRODUCT	346037.	424861.	518851.	591360.	4.1	4.0	2.6	3.6
PERSONAL CONSUMPTION EXPENDITURES	212705.	266761.	343322.	401857.	4.5	5.0	3.1	4.2
PRIVATE INVESTMENT	40108.	53478.	65473.	73923.	5.8	4.0	2.4	4.1
GOVERNMENT EXPENDITURES	58768.	62005.	68686.	75005.	1.1	2.0	1.8	1.6

SMSA TOTAL: SUBURBAN COUNTIES

JOBS BY INDUSTRY	1970	1975	1980	1985	1970-1975	1975-1980	1980-1985	1970-1985
1 NATURAL RESOURCES (1-10)	201.	191.	170.	151.	-1.0	-2.3	-2.3	-1.9
2 CONSTRUCTION (11,12)	501.	631.	696.	761.	4.6	2.0	1.8	2.8
3 MANUFACTURING (13-74)	2597.	2836.	3011.	3050.	1.8	1.2	.3	1.1
4 PUBLIC UTILITIES (75-80)	452.	513.	571.	611.	2.5	2.1	1.4	2.0
5 WHOLESALE TRADE (81)	457.	569.	668.	750.	4.4	3.2	2.3	3.3
6 RETAIL TRADE (86,89-99)	1849.	2165.	2498.	2756.	3.2	2.9	2.3	2.7
7 FINANCE, INS., & REAL ESTATE (82,83)	351.	473.	613.	745.	6.0	5.2	3.9	5.0
8 SERVICES (84,85,87,88,102)	1627.	2028.	2525.	2946.	4.4	4.4	3.1	4.0
9 STATE & LOCAL GOVT. (101)	1222.	1392.	1529.	1656.	2.6	1.9	1.6	2.0
10 FEDERAL GOVERNMENT (100)	332.	356.	396.	433.	1.4	2.1	1.8	1.8
11 MILITARY (103)	226.	183.	183.	183.	-4.3	.0	.0	-1.4
TOTAL JOBS	9816.	11338.	12859.	14042.	2.9	2.5	1.8	2.4
CIVILIAN UNEMPLOYMENT RATE	3.7	3.8	3.3	3.6				
POPULATION	29389.	31984.	35010.	38340.	1.7	1.8	1.8	1.8
PERCENT NON-WHITE	5.4	5.6	5.8	6.1				
PER CAPITA INCOME	3725.	4385.	4995.	5449.	3.3	2.6	1.7	2.5
GROSS REGIONAL PRODUCT	116828.	153434.	197346.	237385.	5.5	5.0	3.7	4.7
PERSONAL CONSUMPTION EXPENDITURES	79760.	99682.	128303.	153318.	4.5	5.0	3.6	4.4
PRIVATE INVESTMENT	18602.	26484.	32314.	37177.	7.1	4.0	2.8	4.6
GOVERNMENT EXPENDITURES	28214.	32876.	36846.	40697.	3.1	2.3	2.0	2.4

JOBS AND POPULATION IN THOUSANDS, GROSS REGIONAL PRODUCT IN MILLIONS (1969 PRICES)

6-13. The overall output drops 1.6 percent but some industries have rather large adjustments. For example, the ordnance industry output is down 46 percent, and the aircraft output is down 34 percent.

Because of the shift to lower productivity industries, the 1985 Gross National Product is approximately 20 billion dollars less under the minimum deterrence budget than it is under the normal budget, even though employment is approximately the same. This change in GNP is approximately equal to the decrease in federal expenditures. As a result of this decrease in federal expenditures, taxes would be lower and disposable income higher; therefore, consumers would spend more for consumer goods. The increased personal consumer expenditures, however, are offset by lower private investment, since the shift away from manufacturing requires fewer capital goods to be produced.

Under the assumption of a gradual decrease in defense expenditures and compensating nondefense expenditures, there is little impact on the urban economies. This occurs even though it was assumed that urban counties with heavy dependency on defense expenditures would have greater cutbacks in defense expenditures than other counties. The defense expenditures for procurement and for military compensation were assumed to decrease 60 percent in urban counties and 46 percent in nonurban counties. If the defense expenditures for a given industry in an urban county were greater than 2 percent of the national defense expenditures for that industry, then the urban county received a greater percentage cutback in defense expenditures for that industry's output than the other counties in the U.S. For the ordnance industry, for example, counties with over 2 percent of the national defense expenditures for ordnance had their relative share cut approximately 17 percent, and the share of other counties was increased approximately 17 percent.

The overall shift to services away from manufacturing is beneficial to the urban areas since urban areas produce higher per capita services. For all SMSA counties, the manufacturing jobs dropped 3.1 percent under the minimum deterrence budget, but the total jobs only dropped 0.2 percent. The increase in services and light manufacturing almost fully compensated for the decreases in heavy manufacturing jobs caused by the lower defense expenditures.

Table 6-14 summarizes the 1985 impact of the lower defense budget on the urban economies by state and region. As can be seen by this table, the percent changes in population, jobs, per capita income, and gross regional product are small. The Southeast and Rocky Mountain regions gain a small number of jobs under the low defense budget and other regions lose jobs. The states earning the highest percentage of their gross regional product from defense procurement and military compensation under the normal budget were New Mexico and Connecticut. The urban economies in New Mexico are almost fully compensated for the loss in defense expenditures, but Connecticut is expected to lose 3.6 percent of its jobs.

Even individual metropolitan areas do not suffer greatly. The largest expected

Table 6-13
Industry Sector Outputs in 1985 under Normal and Minimum Deterrence Defense Budgets (Millions of Dollars (1969 Prices))

INDUSTRY GROUPS	NORMAL	MIN. DET.	% CHANGE
AGRICULTURE (1-4)	103636.	103716.	.1
NON-FERROUS ORE MINING (6)	3311.	2968.	-10.4
OTHER MINING (5,7-10)	38792.	38054.	-1.9
CONSTRUCTION (11,12)	105653.	105393.	-.2
ORDNANCE (13)	12816.	6920.	-46.0
FOOD AND KINDRED PRODUCTS (14-22)	155531.	156145.	.4
COPPER (46)	9002.	8531.	-5.2
ALUMINUM (47)	12647.	11937.	-5.6
OTHER NON-FERROUS METALS (48)	10583.	9982.	-5.7
METALWORKING MACH. & EQUIP. (57)	9512.	9027.	-5.1
MACHINE SHOPS & MISC. MACH. (60)	10330.	9192.	-11.0
COMMUNICATION EQUIPMENT (66)	30262.	26791.	-11.5
ELECTRONIC COMPONENTS (67)	20453.	18475.	-9.7
AIRCRAFT & PARTS (70)	27215.	18076.	-33.6
OTHER MFG. (13-74 NOT INCLUDED ABOVE)	847698.	833277.	-1.7
TRANSPORTATION & COMMUNICATION (75-77)	136960.	135677.	-.9
UTILITIES (78-80)	88049.	87289.	-.9
TRADE (81,88-99)	524440.	523561.	-.2
BUSINESS SERVICES (85)	128277.	125048.	-2.5
OTHER SERVICES (INCLUDING HOUSEHOLDS)	446555.	447554.	.2
FEDERAL GOVERNMENT	35266.	41334.	17.2
STATE & LOCAL GOVERNMENT	85871.	85871.	.0

decrease in total jobs occurs in Fort Worth, Texas, followed by Texarkana, Texas and New London, Connecticut. All three of these areas depend heavily on defense expenditures, but there are other areas that also depend heavily on defense expenditures which are not expected to lose a large number of the jobs. Table 6-15 summarizes the changes in population, jobs, per capita income and gross regional product for those SMSAs that had defense expenditures greater than 5 percent of the gross regional product under the normal defense budget.

Future Research

The results of this study demonstrate the feasibility and usefulness of a large-sized regional forecasting model. The model accounts for major interrelationships among economic and demographic variables, and it has produced a set of reasonable forecasts. It demonstrates that the interrelationships among variables need to be specified. For example, the demographic forecasts depend on the economic forecasts; if they did not, it would be possible to forecast the movement of people in one direction and the movement of jobs in another. Not only is the model useful in making reasonable forecasts, it is also useful in impact analysis. The low defense budget evaluated with the model did cause some geographic redistribution of economic activity.

Reducing defense expenditures is only one of the many possible types of impact analysis. As mentioned in the introduction, the model could be used to evaluate new towns, the effect of industry relocation on economic development, and the regional impacts of alternative transportation systems. The number of other applications is almost unlimited, for it is possible to predetermine the value of any national or regional variable in the model and to study the impact of these predetermined changes.

One of the major shortcomings of the model is the data base. For each county nearly a thousand data items were estimated and the quality of these estimates varies considerably. For example, there are relatively good data available on employment but poor data available on investment. There is need for an organized effort to make this data available annually, and since it is a costly endeavor, it would be appropriate if the estimates were undertaken by a federal agency. With more data and better quality data the forecasts could be improved. For example, with additional years of data the industry location equations would be more reliable because many of the industry relocations are planned several years ahead of time. With additional years of data the appropriate lag structure to plan and construct facilities could be determined separately for each industry.

While some of the impact analysis applications are easily handled by predetermining variables in the model, others would require additional data

Table 6-14
The Effect of the Minimum Deterrence Defense Budget on the 1985 Urban Economies Summarized by State and Region

(PERCENT CHANGE)

STATE AND REGION	DEFENSE EXPEND. *	POPULATION	TOTAL JOBS	MFG. JOBS	PER CAP. INCOME	GR. REG. PRODUCT	DEF. EXP./ GRP #
CONNECTICUT	-69.1	-2.8	-3.6	-10.7	-1.6	-4.8	9.2
MAINE	-37.2	-.4	.5	-1.1	.3	-.9	.9
MASSACHUSETTS	-63.7	-.4	-.4	-3.5	-.1	-1.2	3.7
NEW HAMPSHIRE	-65.4	-.8	-1.2	-3.3	.4	-2.3	6.0
RHODE ISLAND	-58.3	.4	.3	-1.5	.3	-.1	1.3
NEW ENGLAND	-66.5	-1.0	-1.3	-5.5	-.6	-2.2	5.2
DELAWARE	-63.3	-.1	.5	-1.4	.6	.0	.4
DISTRICT OF COLUMBIA	-69.7	-.1	.2	-1.7	-1.3	-3.3	6.8
MARYLAND	-53.3	.7	1.2	-3.0	1.8	1.1	3.2
NEW JERSEY	-52.5	-.1	.3	-1.8	.3	-.1	2.1
NEW YORK	-70.1	.0	-.5	-2.3	-.3	-1.4	2.3
PENNSYLVANIA	-64.3	.0	.2	-2.1	.2	-.6	2.5
MIDEAST	-64.7	.1	-.0	-2.1	.1	-.9	2.6
ILLINOIS	-58.3	-.7	-.0	-1.9	.6	-.7	1.4
INDIANA	-63.1	-.5	-.2	-2.6	.3	-1.2	2.5
MICHIGAN	-66.2	-.0	-.0	-2.1	-.0	-.9	1.2
OHIO	-62.3	-.4	-.5	-2.8	-.1	-1.2	2.4
WISCONSIN	-61.6	-.0	-.3	-1.5	.2	-.3	1.0
GREAT LAKES	-62.1	-.4	-.1	-2.2	.2	-.9	1.7
IOWA	-63.5	.2	.4	-1.3	.3	-.4	1.8
KANSAS	-55.7	-.1	.2	-4.1	.2	-1.0	2.7
MINNESOTA	-67.4	-.9	-.8	-3.4	.1	-2.4	4.2
MISSOURI	-71.1	-.8	-1.1	-3.3	-.5	-2.8	5.3
NEBRASKA	-36.8	.2	.7	-.7	.6	.1	2.2
NORTH DAKOTA	-57.9	.4	.4	-2.3	.6	-1.0	1.1
SOUTH DAKOTA	-54.1	1.0	1.3	.3	.7	.9	.4
PLAINS	-67.0	-.5	-.5	-2.9	-.1	-1.9	4.0

* PROCUREMENT AND MILITARY COMPENSATION
# NORMAL 1985 DEFENSE EXPENDITURES AS A PERCENT OF GROSS REGIONAL PRODUCT

ALABAMA	-57.3	.2	.8	-1.9	.9	-.1	3.8
ARKANSAS	-39.5	.6	1.1	-1.7	.8	.6	1.6
FLORIDA	-51.3	.5	.8	-2.8	.5	.2	2.3
GEORGIA	-31.2	.1	.3	-1.8	.4	.0	3.8
KENTUCKY	-45.3	.9	1.4	-1.1	.6	.8	.3
LOUISIANA	-61.5	.3	1.6	-1.8	.4	.6	2.5
MISSISSIPPI	-52.4	1.1	1.6	-.2	.8	1.4	.4
NORTH CAROLINA	-36.1	.2	.4	-.5	.6	-.1	2.2
SOUTH CAROLINA	-32.3	.9	.3	-1.6	.2	-.1	5.3
TENNESSEE	-57.0	.5	.6	-1.2	.3	.0	1.4
VIRGINIA	-32.5	1.0	1.5	-2.1	1.5	1.6	5.0
WEST VIRGINIA	-68.9	.2	.2	-1.4	.6	-1.0	1.9
SOUTHEAST	-42.6	.5	.7	-1.5	.6	.3	2.8
ARIZONA	-51.3	-.8	-.7	-6.4	.1	-1.8	3.3
NEW MEXICO	-59.1	.0	-.4	-4.7	.3	-2.2	9.7
OKLAHOMA	-38.0	.9	-.7	-3.3	.4	.2	3.1
TEXAS	-62.0	-.4	-.8	-4.9	-.7	-2.0	5.5
SOUTHWEST	-59.7	.3	-.6	-4.9	.3	-1.7	5.1
COLORADO	-38.8	.1	.3	-2.0	.3	-.5	3.6
IDAHO	-29.1	1.2	1.4	-.3	.9	1.0	.5
MONTANA	-31.2	1.1	1.8	-.6	.3	.0	2.0
UTAH	-56.1	1.6	1.6	-2.1	1.0	.5	2.5
ROCKY MOUNTAIN	-41.7	.6	.7	-1.8	.4	-.2	3.1
CALIFORNIA	-61.4	.6	-1.1	-6.2	.6	-2.1	6.3
HAWAII	-28.2	1.3	.9	-.8	.6	.9	6.5
NEVADA	-35.2	1.0	1.2	-.9	.5	.9	1.8
OREGON	-58.9	.8	.7	-1.2	.2	.1	1.8
WASHINGTON	-53.6	.0	-.5	-7.1	.4	-.7	3.1
FAR WEST	-59.6	.4	-.8	-5.9	.4	-1.7	5.6
SMSA TOTAL	-59.7	.1	-.2	-3.1	.0	-1.1	3.3
NON-SMSA COUNTIES	-45.8	.3	.3	-.9	.6	-.3	2.3
UNITED STATES	-57.6	-.0	-.1	-2.5	.1	-.9	3.1

Table 6-15

The Effect of the Minimum Deterrence Defense Budget on the 1985 Economies of the Standard Metropolitan Statistical Areas (Percent Change)

(PERCENT CHANGE)

SMSA	DEFENSE EXPEND. *	POPULATION	TOTAL JOBS	MFG. JOBS	PER CAP. INCOME	GR. REG. PRODUCT	DEF. EXP./ GRP #
TEXARKANA, TEX.-ARK.	-70.7	-4.6	-6.7[b]	-17.9	-6.6	-20.3	58.1
LAWTON, OKLA.	-18.4	.6	2.5	-.7	1.6	-1.0	25.4
FORT WORTH, TEX.	-71.8	-6.8	-8.9[b]	-13.1	-4.4	-14.6	24.4
COLUMBUS, GA.-ALA.	-12.9	.9	-.8	-.0	-1.5	-.4	22.4
ORLANDO, FLA.	-66.3	-2.3	-2.6	-16.3	-1.4	-7.1	21.1
NEW LONDON-GROTON-NORWICH, CONN.	-60.8	-4.7	-6.2	-10.4	-6.5	-6.5	21.1
FAYETTEVILLE, N.C.	-16.1	-.9	-2.3	-.1	.2	-1.2	19.8
SAN DIEGO, CALIF.	-45.8	-1.2	-2.4	-13.1	-1.3	-3.7	17.9
HUNTSVILLE, ALA.	-62.6	.3	.9	-6.7	.4	-3.7	16.9
WICHITA FALLS, TEX.	-19.5	.9	-1.0	-3.3	-.7	-.6	14.5
SALINAS-MONTEREY, CALIF.	-21.4	.3	-1.4	-2.0	-.4	-1.1	14.4
NORFOLK-PORTSMOUTH, VA.	-23.3	1.0	1.1	-8.8	2.8	3.2	13.2
COLORADO SPRINGS, COLO.	-23.2	-.3	-1.4	-6.6	.5	-1.4	13.0
BRIDGEPORT, STAMFORD, NORWALK, CONN.	-71.0	-4.7	-4.4	-11.6	-.1	-5.2	11.5
NEWPORT NEWS-HAMPTON, VA.	-37.2	1.9	.8	-2.1	1.2	2.7	11.4
AUGUSTA, GA.-S.C.	-28.7	1.1	-.3	-.8	-.6	-1.1	11.2
SOUTH BEND, IND.	-64.5	-1.8	1.7	-4.8	-.3	-4.2	11.2
SAN JOSE, CALIF.	-68.3	-2.5	-3.6	-8.2	-1.2	-5.4	10.8
MUSKEGON-MUSKEGON HEIGHTS, MICH.	-69.3	-2.6	-3.0	-4.0	-.6	-6.3	10.6
HARTFORD, NEW BRITAIN, CONN.	-71.1	-2.5	-3.9	-14.1	-2.4	-5.6	9.9
ALBUQUERQUE, N. MEX.	-59.1	-.0	-.4	-4.7	-.3	-2.2	9.7
PENSACOLA, FLA.	-11.7	1.9	1.0	-.7	.4	1.6	8.8
SANTA BARBARA, CALIF.	-55.3	1.2	1.9	-3.9	1.6	1.3	8.7
WACO, TEX.	-56.8	-.4	.4	-4.6	.1	-2.0	8.6
CHARLESTON, S.C.	-35.0	1.5	.9	-6.9	.7	.7	8.6
COLUMBIA, S.C.	-10.8	1.2	.0	-.8	.1	.4	7.9
WATERLOO, IOWA	-59.6	-.5	.4	-1.4	.4	-2.6	7.8
SAN ANTONIO, TEX.	-26.8	2.2	.9	-1.3	.5	1.2	7.8
VALLEJO-NAPA, CALIF.	-28.7	-.1	-.5	.3	1.1	-.5	7.5
BAY CITY, MICH.	-64.6	-1.0	-1.2	-3.0	-.2	-3.1	7.5
ANAHEIM-SANTA ANA-GARDEN GROVE, CALIF.	-68.0	-2.3	-1.9	-9.1	.1	-2.7	7.0
AMARILLO, TEX.	-22.2	-.1	-.3	-.6	-.5	-.5	6.8
WICHITA, KANS.	-61.0	-1.4	-2.1	-8.5	-.9	-3.4	6.7
ABILENE, TEX.	-32.4	-.7	-.7	-2.7	-.8	-1.2	6.7
HONOLULU, HAWAII	-28.2	1.3	.9	-.8	.6	.9	6.5

PITTSFIELD, MASS.	-68.1	-1.1	-2.1	-4.5	-1.1	-3.6	6.1
LOS ANGELES-LONG BEACH, CALIF.	-69.6	-1.0	-2.0	-6.4	-1.2	-3.1	6.0
MANCHESTER, N.H.	-65.4	-.8	-1.2	-3.3	-.4	-2.3	6.0
BEAUMONT-PORT ARTHUR, TEX.	-70.7	-.2	.1	-1.3	.2	-1.5	6.0
TACOMA, WASH.	-29.0	1.3	-.3	-2.2	-.1	.3	5.8
CORPUS CHRISTI, TEX.	-51.7	-.0	.2	-2.6	.2	-1.0	5.6
CHAMPAIGN-URBANA, ILL.	-36.9	-.5	-.8	-3.7	.2	-.8	5.6
OXNARD-VENTURA, CALIF.	-41.8	1.9	.6	-8.1	.7	.2	5.5
ST. LOUIS, MO.-ILL.	-69.8	-.8	-1.4	-3.1	-.6	-3.3	5.3
MACON, GA.	-54.8	.5	1.7	-1.2	.9	.0	5.3
LAKE CHARLES, LA.	-70.8	-.6	.0	-2.3	.3	-1.5	5.2

* PROCUREMENT AND MILITARY COMPENSATION
# NORMAL 1985 DEFENSE EXPENDITURES AS A PERCENT OF GROSS REGIONAL PRODUCT

and modifications of the model. For example, as the model now stands, there are no resource limitations other than the fact that output mining cannot start up in new areas. Perhaps a more important type of resource restriction would be a restriction on the availability of land and water. If an area has unsuitable land for additional development or if land use is controlled by zoning regulations, then there would be a limit on the growth of the area. Also, the pollution of land, air, and water is associated with economic activity, and if pollution controls are instituted, they could limit the growth of an area and cause a geographic distribution of economic activity.

Work has already been started to add pollution emissions to the model, and to specify the relationship between pollution controls and economic activity. Additions to the model also include a state and local revenue and expenditures submodel, so that the model can be used for state planning.

Appendix

Appendix Table

Appendix Table
Selected Projections of Standard Metropolitan Statistical Areas with a 1970 Population Over One Million

NEW YORK, N.Y.

JOBS BY INDUSTRY	1970	1975	1980	1985	AVERAGE ANNUAL RATE OF GROWTH			
					1970–1975	1975–1980	1980–1985	1970–1985
1 NATURAL RESOURCES (1-10)	15.	15.	15.	13.	.9	-1.1	-2.4	-.9
2 CONSTRUCTION (11,12)	183.	201.	219.	233.	2.0	1.7	1.2	1.6
3 MANUFACTURING (13-74)	1131.	1223.	1278.	1254.	1.5	.9	-.4	.7
4 PUBLIC UTILITIES (75-80)	438.	463.	485.	492.	1.1	.9	.3	.8
5 WHOLESALE TRADE (81)	413.	481.	534.	568.	3.0	2.1	1.2	2.1
6 RETAIL TRADE (86,89-99)	791.	858.	936.	976.	1.6	1.7	.8	1.4
7 FINANCE, INS. & REAL ESTATE (82,83)	542.	669.	795.	890.	4.2	3.4	2.3	3.3
8 SERVICES (84,85,87,88,102)	1193.	1384.	1602.	1760.	3.0	2.9	1.9	2.6
9 STATE & LOCAL GOVT. (101)	664.	716.	730.	756.	1.5	.4	.7	.9
10 FEDERAL GOVERNMENT (100)	130.	120.	123.	131.	-1.5	.4	1.3	.1
11 MILITARY (103)	8.	6.	6.	6.	-4.3	.0	.0	-1.4
TOTAL JOBS	5507.	6139.	6721.	7077.	2.2	1.8	1.0	1.7
CIVILIAN UNEMPLOYMENT RATE	4.7	4.4	3.5	3.4				
POPULATION	11529.	12060.	12620.	13180.	.9	.9	.9	.9
PERCENT NON-WHITE	18.0	19.0	19.8	20.6				
PER CAPITA INCOME	4881.	6208.	7575.	8699.	4.8	4.0	2.8	3.9
GROSS REGIONAL PRODUCT	80365.	95098.	112523.	124336.	3.4	3.3	2.0	2.9
PERSONAL CONSUMPTION EXPENDITURES	47338.	59772.	77754.	91794.	4.7	5.3	3.3	4.4
PRIVATE INVESTMENT	8514.	11279.	14058.	15897.	5.6	4.4	2.5	4.2
GOVERNMENT EXPENDITURES	12915.	14051.	15028.	16250.	1.7	1.3	1.6	1.5

LOS ANGELES-LONG BEACH, CALIF.

JOBS BY INDUSTRY	1970	1975	1980	1985	AVERAGE ANNUAL RATE OF GROWTH			
					1970–1975	1975–1980	1980–1985	1970–1985
1 NATURAL RESOURCES (1-10)	32.	27.	23.	20.	-3.0	-3.3	-3.2	-3.2
2 CONSTRUCTION (11,12)	132.	153.	170.	183.	2.9	2.1	1.5	2.2
3 MANUFACTURING (13-74)	868.	956.	1026.	1037.	1.9	1.4	1.2	1.2
4 PUBLIC UTILITIES (75-80)	184.	195.	200.	196.	1.1	.5	-.4	.4

	1970	1975	1980	1985	AVERAGE ANNUAL RATE OF GROWTH			
					1970-1975	1975-1980	1980-1985	1970-1985
5 WHOLESALE TRADE (81)	214.	254.	285.	305.	3.4	2.3	1.4	2.4
6 RETAIL TRADE (86,89-99)	534.	598.	663.	696.	2.3	2.0	1.0	1.8
7 FINANCE, INS. & REAL ESTATE (82,83)	181.	189.	190.	181.	.9	.1	-.9	.0
8 SERVICES (84,85,87,88,102)	616.	756.	918.	1029.	4.1	3.9	2.3	3.4
9 STATE & LOCAL GOVT. (101)	334.	346.	372.	394.	.7	1.4	1.2	1.1
10 FEDERAL GOVERNMENT (100)	69.	66.	72.	74.	-.8	1.6	.7	.5
11 MILITARY (103)	10.	8.	8.	8.	-4.3	.0	.0	-1.4
TOTAL JOBS	3174.	3548.	3927.	4124.	2.2	2.0	1.0	1.7
CIVILIAN UNEMPLOYMENT RATE	5.4	4.7	4.3	4.8				
POPULATION	7032.	7481.	8183.	8905.	1.2	1.8	1.7	1.6
PERCENT NON-WHITE	14.6	15.6	16.6	17.4				
PER CAPITA INCOME	4793.	5775.	6617.	7130.	3.7	2.7	1.5	2.6
GROSS REGIONAL PRODUCT	41888.	51713.	63220.	71639.	4.2	4.0	2.5	3.6
PERSONAL CONSUMPTION EXPENDITURES	27188.	33542.	42921.	49616.	4.2	4.9	2.9	4.0
PRIVATE INVESTMENT	4904.	6435.	7743.	8478.	5.4	3.7	1.8	3.6
GOVERNMENT EXPENDITURES	10253.	11013.	12245.	13327.	1.4	2.1	1.7	1.7

CHICAGO, ILL.

JOBS BY INDUSTRY

	1970	1975	1980	1985	AVERAGE ANNUAL RATE OF GROWTH			
					1970-1975	1975-1980	1980-1985	1970-1985
1 NATURAL RESOURCES (1-10)	16.	16.	15.	14.	3.1	-1.4	-1.7	-1.0
2 CONSTRUCTION (11,12)	134.	159.	172.	183.	3.5	1.6	1.2	2.1
3 MANUFACTURING (13-74)	986.	1113.	1190.	1206.	2.4	1.3	.3	1.3
4 PUBLIC UTILITIES (75-80)	224.	230.	231.	226.	.6	.1	-.5	.1
5 WHOLESALE TRADE (81)	247.	290.	320.	340.	3.2	2.0	1.2	2.1
6 RETAIL TRADE (86,89-99)	550.	597.	637.	653.	1.6	1.3	.5	1.1
7 FINANCE, INS. & REAL ESTATE (82,83)	193.	222.	246.	256.	2.8	2.0	.8	1.9
8 SERVICES (84,85,87,88,102)	566.	650.	741.	795.	2.8	2.6	1.4	2.3
9 STATE & LOCAL GOVT. (101)	297.	321.	342.	360.	1.5	1.0	1.0	1.3
10 FEDERAL GOVERNMENT (100)	78.	75.	79.	79.	-.9	1.0	.0	.1
11 MILITARY (103)	33.	26.	26.	26.	-4.3	.0	.0	-1.4
TOTAL JOBS	3323.	3699.	3999.	4137.	2.1	1.6	.7	1.5
CIVILIAN UNEMPLOYMENT RATE	3.0	3.4	2.7	3.4				
POPULATION	6979.	7399.	7896.	8447.	1.2	1.3	1.3	1.3
PERCENT NON-WHITE	18.7	19.9	21.3	22.2				
PER CAPITA INCOME	4833.	5854.	6670.	7212.	3.8	2.6	1.6	2.7
GROSS REGIONAL PRODUCT	44384.	53589.	63289.	70165.	3.8	3.3	2.1	3.1
PERSONAL CONSUMPTION EXPENDITURES	26675.	32856.	40699.	46278.	4.2	4.3	2.6	3.7
PRIVATE INVESTMENT	5191.	6961.	8113.	8878.	5.9	3.1	1.8	3.6
GOVERNMENT EXPENDITURES	5142.	5955.	6595.	7117.	2.9	2.0	1.5	2.2

Appendix Table (cont.)

PHILADELPHIA, PA.-N.J.

JOBS BY INDUSTRY	1970	1975	1980	1985	AVERAGE ANNUAL RATE OF GROWTH 1970–1975	1975–1980	1980–1985	1970–1985
1 NATURAL RESOURCES (1-10)	16.	15.	13.	11.	-1.2	-2.8	-2.9	-2.3
2 CONSTRUCTION (11,12)	89.	104.	115.	125.	3.1	2.0	1.6	2.2
3 MANUFACTURING (13-74)	573.	646.	698.	718.	2.4	1.6	.5	1.5
4 PUBLIC UTILITIES (75-80)	117.	120.	124.	125.	1.0	.6	.1	.6
5 WHOLESALE TRADE (81)	115.	140.	160.	175.	3.7	2.6	1.8	2.7
6 RETAIL TRADE (86,89-99)	322.	365.	409.	441.	2.5	2.3	1.5	2.1
7 FINANCE, INS. & REAL ESTATE (82,83)	110.	136.	160.	176.	4.2	3.7	2.0	3.1
8 SERVICES (84,85,87,88,102)	374.	445.	534.	609.	3.4	3.7	2.6	3.2
9 STATE & LOCAL GOVT. (101)	177.	185.	204.	219.	.8	1.9	1.4	1.4
10 FEDERAL GOVERNMENT (100)	87.	79.	86.	93.	-1.8	1.7	1.4	.4
11 MILITARY (103)	51.	41.	41.	41.	-4.3	.0	.0	-1.4
TOTAL JOBS	2032.	2277.	2545.	2733.	2.3	2.2	1.4	2.0
CIVILIAN UNEMPLOYMENT RATE	4.8	4.4	3.6	3.9				
POPULATION	4818.	5128.	5530.	5940.	1.2	1.5	1.4	1.4
PERCENT NON-WHITE	18.1	18.7	19.5	20.3				
PER CAPITA INCOME	4122.	4973.	5777.	6408.	3.8	3.0	2.1	2.9
GROSS REGIONAL PRODUCT	24014.	29746.	36644.	42506.	4.3	4.2	3.0	3.8
PERSONAL CONSUMPTION EXPENDITURES	14901.	18498.	23701.	28037.	4.3	5.0	3.4	4.2
PRIVATE INVESTMENT	2792.	3760.	4514.	5098.	6.0	3.7	2.4	4.0
GOVERNMENT EXPENDITURES	4612.	4900.	5496.	6045.	1.2	2.3	1.9	1.8

DETROIT, MICH.

JOBS BY INDUSTRY	1970	1975	1980	1985	AVERAGE ANNUAL RATE OF GROWTH 1970–1975	1975–1980	1980–1985	1970–1985
1 NATURAL RESOURCES (1-10)	8.	8.	8.	7.	.6	-1.4	-1.9	-.9
2 CONSTRUCTION (11,12)	69.	87.	96.	104.	4.8	2.0	1.5	2.8
3 MANUFACTURING (13-74)	572.	656.	700.	697.	2.7	1.3	-.1	1.3
4 PUBLIC UTILITIES (75-80)	87.	108.	126.	137.	4.3	3.1	1.7	3.1
5 WHOLESALE TRADE (81)	98.	125.	145.	158.	4.9	3.1	1.7	3.2
6 RETAIL TRADE (86,89-99)	287.	347.	398.	427.	3.8	2.7	1.4	2.6
7 FINANCE, INS. & REAL ESTATE (82,83)	76.	107.	144.	179.	7.0	5.9	4.4	5.8
8 SERVICES (84,85,87,88,102)	276.	328.	384.	420.	3.4	3.2	1.8	2.8
9 STATE & LOCAL GOVT. (101)	174.	198.	220.	236.	2.6	2.1	1.4	2.0

	1970	1975	1980	1985	1970–1975	1975–1980	1980–1985	1970–1985
10 FEDERAL GOVERNMENT (100)	31.	35.	39.	40.	2.4	2.0	.7	1.7
11 MILITARY (103)	3.	3.	3.	3.	-4.3	.0	.0	-1.4
TOTAL JOBS	1680.	2001.	2263.	2407.	3.5	2.5	1.2	2.4
CIVILIAN UNEMPLOYMENT RATE	3.5	3.5	3.0	3.0				
POPULATION	4200.	4675.	5087.	5431.	2.1	1.7	1.3	1.7
PERCENT NON-WHITE	18.6	19.6	20.8	21.8				
PER CAPITA INCOME	4506.	5518.	6427.	7073.	4.1	3.0	1.9	3.0
GROSS REGIONAL PRODUCT	22692.	30477.	38761.	45252.	5.9	4.8	3.1	4.6
PERSONAL CONSUMPTION EXPENDITURES	13001.	17535.	22961.	26802.	6.0	5.4	3.1	4.8
PRIVATE INVESTMENT	3303.	5038.	6389.	7612.	8.4	4.8	3.5	5.6
GOVERNMENT EXPENDITURES	2959.	3675.	4183.	4563.	4.3	2.6	1.7	2.9

BOSTON, LAWRENCE-HAVERHILL, LOWELL, MASS.

JOBS BY INDUSTRY	1970	1975	1980	1985	AVERAGE ANNUAL RATE OF GROWTH 1970–1975	1975–1980	1980–1985	1970–1985
1 NATURAL RESOURCES (1-10)	8.	8.	7.	6.	-.5	-2.2	-2.6	-1.8
2 CONSTRUCTION (11,12)	62.	69.	76.	82.	2.2	1.9	1.5	1.9
3 MANUFACTURING (13-74)	411.	441.	456.	447.	1.4	.7	-.4	.6
4 PUBLIC UTILITIES (75-80)	88.	87.	85.	81.	-.2	-.5	-.9	-.5
5 WHOLESALE TRADE (81)	94.	112.	126.	136.	3.4	2.3	1.5	2.4
6 RETAIL TRADE (86,89-99)	274.	308.	342.	364.	2.3	2.1	1.2	1.9
7 FINANCE, INS. & REAL ESTATE (82,83)	104.	120.	130.	129.	2.9	1.5	-.1	1.4
8 SERVICES (84,85,87,88,102)	332.	395.	470.	527.	3.4	3.5	2.3	3.1
9 STATE & LOCAL GOVT. (101)	164.	161.	174.	185.	-.3	1.5	1.3	.8
10 FEDERAL GOVERNMENT (100)	52.	44.	48.	51.	-3.3	1.7	.9	-.2
11 MILITARY (103)	12.	10.	10.	10.	-4.3	.0	.0	-1.4
TOTAL JOBS	1603.	1756.	1924.	2018.	1.8	1.8	1.0	1.5
CIVILIAN UNEMPLOYMENT RATE	4.4	4.4	3.5	4.2				
POPULATION	3375.	3613.	3913.	4226.	1.4	1.6	1.5	1.5
PERCENT NON-WHITE	4.6	4.6	4.6	4.6				
PER CAPITA INCOME	4385.	5294.	6108.	6683.	3.8	2.9	1.8	2.8
GROSS REGIONAL PRODUCT	18866.	23054.	28104.	32098.	4.0	4.0	2.7	3.5
PERSONAL CONSUMPTION EXPENDITURES	13636.	16911.	21504.	25092.	4.3	4.8	3.1	4.1
PRIVATE INVESTMENT	2582.	3212.	3822.	4171.	4.4	3.5	1.7	3.2
GOVERNMENT EXPENDITURES	4024.	4181.	4688.	5142.	.8	2.3	1.9	1.6

Appendix Table (cont.)

SAN FRANCISCO-OAKLAND, CALIF.

JOBS BY INDUSTRY	1970	1975	1980	1985	AVERAGE ANNUAL RATE OF GROWTH 1970-1975	1975-1980	1980-1985	1970-1985
1 NATURAL RESOURCES (1-10)	12.	11.	9.	8.	-2.2	-3.3	-3.5	-3.0
2 CONSTRUCTION (11,12)	72.	81.	89.	96.	2.4	1.9	1.6	2.0
3 MANUFACTURING (13-74)	213.	231.	242.	242.	1.6	.9	.0	.8
4 PUBLIC UTILITIES (75-80)	129.	140.	151.	157.	1.6	1.4	.8	1.3
5 WHOLESALE TRADE (81)	97.	112.	124.	132.	3.0	2.0	1.2	2.1
6 RETAIL TRADE (86,89-99)	221.	238.	256.	264.	1.5	1.4	.6	1.2
7 FINANCE, INS. & REAL ESTATE (82,83)	106.	128.	147.	158.	3.8	2.8	1.5	2.7
8 SERVICES (84,85,87,88,102)	258.	288.	323.	344.	2.2	2.3	1.3	1.9
9 STATE & LOCAL GOVT. (101)	183.	182.	192.	202.	-.1	1.1	.9	.6
10 FEDERAL GOVERNMENT (100)	92.	82.	87.	90.	-2.3	1.1	.6	-.2
11 MILITARY (103)	33.	26.	26.	26.	-4.3	.0	.0	-1.4
TOTAL JOBS	1416.	1520.	1646.	1718.	1.4	1.6	.9	1.3
CIVILIAN UNEMPLOYMENT RATE	6.6	6.0	4.6	5.3				
POPULATION	3110.	3211.	3350.	3513.	.6	.9	.9	.8
PERCENT NON-WHITE	17.2	17.8	18.9	20.1				
PER CAPITA INCOME	5050.	6042.	7025.	7775.	3.6	3.0	2.0	2.9
GROSS REGIONAL PRODUCT	20342.	23829.	28213.	31482.	3.2	3.4	2.2	2.9
PERSONAL CONSUMPTION EXPENDITURES	12697.	15080.	18664.	21370.	3.4	4.3	2.7	3.5
PRIVATE INVESTMENT	2342.	3088.	3762.	4281.	5.5	3.9	2.6	4.0
GOVERNMENT EXPENDITURES	4791.	5020.	5526.	5968.	.9	1.9	1.5	1.5

WASHINGTON, D.C.-MD.-VA.

JOBS BY INDUSTRY	1970	1975	1980	1985	AVERAGE ANNUAL RATE OF GROWTH 1970-1975	1975-1980	1980-1985	1970-1985
1 NATURAL RESOURCES (1-10)	6.	6.	6.	5.	.4	-1.3	-1.7	-.9
2 CONSTRUCTION (11,12)	67.	82.	92.	102.	4.2	2.3	2.1	2.9
3 MANUFACTURING (13-74)	55.	67.	79.	90.	3.7	3.5	2.5	3.2
4 PUBLIC UTILITIES (75-80)	60.	69.	81.	89.	2.8	3.1	2.0	2.6
5 WHOLESALE TRADE (81)	47.	59.	72.	83.	4.7	4.0	2.8	3.8

	1970	1975	1980	1985	AVERAGE ANNUAL RATE OF GROWTH			
					1970–1975	1975–1980	1980–1985	1970–1985
6 RETAIL TRADE (86,89-99)	203.	239.	284.	318.	3.3	3.4	2.3	3.0
7 FINANCE, INS. & REAL ESTATE (82,83)	74.	98.	124.	148.	5.6	4.8	3.5	4.6
8 SERVICES (84,85,87,88,102)	293.	364.	453.	528.	4.4	4.3	3.1	3.9
9 STATE & LOCAL GOVT. (101)	141.	145.	166.	183.	.5	2.7	2.0	1.7
10 FEDERAL GOVERNMENT (100)	326.	313.	330.	353.	-.8	1.1	1.3	.5
11 MILITARY (103)	66.	54.	54.	54.	-4.3	.0	.0	-1.4
TOTAL JOBS	1339.	1495.	1740.	1953.	2.2	3.0	2.3	2.5
CIVILIAN UNEMPLOYMENT RATE	2.0	2.8	2.4	2.6				
POPULATION	2713.	2961.	3334.	3722.	1.8	2.4	2.2	2.1
PERCENT NON-WHITE	26.7	26.0	26.4	26.9				
PER CAPITA INCOME	4498.	5203.	5938.	6535.	2.9	2.6	1.9	2.5
GROSS REGIONAL PRODUCT	17514.	22296.	29338.	35786.	4.8	5.5	4.0	4.8
PERSONAL CONSUMPTION EXPENDITURES	12146.	14899.	19718.	23967.	4.1	5.6	3.9	4.5
PRIVATE INVESTMENT	1931.	2657.	3319.	3870.	6.4	4.4	3.1	4.6
GOVERNMENT EXPENDITURES	6121.	6432.	7164.	7971.	1.0	2.2	2.1	1.8

PITTSBURGH, PA.

	1970	1975	1980	1985	AVERAGE ANNUAL RATE OF GROWTH			
					1970–1975	1975–1980	1980–1985	1970–1985
JOBS BY INDUSTRY								
1 NATURAL RESOURCES (1-10)	17.	16.	14.	13.	-1.6	-2.2	-2.3	-2.0
2 CONSTRUCTION (11,12)	45.	51.	56.	59.	2.8	1.6	1.2	1.9
3 MANUFACTURING (13-74)	294.	312.	311.	298.	1.2	-.1	-.9	-.1
4 PUBLIC UTILITIES (75-80)	61.	63.	63.	61.	.7	.0	-.7	.0
5 WHOLESALE TRADE (81)	55.	64.	70.	73.	3.1	1.8	1.0	1.9
6 RETAIL TRADE (86,89-99)	166.	180.	192.	196.	1.6	1.3	.5	1.1
7 FINANCE, INS. & REAL ESTATE (82,83)	43.	57.	71.	83.	5.4	4.4	3.2	4.3
8 SERVICES (84,85,87,88,102)	168.	175.	183.	180.	.9	.9	-.3	.5
9 STATE & LOCAL GOVT. (101)	99.	100.	102.	103.	.3	.3	.3	.3
10 FEDERAL GOVERNMENT (100)	18.	16.	16.	16.	-2.4	.3	-.3	-1.1
11 MILITARY (103)	2.	2.	2.	2.	-4.3	.0	-1.2	-1.4
TOTAL JOBS	968.	1036.	1079.	1083.	1.4	.8	.1	.8
CIVILIAN UNEMPLOYMENT RATE	5.1	4.8	3.6	3.9				
POPULATION	2401.	2447.	2463.	2476.	.4	.1	.1	.2
PERCENT NON-WHITE	7.3	7.9	8.6	9.1				
PER CAPITA INCOME	4065.	4914.	5694.	6311.	3.8	2.9	2.1	2.9
GROSS REGIONAL PRODUCT	11188.	13296.	15384.	16797.	3.5	2.9	1.8	2.7
PERSONAL CONSUMPTION EXPENDITURES	7107.	8437.	10053.	11077.	3.4	3.5	1.9	3.0
PRIVATE INVESTMENT	1339.	1786.	2055.	2235.	5.8	2.8	1.7	3.4
GOVERNMENT EXPENDITURES	1535.	1663.	1764.	1838.	1.6	1.2	.8	1.2

Appendix Table (cont.)

ST. LOUIS, MO.-ILL.

JOBS BY INDUSTRY	1970	1975	1980	1985	AVERAGE ANNUAL RATE OF GROWTH			
					1970-1975	1975-1980	1980-1985	1970-1985
1 NATURAL RESOURCES (1-10)	14.	14.	13.	12.	-.1	-1.2	-1.3	-.9
2 CONSTRUCTION (11,12)	47.	56.	61.	66.	3.6	1.6	1.4	2.2
3 MANUFACTURING (13-74)	290.	303.	311.	308.	.9	.5	-.2	.4
4 PUBLIC UTILITIES (75-80)	68.	71.	73.	72.	1.0	.4	-.2	.4
5 WHOLESALE TRADE (81)	65.	76.	84.	89.	3.2	2.1	1.2	2.2
6 RETAIL TRADE (86,89-99)	174.	190.	207.	215.	1.8	1.7	.8	1.4
7 FINANCE, INS. & REAL ESTATE (82,83)	54.	65.	76.	82.	3.9	2.9	1.7	2.8
8 SERVICES (84,85,87,88,102)	186.	218.	258.	285.	3.2	3.3	2.0	2.8
9 STATE & LOCAL GOVT. (101)	93.	96.	105.	111.	.7	1.7	1.1	1.2
10 FEDERAL GOVERNMENT (100)	39.	33.	36.	39.	-3.2	1.6	1.3	-.1
11 MILITARY (103)	8.	7.	7.	7.	-4.3	.0	.0	-1.4
TOTAL JOBS	1038.	1130.	1230.	1286.	1.7	1.7	.9	1.4
CIVILIAN UNEMPLOYMENT RATE	3.4	3.6	2.8	2.9				
PERCENT NON-WHITE	16.4	16.9	17.7	18.4				
POPULATION	2363.	2445.	2560.	2695.	.7	.9	1.0	.9
PER CAPITA INCOME	4082.	4914.	5680.	6231.	3.7	2.9	1.9	2.8
GROSS REGIONAL PRODUCT	12896.	15589.	18765.	21127.	3.8	3.7	2.4	3.3
PERSONAL CONSUMPTION EXPENDITURES	6889.	8213.	10123.	11517.	3.5	4.2	2.6	3.4
PRIVATE INVESTMENT	1413.	1979.	2401.	2744.	6.7	3.9	2.7	4.4
GOVERNMENT EXPENDITURES	2175.	2300.	2577.	2819.	1.1	2.3	1.8	1.7

CLEVELAND, OHIO

JOBS BY INDUSTRY	1970	1975	1980	1985	AVERAGE ANNUAL RATE OF GROWTH			
					1970-1975	1975-1980	1980-1985	1970-1985
1 NATURAL RESOURCES (1-10)	7.	7.	7.	5.	1.1	-2.5	-4.3	-1.9
2 CONSTRUCTION (11,12)	39.	45.	49.	52.	2.9	1.9	1.3	2.0
3 MANUFACTURING (13-74)	318.	351.	364.	358.	1.9	.7	-.3	.8
4 PUBLIC UTILITIES (75-80)	54.	65.	75.	84.	3.8	3.1	2.1	3.0
5 WHOLESALE TRADE (81)	65.	76.	84.	89.	3.3	1.9	1.1	2.1
6 RETAIL TRADE (86,89-99)	152.	168.	181.	185.	2.0	1.4	.5	1.3
7 FINANCE, INS. & REAL ESTATE (82,83)	43.	50.	55.	57.	3.0	1.9	.5	1.8
8 SERVICES (84,85,87,88,102)	145.	149.	155.	154.	.6	.7	-.1	.4
9 STATE & LOCAL GOVT. (101)	86.	87.	90.	92.	.2	.8	.3	.5

	1970	1975	1980	1985	1970–1975	1975–1980	1980–1985	1970–1985
10 FEDERAL GOVERNMENT (100)	22.	19.	20.	19.	-2.8	.7	-.6	-.9
11 MILITARY (103)	1.	1.	1.	1.	-4.3	.0	.0	-1.4
TOTAL JOBS	932.	1018.	1081.	1096.	1.8	1.2	.3	1.1
CIVILIAN UNEMPLOYMENT RATE	3.3	3.7	3.5	3.8				
POPULATION	2064.	2217.	2372.	2505.	1.4	1.4	1.1	1.3
PERCENT NON-WHITE	16.6	17.5	18.2	18.9				
PER CAPITA INCOME	4290.	5170.	5854.	6240.	3.7	2.5	1.3	2.5
GROSS REGIONAL PRODUCT	11360.	13855.	16424.	18271.	4.0	3.4	2.1	3.2
PERSONAL CONSUMPTION EXPENDITURES	7410.	9189.	11339.	12606.	4.3	4.2	2.1	3.5
PRIVATE INVESTMENT	1641.	2277.	2760.	3166.	6.6	3.8	2.7	4.4
GOVERNMENT EXPENDITURES	1244.	1350.	1471.	1539.	1.6	1.7	.9	1.4

HOUSTON, TEX.

JOBS BY INDUSTRY	1970	1975	1980	1985	AVERAGE ANNUAL RATE OF GROWTH			
					1970–1975	1975–1980	1980–1985	1970–1985
1 NATURAL RESOURCES (1-10)	37.	33.	30.	26.	-2.3	-2.3	-2.4	-2.3
2 CONSTRUCTION (11,12)	88.	106.	119.	131.	3.7	2.3	1.9	2.6
3 MANUFACTURING (13-74)	162.	205.	246.	278.	4.7	3.7	2.5	3.6
4 PUBLIC UTILITIES (75-80)	68.	82.	95.	103.	3.7	2.8	1.6	2.7
5 WHOLESALE TRADE (81)	69.	88.	104.	117.	4.8	3.4	2.4	3.5
6 RETAIL TRADE (86,89-99)	146.	181.	217.	246.	4.3	3.6	2.4	3.5
7 FINANCE, INS. & REAL ESTATE (82,83)	47.	57.	66.	71.	4.1	2.9	1.3	2.8
8 SERVICES (84,85,87,88,102)	175.	232.	299.	358.	5.6	5.1	3.6	4.8
9 STATE & LOCAL GOVT. (101)	70.	84.	101.	115.	3.6	3.6	2.7	3.3
10 FEDERAL GOVERNMENT (100)	18.	21.	25.	29.	3.1	4.1	2.8	3.3
11 MILITARY (103)	1.	1.	1.	1.	-4.3	-.0	-.0	-1.4
TOTAL JOBS	881.	1090.	1303.	1475.	4.3	3.6	2.5	3.4
CIVILIAN UNEMPLOYMENT RATE	3.6	4.1	3.1	3.5				
POPULATION	1985.	2313.	2681.	3068.	3.1	3.0	2.7	2.9
PERCENT NON-WHITE	20.1	19.6	19.4	19.4				
PER CAPITA INCOME	3934.	4921.	5778.	6413.	4.5	3.2	2.1	3.3
GROSS REGIONAL PRODUCT	10845.	15528.	21131.	26283.	7.2	6.2	4.4	5.9
PERSONAL CONSUMPTION EXPENDITURES	6871.	9647.	13427.	16874.	6.8	6.6	4.6	6.0
PRIVATE INVESTMENT	1598.	2398.	3088.	3685.	8.1	5.1	3.5	5.6
GOVERNMENT EXPENDITURES	1302.	1602.	1908.	2192.	4.1	3.5	2.8	3.5

Appendix Table (cont.)

BALTIMORE, MD.

JOBS BY INDUSTRY	1970	1975	1980	1985	AVERAGE ANNUAL RATE OF GROWTH			
					1970-1975	1975-1980	1980-1985	1970-1985
1 NATURAL RESOURCES (1-10)	7.	6.	5.	4.	-2.6	-4.0	-4.2	-3.6
2 CONSTRUCTION (11,12)	44.	52.	56.	61.	3.0	1.7	1.6	2.1
3 MANUFACTURING (13-74)	198.	214.	221.	216.	1.6	.6	-.5	.6
4 PUBLIC UTILITIES (75-80)	56.	61.	66.	70.	1.7	1.6	1.2	1.5
5 WHOLESALE TRADE (81)	42.	51.	59.	65.	4.0	2.8	1.9	2.9
6 RETAIL TRADE (86,89-99)	139.	160.	182.	197.	2.8	2.6	1.9	2.3
7 FINANCE, INS. & REAL ESTATE (82,83)	42.	58.	74.	89.	6.1	5.1	3.7	5.0
8 SERVICES (84,85,87,88,102)	160.	188.	224.	252.	3.2	3.5	2.4	3.0
9 STATE & LOCAL GOVT. (101)	101.	104.	110.	117.	.6	1.2	1.8	1.0
10 FEDERAL GOVERNMENT (100)	42.	41.	46.	50.	-.3	2.1	1.8	1.2
11 MILITARY (103)	29.	24.	24.	24.	-4.3	.0	.0	-1.4
TOTAL JOBS	861.	958.	1067.	1145.	2.1	2.1	1.4	1.9
CIVILIAN UNEMPLOYMENT RATE	4.2	4.0	3.2	3.6				
POPULATION	1955.	2072.	2238.	2402.	1.2	1.5	1.4	1.4
PERCENT NON-WHITE	25.1	25.4	26.3	26.8				
PER CAPITA INCOME	4509.	5301.	6071.	6687.	3.2	2.7	1.9	2.6
GROSS REGIONAL PRODUCT	9804.	12235.	15385.	18148.	4.4	4.6	3.3	4.1
PERSONAL CONSUMPTION EXPENDITURES	6620.	8005.	10161.	11930.	3.8	4.8	3.2	3.9
PRIVATE INVESTMENT	1155.	1564.	1903.	2188.	6.1	3.9	2.8	4.3
GOVERNMENT EXPENDITURES	2967.	3177.	3531.	3911.	1.4	2.1	2.0	1.8

NEWARK, N.J.

JOBS BY INDUSTRY	1970	1975	1980	1985	AVERAGE ANNUAL RATE OF GROWTH			
					1970-1975	1975-1980	1980-1985	1970-1985
1 NATURAL RESOURCES (1-10)	3.	3.	3.	3.	-.4	-2.0	-2.3	-1.6
2 CONSTRUCTION (11,12)	34.	39.	42.	45.	2.9	1.6	1.3	1.9
3 MANUFACTURING (13-74)	270.	286.	295.	292.	1.2	.6	-.2	.5
4 PUBLIC UTILITIES (75-80)	62.	63.	62.	60.	.1	-.3	-.5	-.3
5 WHOLESALE TRADE (81)	61.	71.	79.	85.	3.1	2.1	1.4	2.2

	1970	1975	1980	1985	1970–1975	1975–1980	1980–1985	1970–1985
					AVERAGE ANNUAL RATE OF GROWTH			
6 RETAIL TRADE (86,89–99)	125.	136.	148.	156.	1.8	1.7	1.0	1.5
7 FINANCE, INS. & REAL ESTATE (82,83)	55.	72.	90.	105.	5.3	4.3	3.1	4.3
8 SERVICES (84,85,87,88,102)	139.	149.	159.	162.	1.3	1.3	.9	1.0
9 STATE & LOCAL GOVT. (101)	81.	86.	90.	94.	1.3	.8	.9	1.0
10 FEDERAL GOVERNMENT (100)	23.	22.	24.	25.	-.1	1.4	-.0	.7
11 MILITARY (103)	1.	1.	1.	1.	-4.3	1.0	-.0	-1.4
TOTAL JOBS	854.	929.	991.	1026.	1.7	1.3	.7	1.2
CIVILIAN UNEMPLOYMENT RATE	4.8	4.6	4.2	4.8				
POPULATION	1857.	1952.	2061.	2190.	1.0	1.1	1.2	1.1
PERCENT NON-WHITE	19.5	20.6	22.1	23.7				
PER CAPITA INCOME	5154.	6124.	7028.	7677.	3.4	2.8	1.8	2.7
GROSS REGIONAL PRODUCT	10481.	12641.	15035.	16925.	3.7	3.5	2.7	3.2
PERSONAL CONSUMPTION EXPENDITURES	6752.	8114.	9981.	11440.	3.7	4.1	2.7	3.5
PRIVATE INVESTMENT	1343.	1757.	2067.	2266.	5.4	3.3	1.8	3.5
GOVERNMENT EXPENDITURES	1560.	1803.	1982.	2162.	2.9	1.9	1.7	2.2

MINNEAPOLIS–ST. PAUL, MINN.

JOBS BY INDUSTRY

	1970	1975	1980	1985	1970–1975	1975–1980	1980–1985	1970–1985
					AVERAGE ANNUAL RATE OF GROWTH			
1 NATURAL RESOURCES (1–10)	7.	7.	5.	4.	-2.4	-4.0	-3.9	-3.4
2 CONSTRUCTION (11,12)	44.	51.	57.	62.	3.1	2.2	1.7	2.3
3 MANUFACTURING (13–74)	224.	258.	276.	275.	2.8	1.3	-.0	1.4
4 PUBLIC UTILITIES (75–80)	59.	66.	71.	74.	2.3	1.5	.6	1.5
5 WHOLESALE TRADE (81)	68.	82.	94.	102.	4.0	2.6	1.7	2.8
6 RETAIL TRADE (86,89–99)	172.	203.	233.	254.	3.3	2.8	1.7	2.6
7 FINANCE, INS. & REAL ESTATE (82,83)	54.	65.	81.	81.	3.7	2.8	1.7	2.7
8 SERVICES (84,85,87,88,102)	174.	196.	221.	236.	2.3	2.5	1.2	2.0
9 STATE & LOCAL GOVT. (101)	92.	96.	105.	111.	-.7	1.8	1.1	1.2
10 FEDERAL GOVERNMENT (100)	19.	15.	17.	17.	-4.5	2.6	.0	-.6
11 MILITARY (103)	1.	1.	1.	1.	-4.3	.0	.0	-1.4
TOTAL JOBS	915.	1040.	1156.	1218.	2.6	2.1	1.0	1.9
CIVILIAN UNEMPLOYMENT RATE	3.0	3.2	2.6	2.9				
POPULATION	1814.	1951.	2104.	2235.	1.5	1.5	1.2	1.4
PERCENT NON-WHITE	2.8	2.9	3.1	3.3				
PER CAPITA INCOME	4597.	5641.	6531.	7195.	4.1	2.9	1.9	3.0
GROSS REGIONAL PRODUCT	10843.	13980.	17453.	20181.	5.1	4.4	2.9	4.1
PERSONAL CONSUMPTION EXPENDITURES	7066.	9034.	11568.	13432.	4.9	4.9	3.0	4.3
PRIVATE INVESTMENT	1523.	2100.	2652.	3030.	6.4	4.7	2.7	4.6
GOVERNMENT EXPENDITURES	2213.	2347.	2651.	2882.	1.2	2.4	1.7	1.8

Appendix Table (cont.)

DALLAS, TEX.

JOBS BY INDUSTRY	1970	1975	1980	1985	AVERAGE ANNUAL RATE OF GROWTH 1970-1975	1975-1980	1980-1985	1970-1985
1 NATURAL RESOURCES (1-10)	16.	15.	14.	12.	-1.4	-2.1	-2.2	-1.9
2 CONSTRUCTION (11,12)	48.	54.	59.	64.	2.6	1.8	1.5	2.0
3 MANUFACTURING (13-74)	184.	197.	209.	216.	1.3	1.3	.6	1.1
4 PUBLIC UTILITIES (75-80)	52.	53.	53.	51.	.2	-.1	-.6	-.1
5 WHOLESALE TRADE (81)	67.	81.	93.	101.	3.7	2.7	1.8	2.7
6 RETAIL TRADE (86,89-99)	140.	160.	181.	195.	2.6	2.4	1.5	2.2
7 FINANCE, INS. & REAL ESTATE (82,83)	61.	72.	81.	85.	3.5	2.3	.9	2.2
8 SERVICES (84,85,87,88,102)	142.	155.	173.	184.	1.9	2.1	1.2	1.7
9 STATE & LOCAL GOVT. (101)	60.	59.	63.	68.	-.5	1.5	1.3	.8
10 FEDERAL GOVERNMENT (100)	14.	11.	13.	13.	-3.8	1.8	.8	.8
11 MILITARY (103)	1.	1.	1.	1.	-4.3	-1.0	-.0	-1.4
TOTAL JOBS	786.	859.	940.	989.	1.8	1.8	1.0	1.5
CIVILIAN UNEMPLOYMENT RATE	3.8	4.2	3.2	4.1				
POPULATION	1517.	1609.	1738.	1898.	1.2	1.5	1.8	1.5
PERCENT NON-WHITE	16.6	17.1	17.5	17.8				
PER CAPITA INCOME	4171.	5025.	5779.	6275.	3.7	2.8	1.6	2.7
GROSS REGIONAL PRODUCT	10097.	12915.	16460.	19483.	4.9	4.9	3.4	4.4
PERSONAL CONSUMPTION EXPENDITURES	6425.	7960.	10166.	11962.	4.3	4.9	3.3	4.1
PRIVATE INVESTMENT	1469.	1907.	2270.	2518.	5.2	3.5	3.3	3.6
GOVERNMENT EXPENDITURES	1629.	1650.	1847.	2028.	.3	2.3	1.9	1.5

SEATTLE-EVERETT, WASH.

JOBS BY INDUSTRY	1970	1975	1980	1985	AVERAGE ANNUAL RATE OF GROWTH 1970-1975	1975-1980	1980-1985	1970-1985
1 NATURAL RESOURCES (1-10)	9.	9.	8.	7.	-.7	-2.6	-3.1	-2.1
2 CONSTRUCTION (11,12)	30.	39.	44.	49.	5.1	2.5	2.1	3.2
3 MANUFACTURING (13-74)	140.	140.	142.	139.	-.1	.3	-.4	-.0
4 PUBLIC UTILITIES (75-80)	41.	45.	49.	50.	2.1	1.6	.6	1.4
5 WHOLESALE TRADE (81)	40.	51.	61.	69.	4.8	3.7	2.6	3.7
6 RETAIL TRADE (86,89-99)	99.	122.	148.	168.	4.1	3.8	2.6	3.5
7 FINANCE, INS. & REAL ESTATE (82,83)	39.	56.	77.	96.	7.7	6.2	4.4	6.1
8 SERVICES (84,85,87,88,102)	100.	134.	175.	209.	5.9	5.3	3.6	4.9
9 STATE & LOCAL GOVT. (101)	76.	89.	99.	110.	3.2	2.2	2.0	2.5

	1970	1975	1980	1985	AVERAGE ANNUAL RATE OF GROWTH 1970-1975	1975-1980	1980-1985	1970-1985
10 FEDERAL GOVERNMENT (100)	17.	19.	23.	25.	2.9	3.4	2.1	2.8
11 MILITARY (103)	4.	3.	3.	3.	-4.3	.0	.0	-1.4
TOTAL JOBS	594.	707.	828.	926.	3.5	3.2	2.2	3.0
CIVILIAN UNEMPLOYMENT RATE	4.8	5.2	4.0	4.5				
POPULATION	1422.	1631.	1664.	2130.	2.7	2.7	2.7	2.7
PERCENT NON-WHITE	6.0	5.9	5.9	5.9				
PER CAPITA INCOME	4581.	5338.	6063.	6559.	3.1	2.5	1.6	2.4
GROSS REGIONAL PRODUCT	7256.	10380.	14403.	18139.	7.2	6.6	4.6	6.1
PERSONAL CONSUMPTION EXPENDITURES	4977.	6541.	8855.	10973.	5.5	6.1	4.3	5.3
PRIVATE INVESTMENT	1237.	1751.	2178.	2503.	7.0	4.4	2.8	4.7
GOVERNMENT EXPENDITURES	1408.	1709.	1977.	2239.	3.9	2.9	2.5	3.1

ANAHEIM-SANTA ANA-GARDEN GROVE, CALIF.

JOBS BY INDUSTRY	1970	1975	1980	1985	AVERAGE ANNUAL RATE OF GROWTH 1970-1975	1975-1980	1980-1985	1970-1985
1 NATURAL RESOURCES (1-10)	9.	9.	8.	8.	.6	-.9	-1.3	-.5
2 CONSTRUCTION (11,12)	24.	33.	37.	42.	5.8	2.7	2.2	3.6
3 MANUFACTURING (13-74)	120.	124.	134.	139.	.7	1.5	.8	1.0
4 PUBLIC UTILITIES (75-80)	14.	19.	23.	27.	5.6	4.2	2.4	4.1
5 WHOLESALE TRADE (81)	15.	19.	24.	28.	5.6	4.4	3.2	4.4
6 RETAIL TRADE (86,89-99)	99.	120.	143.	162.	3.8	3.6	2.5	3.3
7 FINANCE, INS. & REAL ESTATE (82,83)	23.	29.	34.	38.	4.5	3.4	1.8	3.2
8 SERVICES (84,85,87,88,102)	77.	108.	147.	180.	6.8	6.2	4.0	5.7
9 STATE & LOCAL GOVT. (101)	58.	70.	80.	88.	3.7	2.6	2.0	2.8
10 FEDERAL GOVERNMENT (100)	8.	10.	13.	16.	3.2	5.1	4.8	4.4
11 MILITARY (103)	10.	8.	8.	8.	-4.3	.0	.0	-1.4
TOTAL JOBS	458.	549.	653.	736.	3.6	3.5	2.4	3.2
CIVILIAN UNEMPLOYMENT RATE	4.2	4.6	4.3	4.8				
POPULATION	1420.	1634.	1893.	2170.	2.8	2.9	2.7	2.8
PERCENT NON-WHITE	2.7	2.9	3.1	3.2				
PER CAPITA INCOME	3945.	4579.	5208.	5624.	3.0	2.6	1.5	2.4
GROSS REGIONAL PRODUCT	6062.	8244.	11015.	13541.	6.1	5.8	4.1	5.4
PERSONAL CONSUMPTION EXPENDITURES	4389.	5663.	7672.	9456.	5.1	6.1	4.2	5.1
PRIVATE INVESTMENT	1116.	1586.	1967.	2253.	7.0	4.3	2.7	4.7
GOVERNMENT EXPENDITURES	1687.	1960.	2270.	2570.	3.0	2.9	2.5	2.8

Appendix Table (cont.)

ATLANTA, GA.

JOBS BY INDUSTRY	1970	1975	1980	1985	AVERAGE ANNUAL RATE OF GROWTH 1970-1975	1975-1980	1980-1985	1970-1985
1 NATURAL RESOURCES (1-10)	5.	5.	5.	4.	-1.3	-2.6	-2.8	-2.2
2 CONSTRUCTION (11,12)	45.	53.	59.	65.	3.4	2.2	1.8	2.5
3 MANUFACTURING (13-74)	130.	132.	135.	133.	.3	.4	-.3	.2
4 PUBLIC UTILITIES (75-80)	59.	62.	64.	65.	1.0	.8	.3	.7
5 WHOLESALE TRADE (81)	70.	86.	101.	112.	4.2	3.1	2.1	3.1
6 RETAIL TRADE (86,89-99)	126.	152.	183.	207.	3.7	3.6	2.5	3.3
7 FINANCE, INS. & REAL ESTATE (82,83)	47.	65.	87.	107.	6.8	5.7	4.2	5.6
8 SERVICES (84,85,87,88,102)	135.	169.	213.	249.	4.6	4.6	3.2	4.1
9 STATE & LOCAL GOVT. (101)	79.	78.	90.	100.	-.3	3.0	2.0	1.6
10 FEDERAL GOVERNMENT (100)	28.	25.	29.	32.	-2.9	3.3	2.2	.9
11 MILITARY (103)	5.	4.	4.	4.	-4.3	-.0	.0	-1.4
TOTAL JOBS	728.	831.	969.	1079.	2.7	3.1	2.1	2.6
CIVILIAN UNEMPLOYMENT RATE	3.2	3.5	2.7	2.7				
POPULATION	1390.	1466.	1595.	1753.	1.1	1.7	1.9	1.5
PERCENT NON-WHITE	22.6	23.2	23.6	24.3				
PER CAPITA INCOME	4220.	5291.	6391.	7230.	4.5	3.8	2.5	3.6
GROSS REGIONAL PRODUCT	8525.	11564.	15663.	19459.	6.1	6.1	4.3	5.5
PERSONAL CONSUMPTION EXPENDITURES	5615.	7244.	9755.	11993.	5.1	6.0	4.1	5.1
PRIVATE INVESTMENT	1303.	1782.	2196.	2530.	6.3	4.2	2.8	4.4
GOVERNMENT EXPENDITURES	1260.	1311.	1550.	1770.	.8	3.3	2.7	2.3

CINCINNATI, OHIO-KY.-IND.

JOBS BY INDUSTRY	1970	1975	1980	1985	AVERAGE ANNUAL RATE OF GROWTH 1970-1975	1975-1980	1980-1985	1970-1985
1 NATURAL RESOURCES (1-10)	8.	7.	6.	5.	-2.2	-3.8	-3.9	-3.3
2 CONSTRUCTION (11,12)	25.	30.	34.	38.	3.7	2.5	2.1	2.8
3 MANUFACTURING (13-74)	173.	191.	204.	206.	2.0	1.3	.3	1.2
4 PUBLIC UTILITIES (75-80)	36.	38.	40.	41.	1.1	.9	.4	.8
5 WHOLESALE TRADE (81)	39.	49.	57.	64.	4.2	3.2	2.3	3.2

	1970	1975	1980	1985	1970-1975	1975-1980	1980-1985	1970-1985
6 RETAIL TRADE (86,89-99)	96.	113.	133.	149.	3.3	3.2	2.3	3.0
7 FINANCE, INS. & REAL ESTATE (82,83)	28.	38.	48.	57.	5.9	4.7	3.2	4.6
8 SERVICES (84,85,87,88,102)	87.	113.	146.	174.	5.3	5.1	3.6	4.7
9 STATE & LOCAL GOVT. (101)	55.	61.	68.	74.	1.9	2.2	1.8	2.0
10 FEDERAL GOVERNMENT (100)	15.	15.	17.	19.	.3	.0	1.8	1.6
11 MILITARY (103)	0.	0.	0.	0.	-4.3			-1.4
TOTAL JOBS	563.	655.	753.	827.	3.0	2.8	1.9	2.6
CIVILIAN UNEMPLOYMENT RATE	3.6	3.7	2.8	3.2				
POPULATION	1385.	1504.	1662.	1842.	1.7	2.0	2.1	1.9
PERCENT NON-WHITE	11.3	11.7	12.1	12.4				
PER CAPITA INCOME	4153.	5070.	5878.	6450.	4.0	3.0	1.9	2.9
GROSS REGIONAL PRODUCT	6855.	9154.	12064.	14764.	5.8	5.5	4.0	5.1
PERSONAL CONSUMPTION EXPENDITURES	4304.	5570.	7401.	9018.	5.2	5.7	4.0	4.9
PRIVATE INVESTMENT	992.	1347.	1654.	1901.	6.1	4.1	2.8	4.3
GOVERNMENT EXPENDITURES	1215.	1383.	1594.	1796.	2.6	2.8	2.4	2.6

PATERSON-CLIFTON-PASSAIC, N.J.

JOBS BY INDUSTRY	1970	1975	1980	1985	AVERAGE ANNUAL RATE OF GROWTH 1970-1975	1975-1980	1980-1985	1970-1985
1 NATURAL RESOURCES (1-10)	2.	2.	2.	2.	1.2	-.6	-1.2	-.2
2 CONSTRUCTION (11,12)	22.	27.	31.	34.	4.6	2.4	2.0	3.0
3 MANUFACTURING (13-74)	192.	215.	236.	245.	2.3	1.8	.8	1.6
4 PUBLIC UTILITIES (75-80)	30.	33.	36.	38.	1.9	1.7	1.2	1.6
5 WHOLESALE TRADE (81)	46.	57.	66.	74.	4.2	3.1	2.2	3.2
6 RETAIL TRADE (86,89-99)	99.	117.	136.	152.	3.3	3.0	2.2	2.8
7 FINANCE, INS. & REAL ESTATE (82,83)	20.	27.	36.	44.	6.4	5.4	3.9	5.2
8 SERVICES (84,85,87,88,102)	80.	112.	153.	195.	6.7	6.3	4.8	5.9
9 STATE & LOCAL GOVT. (101)	45.	52.	60.	71.	2.8	3.2	3.3	3.1
10 FEDERAL GOVERNMENT (100)	6.	7.	9.	11.	3.2	4.3	4.4	4.0
11 MILITARY (103)	0.	0.	0.	0.	-4.3	.0		-1.4
TOTAL JOBS	542.	650.	765.	867.	3.6	3.3	2.5	3.1
CIVILIAN UNEMPLOYMENT RATE	5.0	4.6	3.6	3.9				
POPULATION	1359.	1500.	1679.	1863.	2.0	2.3	2.1	2.1
PERCENT NON-WHITE	6.1	6.4	6.6	6.9				
PER CAPITA INCOME	4944.	6024.	7022.	7865.	3.9	3.1	2.3	3.1
GROSS REGIONAL PRODUCT	6806.	9130.	11968.	14688.	5.9	5.4	4.1	5.1
PERSONAL CONSUMPTION EXPENDITURES	4192.	5569.	7574.	9504.	5.7	6.2	4.5	5.5
PRIVATE INVESTMENT	926.	1309.	1627.	1880.	6.9	4.3	2.9	4.7
GOVERNMENT EXPENDITURES	967.	1227.	1462.	1727.	4.8	3.5	3.3	3.9

Appendix Table (cont.)

SAN DIEGO, CALIF.

JOBS BY INDUSTRY	1970	1975	1980	1985	AVERAGE ANNUAL RATE OF GROWTH			
					1970–1975	1975–1980	1980–1985	1970–1985
1 NATURAL RESOURCES (1-10)	14.	14.	12.	11.	-.4	-2.0	-2.7	-1.7
2 CONSTRUCTION (11,12)	23.	25.	26.	28.	1.5	1.4	1.2	1.3
3 MANUFACTURING (13-74)	75.	75.	77.	75.	.2	.5	-.5	.1
4 PUBLIC UTILITIES (75-80)	20.	22.	24.	25.	1.7	1.8	1.1	1.5
5 WHOLESALE TRADE (81)	15.	17.	19.	20.	2.5	2.0	1.2	1.9
6 RETAIL TRADE (86,89-99)	88.	98.	109.	117.	2.1	2.2	1.3	1.9
7 FINANCE, INS. & REAL ESTATE (82,83)	21.	25.	29.	30.	3.4	2.3	.8	2.2
8 SERVICES (84,85,87,88,102)	83.	92.	105.	113.	2.0	2.7	1.5	2.0
9 STATE & LOCAL GOVT. (101)	61.	55.	57.	59.	-2.1	.5	.7	-.3
10 FEDERAL GOVERNMENT (100)	31.	27.	28.	28.	-3.2	.5	.7	-.7
11 MILITARY (103)	74.	60.	60.	60.	-4.3	.0	.0	-1.4
TOTAL JOBS	507.	510.	546.	566.	.1	1.4	.7	.7
CIVILIAN UNEMPLOYMENT RATE	7.0	6.4	5.4	7.0				
POPULATION	1358.	1376.	1481.	1615.	.3	1.5	1.7	1.2
PERCENT NON-WHITE	7.8	8.2	8.7	9.3				
PER CAPITA INCOME	3828.	4242.	4693.	4955.	2.1	2.0	1.1	1.7
GROSS REGIONAL PRODUCT	5673.	6206.	7246.	8040.	1.8	3.1	2.1	2.3
PERSONAL CONSUMPTION EXPENDITURES	3542.	3787.	4575.	5208.	1.3	3.8	2.6	2.6
PRIVATE INVESTMENT	644.	829.	999.	1109.	5.0	3.7	2.1	3.6
GOVERNMENT EXPENDITURES	2868.	2674.	2846.	3017.	-1.4	1.2	1.2	.3

BUFFALO, N.Y.

JOBS BY INDUSTRY	1970	1975	1980	1985	AVERAGE ANNUAL RATE OF GROWTH			
					1970–1975	1975–1980	1980–1985	1970–1985
1 NATURAL RESOURCES (1-10)	6.	5.	5.	4.	-1.0	-2.9	-3.1	-2.3
2 CONSTRUCTION (11,12)	20.	23.	25.	27.	3.1	1.8	1.6	2.2
3 MANUFACTURING (13-74)	174.	189.	197.	196.	1.7	.8	-.2	.8
4 PUBLIC UTILITIES (75-80)	31.	32.	32.	32.	.5	.8	-.3	.1
5 WHOLESALE TRADE (81)	28.	34.	39.	43.	4.2	2.8	2.0	3.0
6 RETAIL TRADE (86,89-99)	90.	105.	120.	130.	3.1	2.5	1.7	2.4
7 FINANCE, INS. & REAL ESTATE (82,83)	22.	34.	50.	67.	9.3	7.5	5.8	7.6
8 SERVICES (84,85,87,88,102)	82.	96.	113.	125.	3.3	3.3	2.0	2.9
9 STATE & LOCAL GOVT. (101)	76.	79.	85.	90.	.8	1.3	1.3	1.1

	1970	1975	1980	1985	1970-1975	1975-1980	1980-1985	1970-1985
10 FEDERAL GOVERNMENT (100)	10.	11.	12.	13.	2.0	1.2	1.9	1.7
11 MILITARY (103)	2.	1.	1.	1.	-4.3	.0	.0	-1.4
TOTAL JOBS	539.	611.	679.	729.	2.5	2.1	1.4	2.0
CIVILIAN UNEMPLOYMENT RATE	5.3	4.8	3.7	4.0				
POPULATION	1349.	1439.	1540.	1644.	1.3	1.4	1.3	1.3
PERCENT NON-WHITE	8.8	9.2	9.9	10.6				
PER CAPITA INCOME	3379.	4140.	4832.	5430.	4.1	3.1	2.3	3.2
GROSS REGIONAL PRODUCT	5831.	7674.	9753.	11623.	5.5	4.8	3.5	4.6
PERSONAL CONSUMPTION EXPENDITURES	3187.	4091.	5266.	6312.	5.0	5.0	3.6	4.6
PRIVATE INVESTMENT	658.	912.	1095.	1251.	6.5	3.7	2.6	4.3
GOVERNMENT EXPENDITURES	1024.	1184.	1317.	1459.	2.9	2.1	2.1	2.4

MILWAUKEE, WIS.

JOBS BY INDUSTRY	1970	1975	1980	1985	AVERAGE ANNUAL RATE OF GROWTH 1970-1975	1975-1980	1980-1985	1970-1985
1 NATURAL RESOURCES (1-10)	5.	5.	4.	4.	-1.3	-3.0	-3.0	-2.4
2 CONSTRUCTION (11,12)	25.	29.	32.	35.	3.4	1.8	1.6	2.3
3 MANUFACTURING (13-74)	215.	253.	281.	298.	3.3	2.1	1.2	2.2
4 PUBLIC UTILITIES (75-80)	32.	34.	35.	36.	1.0	.7	.3	.7
5 WHOLESALE TRADE (81)	37.	45.	52.	59.	4.3	2.9	2.2	3.1
6 RETAIL TRADE (86,89-99)	114.	135.	156.	173.	3.3	2.8	2.1	2.8
7 FINANCE, INS. & REAL ESTATE (82,83)	31.	41.	51.	60.	5.5	4.4	3.0	4.3
8 SERVICES (84,85,87,88,102)	106.	116.	128.	134.	1.8	2.0	.8	1.5
9 STATE & LOCAL GOVT. (101)	54.	59.	65.	71.	1.8	2.1	1.7	1.9
10 FEDERAL GOVERNMENT (100)	11.	11.	12.	14.	.4	2.2	1.9	1.5
11 MILITARY (103)	1.	0.	0.	0.	-4.3	.0	.0	-1.4
TOTAL JOBS	630.	730.	818.	882.	2.9	2.3	1.5	2.2
CIVILIAN UNEMPLOYMENT RATE	3.4	3.2	3.0	3.3				
POPULATION	1340.	1470.	1613.	1748.	1.8	1.9	1.6	1.8
PERCENT NON-WHITE	8.6	9.2	10.0	10.7				
PER CAPITA INCOME	4351.	5309.	6138.	6799.	4.0	2.9	2.0	3.0
GROSS REGIONAL PRODUCT	7091.	9292.	11807.	14159.	5.4	4.8	3.6	4.6
PERSONAL CONSUMPTION EXPENDITURES	4261.	5587.	7306.	8795.	5.4	5.4	3.7	4.8
PRIVATE INVESTMENT	743.	1021.	1219.	1384.	6.3	3.6	2.5	4.1
GOVERNMENT EXPENDITURES	966.	1146.	1303.	1451.	3.4	2.6	2.1	2.7

Appendix Table (cont.)

MIAMI, FLA.

JOBS BY INDUSTRY	1970	1975	1980	1985	AVERAGE ANNUAL RATE OF GROWTH 1970-1975	1975-1980	1980-1985	1970-1985
1 NATURAL RESOURCES (1-10)	6.	5.	4.	3.	-3.9	-5.4	-5.7	-5.0
2 CONSTRUCTION (11,12)	38.	48.	55.	62.	4.6	2.8	2.4	3.3
3 MANUFACTURING (13-74)	77.	85.	88.	87.	1.9	.9	-.3	.8
4 PUBLIC UTILITIES (75-80)	59.	65.	69.	72.	1.7	1.4	.8	1.3
5 WHOLESALE TRADE (81)	41.	53.	66.	76.	5.4	4.2	2.9	4.2
6 RETAIL TRADE (86,89-99)	122.	153.	189.	217.	4.6	4.2	2.8	3.9
7 FINANCE, INS. & REAL ESTATE (82,83)	44.	67.	94.	119.	8.4	6.7	4.7	6.6
8 SERVICES (84,85,87,88,102)	144.	181.	228.	268.	4.5	4.6	3.2	4.1
9 STATE & LOCAL GOVT. (101)	57.	66.	76.	87.	2.8	2.9	2.7	2.8
10 FEDERAL GOVERNMENT (100)	12.	13.	16.	19.	2.7	4.2	3.3	3.4
11 MILITARY (103)	9.	7.	7.	7.	-4.3	-1.0	-.0	-1.4
TOTAL JOBS	609.	743.	893.	1017.	4.0	3.7	2.6	3.4
CIVILIAN UNEMPLOYMENT RATE	3.5	3.2	3.0	3.0				
POPULATION	1268.	1458.	1692.	1897.	2.8	3.0	2.3	2.7
PERCENT NON-WHITE	15.5	16.0	16.8	17.7				
PER CAPITA INCOME	4463.	5514.	6514.	7390.	4.2	3.3	2.5	3.4
GROSS REGIONAL PRODUCT	8079.	12088.	17414.	22421.	8.1	7.3	5.1	6.8
PERSONAL CONSUMPTION EXPENDITURES	6619.	8904.	12346.	15376.	5.9	6.5	4.4	5.6
PRIVATE INVESTMENT	1331.	1862.	2327.	2702.	6.7	4.5	3.0	4.7
GOVERNMENT EXPENDITURES	1033.	1260.	1507.	1760.	4.0	3.6	3.1	3.5

KANSAS CITY, MO.-KANS.

JOBS BY INDUSTRY	1970	1975	1980	1985	AVERAGE ANNUAL RATE OF GROWTH 1970-1975	1975-1980	1980-1985	1970-1985
1 NATURAL RESOURCES (1-10)	8.	8.	7.	6.	-.9	-2.6	-2.5	-2.0
2 CONSTRUCTION (11,12)	33.	40.	45.	49.	3.5	2.3	2.0	2.6
3 MANUFACTURING (13-74)	135.	154.	170.	177.	2.6	1.9	.8	1.8
4 PUBLIC UTILITIES (75-80)	53.	60.	67.	71.	2.7	2.1	1.3	2.0
5 WHOLESALE TRADE (81)	48.	59.	68.	75.	4.0	2.9	2.0	3.0

	1970	1975	1980	1985	1970–1975	1975–1980	1980–1985	1970–1985
6 RETAIL TRADE (86,89-99)	116.	136.	157.	173.	3.2	2.9	1.9	2.7
7 FINANCE, INS. & REAL ESTATE (82,83)	37.	46.	54.	58.	4.2	3.1	1.7	3.0
8 SERVICES (84,85,87,88,102)	105.	119.	137.	146.	2.6	2.7	1.4	2.2
9 STATE & LOCAL GOVT. (101)	56.	58.	64.	69.	.7	1.9	1.8	1.5
10 FEDERAL GOVERNMENT (100)	23.	21.	23.	25.	-1.8	2.0	1.4	1.5
11 MILITARY (103)	5.	4.	4.	4.	-4.3	.0	.0	-1.4
TOTAL JOBS	619.	704.	794.	854.	2.6	2.4	1.5	2.1
CIVILIAN UNEMPLOYMENT RATE	4.0	3.9	3.5	3.8				
POPULATION	1254.	1360.	1490.	1641.	1.6	1.8	1.9	1.8
PERCENT NON-WHITE	12.6	13.3	14.2	14.7				
PER CAPITA INCOME	4121.	4981.	5780.	6271.	3.8	3.0	1.6	2.8
GROSS REGIONAL PRODUCT	7586.	9820.	12586.	15021.	5.2	5.0	3.5	4.6
PERSONAL CONSUMPTION EXPENDITURES	4711.	5998.	7846.	9352.	4.8	5.4	3.5	4.6
PRIVATE INVESTMENT	1221.	1769.	2277.	2751.	7.4	5.0	3.8	5.4
GOVERNMENT EXPENDITURES	1293.	1384.	1576.	1755.	1.4	2.6	2.1	2.0

DENVER, COLO.

		1970	1975	1980	1985	AVERAGE ANNUAL RATE OF GROWTH			
JOBS BY INDUSTRY						1970–1975	1975–1980	1980–1985	1970–1985
1 NATURAL RESOURCES (1-10)		11.	10.	9.	9.	-1.0	-1.5	-1.8	-1.4
2 CONSTRUCTION (11,12)		32.	38.	41.	44.	3.2	1.7	1.4	2.1
3 MANUFACTURING (13-74)		90.	103.	114.	117.	2.8	1.9	.7	1.8
4 PUBLIC UTILITIES (75-80)		35.	36.	36.	35.	.2	.0	-.3	-.0
5 WHOLESALE TRADE (81)		39.	46.	52.	58.	3.5	2.5	1.8	2.6
6 RETAIL TRADE (86,89-99)		102.	118.	136.	149.	3.0	2.8	1.9	2.5
7 FINANCE, INS. & REAL ESTATE (82,83)		33.	39.	44.	45.	3.4	2.2	.6	2.0
8 SERVICES (84,85,87,88,102)		102.	116.	133.	144.	2.5	2.8	1.6	2.3
9 STATE & LOCAL GOVT. (101)		66.	66.	72.	77.	.0	1.7	1.2	1.0
10 FEDERAL GOVERNMENT (100)		26.	23.	26.	27.	-2.2	1.8	1.0	.2
11 MILITARY (103)		14.	12.	12.	12.	-4.3	.0	.2	-1.4
TOTAL JOBS		550.	608.	674.	716.	2.0	2.1	1.2	1.8
CIVILIAN UNEMPLOYMENT RATE		3.9	4.1	3.5	4.0				
POPULATION		1228.	1320.	1438.	1561.	1.4	1.7	1.6	1.6
PERCENT NON-WHITE		5.5	5.6	5.9	6.0				
PER CAPITA INCOME		4069.	4815.	5505.	5972.	3.4	2.7	1.6	2.6
GROSS REGIONAL PRODUCT		6514.	8044.	9946.	11496.	4.2	4.2	2.9	3.8
PERSONAL CONSUMPTION EXPENDITURES		4402.	5412.	6913.	8093.	4.1	4.9	3.2	4.1
PRIVATE INVESTMENT		984.	1299.	1552.	1713.	5.6	3.6	2.0	3.7
GOVERNMENT EXPENDITURES		1336.	1393.	1549.	1679.	.8	2.1	1.6	1.5

Appendix Table (cont.)

SAN BERNARDINO-RIVERSIDE-ONTARIO, CALIF.

JOBS BY INDUSTRY	1970	1975	1980	1985	AVERAGE ANNUAL RATE OF GROWTH			
					1970-1975	1975-1980	1980-1985	1970-1985
1 NATURAL RESOURCES (1-10)	19.	18.	16.	14.	-.6	-2.5	-2.6	-1.9
2 CONSTRUCTION (11,12)	17.	20.	22.	23.	2.6	1.6	1.5	1.9
3 MANUFACTURING (13-74)	54.	57.	60.	61.	1.4	.9	.3	.8
4 PUBLIC UTILITIES (75-80)	18.	19.	21.	22.	1.3	1.5	1.2	1.3
5 WHOLESALE TRADE (81)	12.	14.	16.	17.	3.3	2.6	2.0	2.6
6 RETAIL TRADE (86,89-99)	67.	75.	84.	91.	2.3	2.3	1.6	2.0
7 FINANCE, INS. & REAL ESTATE (82,83)	11.	15.	20.	24.	6.3	5.4	4.1	5.3
8 SERVICES (84,85,87,88,102)	61.	72.	86.	95.	3.2	3.5	2.2	2.9
9 STATE & LOCAL GOVT. (101)	59.	61.	64.	67.	.5	.9	1.2	.9
10 FEDERAL GOVERNMENT (100)	15.	14.	15.	16.	-.5	.6	1.1	.4
11 MILITARY (103)	27.	22.	22.	22.	-4.3	.0	.0	-1.4
TOTAL JOBS	360.	388.	424.	454.	1.5	1.8	1.3	1.5
CIVILIAN UNEMPLOYMENT RATE	9.3	8.6	7.9	8.7				
POPULATION	1143.	1226.	1341.	1496.	1.4	1.8	2.2	1.8
PERCENT NON-WHITE	6.5	6.5	6.6	6.7				
PER CAPITA INCOME	3338.	3794.	4223.	4458.	2.6	2.1	1.1	1.9
GROSS REGIONAL PRODUCT	3655.	4325.	5187.	5990.	3.4	3.6	2.9	3.3
PERSONAL CONSUMPTION EXPENDITURES	2814.	3314.	4119.	4832.	3.3	4.4	3.2	3.6
PRIVATE INVESTMENT	518.	722.	875.	1008.	6.6	3.8	2.8	4.4
GOVERNMENT EXPENDITURES	1309.	1405.	1511.	1630.	1.4	1.5	1.5	1.5

INDIANAPOLIS, IND.

JOBS BY INDUSTRY	1970	1975	1980	1985	AVERAGE ANNUAL RATE OF GROWTH			
					1970-1975	1975-1980	1980-1985	1970-1985
1 NATURAL RESOURCES (1-10)	8.	8.	6.	5.	-1.9	-3.7	-3.7	-3.1
2 CONSTRUCTION (11,12)	25.	30.	32.	34.	3.2	1.6	1.3	2.0
3 MANUFACTURING (13-74)	132.	140.	141.	135.	1.2	.2	-1.0	.1
4 PUBLIC UTILITIES (75-80)	28.	28.	27.	26.	.0	-.5	-1.2	-.6
5 WHOLESALE TRADE (81)	36.	44.	50.	54.	4.0	2.6	1.6	2.7
6 RETAIL TRADE (86,89-99)	85.	100.	114.	123.	3.2	2.7	1.6	2.5
7 FINANCE, INS. & REAL ESTATE (82,83)	31.	43.	55.	65.	6.3	5.0	3.5	4.9
8 SERVICES (84,85,87,88,102)	72.	91.	110.	121.	4.5	3.8	2.0	3.4
9 STATE & LOCAL GOVT. (101)	55.	61.	64.	67.	2.0	1.0	1.0	1.3

10 FEDERAL GOVERNMENT (100)	17.	17.	18.	19.	.1	1.0	.7	.6
11 MILITARY (103)	3.	2.	2.	2.	-4.3	.0	.0	-1.4
TOTAL JOBS	493.	562.	620.	652.	2.6	1.9	1.0	1.0
CIVILIAN UNEMPLOYMENT RATE	2.4	2.7	2.5	2.8				
POPULATION	1079.	1162.	1257.	1364.	1.5	1.6	1.6	1.6
PERCENT NON-WHITE	13.0	13.8	14.7	15.2				
PER CAPITA INCOME	4256.	5106.	5793.	6185.	3.6	2.5	1.3	2.5
GROSS REGIONAL PRODUCT	5690.	7537.	9607.	11297.	5.6	4.9	3.2	4.6
PERSONAL CONSUMPTION EXPENDITURES	3438.	4321.	5451.	6268.	4.6	4.6	2.8	4.0
PRIVATE INVESTMENT	952.	1310.	1576.	1772.	6.4	3.7	2.3	4.1
GOVERNMENT EXPENDITURES	974.	1110.	1213.	1311.	2.6	1.8	1.5	2.0

SAN JOSE, CALIF.

JOBS BY INDUSTRY	1970	1975	1980	1985	AVERAGE ANNUAL RATE OF GROWTH 1970-1975	1975-1980	1980-1985	1970-1985
1 NATURAL RESOURCES (1-10)	8.	8.	7.	6.	-1.1	-2.4	-3.2	-2.2
2 CONSTRUCTION (11,12)	18.	21.	23.	25.	3.2	1.7	1.4	2.1
3 MANUFACTURING (13-74)	133.	150.	168.	177.	2.4	2.2	1.1	1.9
4 PUBLIC UTILITIES (75-80)	16.	17.	17.	17.	.7	.6	-.2	.4
5 WHOLESALE TRADE (81)	15.	19.	22.	24.	4.0	3.0	2.0	3.0
6 RETAIL TRADE (86,89-99)	66.	75.	85.	92.	2.7	2.5	1.5	2.2
7 FINANCE, INS. & REAL ESTATE (82,83)	16.	15.	14.	12.	-.9	-2.0	-2.8	-1.9
8 SERVICES (84,85,87,88,102)	76.	89.	104.	114.	3.2	3.1	1.9	2.7
9 STATE & LOCAL GOVT. (101)	47.	48.	51.	54.	.5	1.4	1.2	1.0
10 FEDERAL GOVERNMENT (100)	9.	9.	9.	10.	-.8	1.5	1.0	.6
11 MILITARY (103)	2.	2.	2.	2.	-4.3	-1.0	.0	-1.4
TOTAL JOBS	406.	451.	501.	532.	2.1	2.1	1.2	1.8
CIVILIAN UNEMPLOYMENT RATE	5.6	5.1	4.7	5.2				
POPULATION	1065.	1146.	1267.	1409.	1.5	2.0	2.1	1.9
PERCENT NON-WHITE	5.7	6.1	6.6	7.0				
PER CAPITA INCOME	4071.	4822.	5446.	5760.	3.4	2.4	1.1	2.3
GROSS REGIONAL PRODUCT	5809.	7218.	8918.	10296.	4.3	4.2	2.9	3.8
PERSONAL CONSUMPTION EXPENDITURES	3544.	4356.	5583.	6533.	4.1	5.0	3.1	4.1
PRIVATE INVESTMENT	911.	1274.	1590.	1811.	6.7	4.4	2.6	4.6
GOVERNMENT EXPENDITURES	1689.	1778.	1994.	2195.	1.0	2.3	1.9	1.7

Appendix Table (cont.)

NEW ORLEANS, LA.

JOBS BY INDUSTRY	1970	1975	1980	1985	AVERAGE ANNUAL RATE OF GROWTH			
					1970–1975	1975–1980	1980–1985	1970–1985
1 NATURAL RESOURCES (1-10)	17.	19.	22.	26.	3.0	3.0	2.8	2.9
2 CONSTRUCTION (11,12)	26.	33.	39.	48.	4.9	3.8	4.2	4.3
3 MANUFACTURING (13-74)	56.	65.	72.	76.	3.2	2.1	1.0	2.1
4 PUBLIC UTILITIES (75-80)	46.	47.	47.	48.	.3	.1	.1	.2
5 WHOLESALE TRADE (81)	33.	39.	45.	51.	3.7	2.9	2.2	2.9
6 RETAIL TRADE (86,89-99)	72.	81.	93.	104.	2.6	2.8	2.2	2.5
7 FINANCE, INS. & REAL ESTATE (82,83)	24.	31.	38.	45.	5.3	4.3	3.1	4.2
8 SERVICES (84,85,87,88,102)	76.	85.	98.	106.	2.4	2.8	1.6	2.3
9 STATE & LOCAL GOVT. (101)	50.	51.	57.	63.	.7	2.0	2.2	1.6
10 FEDERAL GOVERNMENT (100)	14.	13.	14.	15.	-1.3	1.5	1.9	.7
11 MILITARY (103)	1.	1.	1.	1.	-4.3	.0	.0	-1.4
TOTAL JOBS	412.	466.	528.	584.	2.5	2.5	2.0	2.3
CIVILIAN UNEMPLOYMENT RATE	4.4	4.6	3.5	3.7				
POPULATION	1046.	1119.	1213.	1326.	1.3	1.6	1.8	1.6
PERCENT NON-WHITE	31.4	31.4	32.0	32.3				
PER CAPITA INCOME	3352.	4047.	4736.	5337.	3.8	3.1	2.4	3.1
GROSS REGIONAL PRODUCT	5182.	6497.	8272.	10122.	4.5	4.8	4.0	4.5
PERSONAL CONSUMPTION EXPENDITURES	3093.	3850.	5026.	6164.	4.4	5.3	4.1	4.6
PRIVATE INVESTMENT	721.	1020.	1317.	1628.	6.9	5.1	4.2	5.4
GOVERNMENT EXPENDITURES	966.	1055.	1188.	1327.	1.8	2.4	2.2	2.1

TAMPA-ST. PETERSBURG, FLA.

JOBS BY INDUSTRY	1970	1975	1980	1985	AVERAGE ANNUAL RATE OF GROWTH			
					1970–1975	1975–1980	1980–1985	1970–1985
1 NATURAL RESOURCES (1-10)	11.	10.	9.	9.	-.7	-1.9	-1.7	-1.4
2 CONSTRUCTION (11,12)	30.	35.	40.	44.	3.6	2.3	2.0	2.6
3 MANUFACTURING (13-74)	54.	62.	69.	72.	2.7	2.1	1.1	1.9
4 PUBLIC UTILITIES (75-80)	21.	25.	28.	30.	3.4	2.6	1.4	2.4
5 WHOLESALE TRADE (81)	25.	31.	37.	41.	4.4	3.3	2.3	3.3

	1970	1975	1980	1985	1970–1975	1975–1980	1980–1985	1970–1985
6 RETAIL TRADE (86,89-99)	75.	88.	102.	113.	3.2	3.0	2.0	2.7
7 FINANCE, INS. & REAL ESTATE (82,83)	19.	26.	32.	38.	5.7	4.6	3.1	4.5
8 SERVICES (84,85,87,88,102)	74.	87.	104.	116.	3.3	3.5	2.3	3.0
9 STATE & LOCAL GOVT. (101)	48.	53.	58.	63.	1.8	1.8	1.8	1.8
10 FEDERAL GOVERNMENT (100)	7.	8.	9.	11.	3.2	3.0	2.6	3.0
11 MILITARY (103)	9.	7.	7.	7.	-4.3	-.7	-.0	-1.4
TOTAL JOBS	372.	432.	495.	545.	3.0	2.7	1.9	2.5
CIVILIAN UNEMPLOYMENT RATE	3.5	4.1	3.4	4.3				
POPULATION	1013.	1151.	1303.	1473.	2.6	2.5	2.4	2.5
PERCENT NON-WHITE	11.1	10.8	10.8	10.9				
PER CAPITA INCOME	3650.	4338.	4963.	5403.	3.5	2.7	1.7	2.6
GROSS REGIONAL PRODUCT	3619.	4957.	6650.	8250.	6.3	5.9	4.3	5.5
PERSONAL CONSUMPTION EXPENDITURES	3296.	4271.	5658.	6914.	5.2	5.6	4.0	4.9
PRIVATE INVESTMENT	645.	918.	1172.	1391.	7.0	4.9	3.4	5.1
GOVERNMENT EXPENDITURES	797.	936.	1066.	1201.	3.2	2.6	2.4	2.7

PORTLAND, OREG.-WASH.

JOBS BY INDUSTRY	1970	1975	1980	1985	AVERAGE ANNUAL RATE OF GROWTH 1970–1975	1975–1980	1980–1985	1970–1985
1 NATURAL RESOURCES (1-10)	16.	14.	12.	10.	-1.9	-3.7	-3.9	-3.1
2 CONSTRUCTION (11,12)	21.	24.	27.	29.	3.3	1.8	1.5	2.2
3 MANUFACTURING (13-74)	89.	104.	115.	120.	3.1	2.0	.9	2.0
4 PUBLIC UTILITIES (75-80)	32.	33.	33.	32.	.6	.0	-.7	-.1
5 WHOLESALE TRADE (81)	35.	42.	48.	52.	3.7	2.5	1.6	2.6
6 RETAIL TRADE (86,89-99)	73.	83.	91.	97.	2.4	2.0	1.2	1.9
7 FINANCE, INS. & REAL ESTATE (82,83)	25.	37.	52.	67.	7.6	6.7	5.3	6.5
8 SERVICES (84,85,87,88,102)	80.	91.	103.	110.	2.5	2.6	1.3	2.1
9 STATE & LOCAL GOVT. (101)	49.	52.	56.	61.	1.2	1.8	1.6	1.5
10 FEDERAL GOVERNMENT (100)	15.	14.	15.	17.	-1.2	1.6	1.5	.7
11 MILITARY (103)	0.	0.	0.	0.				
TOTAL JOBS	435.	494.	552.	595.	2.6	2.2	1.5	2.1
CIVILIAN UNEMPLOYMENT RATE	4.6	4.4	3.9	3.8				
POPULATION	1009.	1081.	1167.	1242.	1.4	1.5	1.2	1.4
PERCENT NON-WHITE	3.8	3.9	4.1	4.3				
PER CAPITA INCOME	3997.	4918.	5794.	6548.	4.1	3.3	2.4	3.3
GROSS REGIONAL PRODUCT	5053.	6325.	7770.	8963.	4.5	4.1	2.9	3.8
PERSONAL CONSUMPTION EXPENDITURES	3361.	4271.	5538.	6589.	4.8	5.2	3.5	4.5
PRIVATE INVESTMENT	769.	1055.	1251.	1395.	6.3	3.4	2.2	4.0
GOVERNMENT EXPENDITURES	747.	845.	955.	1063.	2.5	2.5	2.1	2.4

JOBS AND POPULATION IN THOUSANDS, GROSS REGIONAL PRODUCT IN MILLIONS (1969 PRICES)

Index

Index

Age: 61; and employment, 41, 44; and migration, 42, 43
Age-Color-Specific-Death Rate method, 60
Age-Race estimates, 57-61
Agglomeration variables, 2, 23, 24, 38
Agriculture, 48, 55, 56, 58-59, 135, 144
Aircraft industry, 191
Almon, Clopper, Jr., xvi, 1n., 31, 49, 72, 136
Anaheim, Cal., 154
Anderson, Ind., 147, 154
Ann Arbor, Mich., 147
Annual Survey of Manufactures, 48, 53
Appalachia, 1
Area Trends in Employment and Unemployment, 56
Arizona, 154
Arkansas, 154
Armed forces: 16, 27; employment, 54, 55, 58, 63, 169; *see also* Defense expenditures
Arms Control and Disarmament Agency, 1

BEA, *see* Bureau of Economic Analysis
Bakersfield, Cal., 154
Beaumont-Port Arthur, Tex., 147, 154
Binghamton, N.Y., 147, 154
Birth rates: 15, 27, 63, 116; forecasts, 143
Buckler, Margaret, xvi
Bureau of Census, 59, 60, 71, 136
Bureau of Economic Analysis (BEA), 154, 155
Bureau of Labor Statistics, 136
Bureau of Public Roads, 66

Canadian imports, 47, 48
Capital costs: 37-38; *see also* Equipment
Capital equipment, *see* Equipment
Capital expenditures, 24
Census data: state, 42; adjustment, 52; *see also* Bureau of Census
Census of Agriculture, 48, 56

Census of Business, 48, 52
Census of Government, 53-54, 56
Census of Manufacturers, 137
Census of Population, 56
Central cities, 159, 165
Charleston, W.Va., 147
Chemical industry, 75
Columbia, 2
Commerce Department: 2; Economic Development Administration, xvi, 56
Commodity Credit Corporation, 23
Commuters: 16, 27, 29, 54, 56n., 57, 59; forecasts, 143
CONUS defense, 169
Connecticut, 191
Construction: 15, 16, 17, 18, 25-26, 48, 99, 142; equations, 19, 74, 99-103; expenditures, 37, 39; maintenance, 26; military, 103; public, 26, 99-103; residential, 25, 99
Cost of Transporting Freight by Class I and Class II Motor Carriers, 67
County Business Patterns, 48, 49, 54, 56, 59, 71, 136
Crops, 23, 58
Cumberland, John H., xvi
Current Population Reports, 60
Customs districts, 48-49, 54

Davis, Richard, xvi
Death rates: 15, 16, 27, 60, 61-62, 116; forecasts, 143
Defense expenditures, 9, 16, 22, 23, 25, 53, 74, 135, 142, 165, 169, 191, 193
Demand, 49-52
Depreciation costs, 38, 39, 40
Depressed areas, 2
Discrimination in employment, 41
Distribution of Rail Revenue Contribution by Commodity Group, 66
District of Columbia, 61, 154
Domestic service, 26, 29, 54, 55, 58, 59
Donnely, William, III, xvi

227

Earnings, *see* Wage rate
Economic base projections, 5
Economic Development
 Administration, *see* Commerce
 Department
Employment: 26-27, 28, 38, 40,
 54-57, 135; analysis, 4-5, 193;
 equations, 19-20, 103-116; federal,
 26; growth rates, 43; regional, 38,
 42, 45, 54, 71; *see also*
 Unemployment
Employment and Earnings, 56
Equipment: 7, 17, 24, 28-29, 37-38;
 depreciation, 39, 40; and
 employment, 40; equations, 75, 99,
 103; as variable, 135
Equipment purchase, 12-15, 25, 26,
 28-29, 141-142
Erie, Pa., 154
Exports, 3, 16, 29, 54, 121, 132, 136,
 144

F.W. Dodge Division, 52, 53
Far West: employment, 165; per
 capita income, 155; population
 growth, 155
Farm equipment: exports, 29;
 purchases, 52
Farm Income Situation, 48
Farm Labor, 56
Federal government expenditures: 1-2,
 73; equations, 18; and employment,
 54, 55, 56, 58; and population
 distribution, 2, 22-23, 53-54; *see
 also* Defense expenditures
Fishing Statistics, , 48
Forestry, 23, 38, 53, 58
Fort Worth, Tex., 193

General Purpose Force planning, 169
Government expenditures: 15, 22-23,
 26, 142-143; equations, 18; growth
 rates, 159; wage rates, 121, 143; *see
 also* Federal government
 expenditures *and* State government
 expenditures
Great Lakes region, 159
Gross investment, 18, 25-26, 39
Gross National Product, 191
Gross Regional Product, 147, 159

Hartford, Conn., 147
*Highlights of U.S. Export and Import
 Trade*, 48, 49, 54
Highway construction, 2
Highway transportation, 3, 64-66
Hopkins, Frank E., xvi
Housing and Urban Development
 Department, 2

Idaho, 155
Imports: 9-10, 16, 20, 30, 47-48,
 57-59, 121, 136, 144; competitive,
 30, 47, 49
Income, 3, 17, 23, 25, 26, 57, 141;
 equation, 21, 117, 122-23; and construction, 99; regional, 27, 29, and
 residence, 27; and tax revenues, 26;
 see also Per capita income *and* Wage
 rate
Input prices, 3
Input-output projection models, 5-7,
 31, 72, 135
Input-output sectors: 47-48, 49; coefficients, 136; national, 49, 52; and
 sales, 52
Insurance industry, 147, 155, 165
Interest rates: 24, 37; forecasts, 135-
 36
International trade: equation, 21, 29;
 see also *Exports* and *Imports*
Interstate Commerce Commission, 64,
 66-67
Investment tax credit, 135

Johnstown, N.Y., 154

Kanoska, Wis., 147
Kaufmann, William W., 169
Klein, Lawrence, 1n.

Labor force, 20-21, 44-45, 54-57, 135;
 equations, 116-117; forecasts, 140,
 143; surplus, 17, 28, 44
Lafayette, Ind., 154
Lake Charles, La., 147
Land resources, 198
Land values: 17, 24, 31, 34n., 75, 121,
 132; forecasts, 143
Linear programming algorithm, 35, 37,
 132

Line-haul costs, 66
Livestock, 23, 55, 58
Loans, 2, 37

McConnell, Kenneth, xvi
Macroeconomic forecasting models, 5
Maintenance construction, *see* Construction
Manufacturing industry, 47-48, 169, 191
Marginal transport costs: equation, 22, 30-31; *see also* Shadow prices
Market price equation, 36
Markup ratios, 64, 65-66
Maryland, University of, xvi, 31
Maryland Interindustry Forecasting Project, xvi
Menominee County, Wis., 57
Merchant, Stephen, xvi
Mexican imports, 48
Midland, Tex., 147, 154
Mideast, 155
Migration: 16, 27, 40-44; by age group, 28, 43, 116-17, 140; equation, 42-43, 116-17, 140; forecasts, 59, 63; and race, 43-44, 59
Mining industry, 49, 58, 103, 137, 198
Minuteman, 169
Mississippi, 154
Montana, 154
Moving costs, 41-44
Multicollinearity, 69-70, 103
Multijob holders, 16, 27, 54, 55, 56n., 143

NASA, 23, 53, 142
National Planning Association (NPA), 154, 155
National Transportation Acts, 64
Nevada, 154
New England: government expenditures, 159; income growth, 155; population, 165
New London, Conn., 193
New Mexico, 191
New towns, 2
North Dakota, 154, 155
Northeast Corridor, 1

OBE, *see* Office of Business Economics
OMB, *see* Office of Management and Budget

Office of Business Economics, 9, 29, 57-58
Office of Economic Opportunity, 44
Office of Management and Budget, 53
Oklahoma, 154
Ordnance industry, 191
Output equations, 74-75, 103, 137, 146-47
Overseas population, 136

Pensions, 29
Peoria, Ill., 147
Per capita income, 43, 44, 147, 165
Personal consumption expenditures: 7, 17, 24-25, 29, 52, 121; equation, 21; by industry sector, 141
Pipeline transportation costs, 65
Plains States, 155, 159, 165
Plant-size factor, 137
Polaris-Poseidon force, 169
Pollution, 2, 198
Population: 16, 17, 27-28, 147-55; county, 61-64; declines, 147; density, 25, 38; equations, 20, 116-17; forecasts, 5, 15, 59-64, 136, 140, 147; overseas, 136; social costs, 2; state, 60-61
Post offices, 22
Port activities, 121
Prices, 23
Procedures for Developing Rail Revenue Contribution by Commodity Group (ICC), 66-67
Production costs, 33
Productivity rates, 13
Property income, 17, 29, 31, 57, 117, 121, 132
Public Health Service, 60
Public works grants, 2

Race: 15, 17, 60; and employment, 40; and migration, 42, 43
Railroads: 3, 55, 56, 64, 143, 144; costs, 64, 66-67
Railroad Retirement Board, 56
Real estate industry, 155, 165
Regression analysis, 5, 69
Regression line equations, 145-47
Relative income, 43
Rents: and business location, 33-34, 36; equations, 37; as income, 29
Residuals, 145-147
Reston, 2

Ricardian theory of rents, 33
Roberts, Merrill J., 66, 67
Rochester, N.Y., 154
Rocky Mountains area, 165, 191
Russek, Marianne, xvi

SIC groups, 10-15, 47
SMSA, *see* Standard Metropolitan
    Statistical Areas
Sales, 5, 17
Sectoring scheme, 9-19
Series "C" projections, 136
Service industries, 165, 169, 191
Shadow prices: 3, 22, 30-31, 35-36,
    75, 121, 132-34; equation, 22
Shift-share analysis, 4-5
Social insurance, 17, 57, 117
Social Security, 29, 54, 55
Social Security Bulletin, 56, 143
South Dakota, 155
Southeast area: employment, 191;
    gross regional product, 159; per
    capita income growth, 155; popula-
    tion growth, 155, 168
Southwest area: employment, 155;
    gross regional product, 159; popula-
    tion growth, 155
Standard Metropolitan Statistical
    Areas, 52, 57, 58, 135, 147, 155,
    159, 191
State government expenditures: 23,
    143, 144; employment, 54, 55, 56,
    58
Statistical Abstract of the U.S., 48
*Statistics of Communications Com-
    mon Carriers*, 48
Statistics of Electric Utilities, 48
Steel industry, 3, 49, 75
Stepwise regression, 69

Suburban growth, 159, 165

Taxes, rates, 2, 191
Terminal costs, 66
Texarkana, Tex., 193
Textile industry, 49
Theil, Henri, 69
Transfer payments, 17, 29, 57, 117,
    121
Transportation: 2-3, 29, 58, 78, 193;
    costs, 17, 23, 34-37, 64-66; equa-
    tions, 22, 30-31, 121; statistical vari-
    ables, 71
Transportation Department, 2

Unemployment: 2; in cities, 165;
    equations, 20-21, 28; forecasts, 140,
    155-59; regional, 45, 54, 56, 71-72,
    155; *see also* Employment
Unemployment insurance, 17, 29
Utah, 154
Utilities industry, 48, 58, 155

Variables: 69-70, 74, 75, 193; ag-
    glomeration, 24; dependent, 74;
    dummy, 43-44, 146; independent,
    73, 74; regional, 28
Virginia, 57

Wage rates: 24, 27, 29, 34, 41, 73, 75,
    116; forecasts, 140; and investment,
    116-17
Waterborne Commerce, 48, 54
Welfare, 29
West Virginia, 155
Wheeling, W.Va., 147
Wolfson, Stanley, xvi
Women: 28; employment, 40, 44-45;
    and moving, 41

About the Author

Curtis C. Harris, Jr. is Associate Professor of Economics at the Bureau of Business and Economic Research and at the Economics Department of the University of Maryland. He has been with the U.S. Department of Commerce and the University of California, Davis. Professor Harris received the B.S. in economics from the University of Florida in 1956, and the M.A. and Ph.D. from Harvard.

Professor Harris has published numerous articles in professional journals and he is co-author of a recent Lexington book on *Locational Analysis*. He has served as a consultant to the federal government and private industry. Professor Harris specialized in regional and urban economics at the University of Maryland.